The Crime Victim's Book

Second Edition

BRUNNER/MAZEL PSYCHOSOCIAL STRESS SERIES NO. 6

The Crime Victim's Book

Second Edition

MORTON BARD

&

DAWN SANGREY

BRUNNER/MAZEL Publishers • *New York*

SECOND PRINTING

Four lines from William Butler Yeats' "The Second Coming," reprinted with permission of Macmillan Publishing Company, from The Poems by W. B. Yeats, edited by Richard J. Finneran. Copyright © 1924 by Macmillian Publishing Company, renewed 1952 by Bertha Georgie Yeats. And with permission of Michael B. Yeats and Macmillan London Ltd.

Lines from Robert Bolt's A Man for All Seasons reprinted by permission of Random House, Inc. Copyright © 1962 by Robert Bolt.

Library of Congress Cataloging-in-Publication Data

Bard, Morton, 1924-
    The crime victim's book.

  (Brunner/Mazel psychosocial stress series; no. 6)
  Bibliography: p.
  Includes index.
    1. Victims of crimes. 2. Victims of crimes—United
States. I. Sangrey, Dawn. II. Title. III. Series.
HV6250.25.B37 1985   362.8'8   85-21258
ISBN 0-87630-415-3

Published by
BRUNNER/MAZEL, INC.
19 Union Square West
New York, New York 10003

MANUFACTURED IN THE UNITED STATES OF AMERICA

for Arlene

and

for Paul

EDITORIAL NOTE

"You're not the only one." This one simple phrase, at least for one female victim, could have significantly lessened the emotional pain of her memories, the realities of her brother's murder. Indeed, she is not the only one. According to a recent report of the President's Task Force on Victims of Crime, every 23 minutes someone is murdered. The female victim mentioned above was among the first crime victims interviewed by the authors of this remarkable book. Her observations, note the authors, "... became a touchstone for our work, the test against which we have measured everything that is written here."

Morton Bard and Dawn Sangrey, authors of *The Crime Victim's Book,* have produced one of the most significant contributions to understanding and treating crime victims and co-victims (friends and close family members of the victim). The first edition is already a classic among victimology specialists. This second edition is intended for a wider audience.

The Crime Victim's Book is the sixth book in the Brunner/Mazel Psychosocial Stress Book Series. The purpose of the Series is to produce books that expand knowledge about the development, prevention, or effective management of psychosocial stress. The primary readership of this Series includes those mental health practitioners, scholars, and their students who are committed to this purpose.

Books in the Series have focused on the stress associated with a wide variety of psychosocial stressors. Together they form a new wave of thinking about human behavior under extraordinary conditions.

The Crime Victim's Book is the first in the Series to discuss the special psychosocial stress of victims of crime, though it was first published in 1979, a year after the first book in this Series, *Stress Disorders Among Vietnam Veterans.*

In contrast to the other books published in this Series, *The Crime Victim's Book* is just that: a book written from the point of view of the victim *for* the victim. Yet, it is my opinion that this book will be read and referenced by an equal number of professionals. Clinicians, scholars, and others interested in the psychosocial consequences of traumatic events will benefit from this well-written book. One major reason for the interest is the extraordinary number of people victimized by crime, including the President of the United States and his family.

In recent years there has been a surge of concern for the plight of the crime victim in this country. This new sensitivity emerged in part by the influence of this book. Dr. Morton Bard, Professor of Psychology at the Graduate School of the City University of New York, chaired and contributed to the final report of the American Psychological Association's Task Force on the Victims of Crime and Violence.

The new elements of this second edition of their book are, in some ways, a by-product of the first edition. The appendix includes excerpts from two of the most important final reports in the area of crime victimization. The 1982 report of the President's Task Force on Victims of Crime, chaired by Lois Haight Herrington, includes 75 recommendations to segments of society which are relevant to the victims of crime. Included, for example, are recommendations to hospitals to improve the quality of medical and emergency care of the crime victims and co-victims. The Task Force recommended five methods to relieve the severe psychological suffering. The mental health community should:

1. Develop and provide immediate and long-term psychological treatment programs for victims of crime and their families.
2. Establish training programs that will enable practitioners to treat crime victims and their families.
3. Study the immediate and long-term psychological effects of criminal victimization.
4. Work with public agencies, victim compensation boards, and private insurers to make psychological treatment readily available to crime victims and their families.

5. Establish and maintain direct liaison with other victim service agencies.

The 1984 Task Force Report to the American Psychological Association's Board of Directors proposed seven objectives:

1. Psychologists involved in service delivery should acquire specific, identifiable skills in direct intervention with victims.
2. More psychologists should acquire specialized consultative skills to increase the capacity of indigenous workers to help victims.
3. More psychologists should become involved in initiating and evaluating changes in the criminal justice system designed to ameliorate the problems victims experience in that system.
4. More psychologists who are prepared to do so should actually provide service directly to victims, to indigenous helping systems, and in the criminal justice system.
5. Psychologists should be more involved in gaining helpful interventions for victims.
6. There should be more public awareness about the mental health needs of victims, and the roles of psychology and psychologists can serve in helping victims.
7. The APA should endorse laws and legal arrangements that facilitate the realization of victims' interests and encourage the formal evaluation of these arrangements.

There continue to be significant and far-reaching changes in both the public and private sector. One major effort was the recently enacted Federal crime victim-assistance program. This program will provide funds for psychotherapy for crime victims to promote more immediate emotional recovery.

The sensitive men and women who developed these recommendations were influenced by Bard and Sangrey's important work. Among other things, *The Crime Victim's Book* provides the scholarly insights, sets the political agenda, and reminds us all to say to crime victims, at the very least, "You are not the only one."

Charles R. Figley, Ph.D.
Series Editor

CONTENTS

ACKNOWLEDGMENTS

This book could not have been written without the interest and support of many people. We are indebted, first of all, to the many victims of personal crime who were willing to share their experiences with us. Their openness and clarity has deepened our perception. Their insight has confirmed our faith in the ability of people to understand and deal with the adversity in their lives. Their strength has encouraged us. We are grateful for their trust and for their courage.

We would like to thank James Garofalo, Project Director at the Criminal Justice Research Center (Albany, New York), for his help with statistical matters; Edwin J. Donovan of Pennsylvania State University and Harry O'Reilly, Director of the Institute for the Study of Investigative Services at the Criminal Justice Center, John Jay College, the City University of New York, for their insights into the role of the police; James Rowland, Chief Probation Officer of the County of Fresno (California), for his help in exploring the work of victim advocates; and Leslie Crocker Snyder, Special Assistant Attorney General and Chief of Trials in the office of Special New York State Prosecuter John F. Keenan, for her help with the material on the criminal-justice system.

Portions of the manuscript were read by Lady Borton; Harriet Connolly of the Center for Social Research, the City University of New York; Myra Damsky; Irwin Katz of the Graduate School, the City University of New York; Sandra Kiersky; Patrick V. Murphy of the Police Foundation; Alice Napier; Mario Riservato; Charles H. Rogovin of the Temple University Law School; David Z. Rosensweig; William Ryan of Boston College; Elletta Sangrey; Madeline Schroth; Saul Touster of the Graduate School, the City University of New York; and Janet Vrchota. We are grateful for their comments and support.

We would like to thank D. Ellen Boyle, Maureen Mahany, and Jacqueline Williams for assistance with research and interviewing; Mimi Eisenberg, who typed the final manuscript, bringing order out of chaos; and Myra Damsky, who kept the wolves at bay so we could work.

The dedication acknowledges our greatest personal debt, to Arlene and Paul, who have nourished us through this long process of making a book by believing in it and in us every day of the way.

MORTON BARD
DAWN SANGREY
September 1978

The work of the Second Editon has been supported by many people: those who encouraged us to persist in our efforts to bring out a revision; those who helped us to document the many changes that have occurred in victim rights and services in the past six years; those who told us that *The Crime Victim's Book* has been helpful to them. We want to extend special thanks to: Gregory Brady, Director, Office of Victims, U.S. Department of Justice; Lois Haight Herrington, Assistant U.S. Attorney General; Charles R. Figley, Editor of the Brunner/Mazel Psychosocial Stress Series of which this revision is a part, without whom we would not have the second edition; James Garofalo, Executive Director of the Hindelang Criminal Justice Research Center, SUNY Albany; Arnold S. Kahn, who edited the Final Report of the American Psychological Association Task Force on the Victims of Crime and Violence; Dorine Rootsaert, Reference Specialist, National Victims Resource Center; Max Siegel, Past President, American Psychological Association; John Stein, Director of Public Affairs, National Organization for Victim Assistance; Eileen M. Wall, Manager, National Victims Resource Center; and Marlene Young, Executive Director, National Organization for Victim Assistance. Joanne Modlin helped with the research for this second edition, and Myra Damsky is still the world's champion at keeping the wolves at bay.

MORTON BARD
DAWN SANGREY
April 1985

INTRODUCTION

It would have been easier if there had been someone to tell me what was going on and to prepare me for the things that happened after—with my family, my friends, the police, the courts. Someone to help sort it out, to say:"You're not the only one." I felt so terribly alone. If only there had been some way to find out about other people in the same situation, to hear what they were going through so I could compare it to what I was going through. More than anything else, I just needed to understand what was happening.
—Sister of a murder victim

We were just beginning to work on this book when we talked with a woman whose sister had been murdered several years earlier. It was a long story, and most of it was sad. She told us about the phone call in the middle of the night from the police. "Come down to the station," they said. "It's about your sister." She told us about identifying the body. She told us about the family members who were suddenly distant, about the friends who did nothing because they didn't know what to do. She told us about the trial and the judge who gave a light sentence because the murderer had never been in trouble before. She said that it was still hard for her to accept the loss and go on with her life.

She talked for more than three hours, filling reels of tape, and we had the feeling—as we would have again in conversations with other victims—that she had never had a chance to say these things before. At the end of the interview, we asked her if there was anything that might have helped in the first weeks and months after the crime. Her reply, which is quoted above, was so remarkable that it became a touchstone for our work, the test against which we have measured everything that is written here. We believe that some of her suffering was unnecessary. We have written this book so that victims and those who care about them can understand and overcome the isolation, confusion, and distress that follows victimization.

Every victim of personal crime is confronted with a brutal reality: the deliberate violation of one human being by another. The crime may be a murder or a rape, a robbery or a burglary, the theft of an automobile, a pocket picking or a purse snatching—but the essential internal injury is the same. Victims have been assaulted—emotionally and sometimes physically—by a predator who has shaken their world to its foundations.

There is nothing more isolating than the pain of violation. It forces victims to question themselves and their world because it destroys two essential beliefs: their sense of trust and their sense of control over their lives. After the crime is over, victims begin to struggle with their reactions to the experience. They are often almost overcome with fear, anger, guilt, and shame. They may feel contaminated and unworthy of help. Their relationships with family and friends can be seriously disrupted, and if they become involved with the police and the courts, they may come to believe that no one understands or cares about what has happened to them.

The pain of victimization is compounded by the victim's belief that he or she is the only person who has ever experienced these reactions. Victims commonly think that their feelings are unique, peculiar, weird, even crazy. This conviction can intensify their sense of isolation, bringing them to the edge of panic. But their feelings are not crazy. Everything we know about the stress of victimization indicates that the reactions of victims are both logical and understandable.

Even with the best support, the victim of a serious personal crime will go through a difficult period of adjustment. Some victims are disabled by the scars of their experience for the rest of their lives. We do not intend to belittle the victim's pain or to discount its effects. But some of the pain is unnecessary. Victims need not be imprisoned in their own fear and self-doubt. The purpose of this book is to liberate them from these feelings so that they can renew the most healing of all discoveries: None of us is alone.

Repairing the damage of victimization is an intricate and highly individual process. People react to the stress in many different ways. The victim's experience cannot be reduced to a set of formulas; it's more complicated than that. There are no prescriptions here, no inspirational peptalks.

But the healing process can be supported. Victims need to understand what's going on, what's happening to them. They need to know what they are experiencing is a normal, appropriate reaction. They need specific information about the reasons for their feelings. They need to know how their loved ones will react, what they can expect from the police and the courts, and how to get help when they need it. All of this information is included here.

We begin in Chapter 1 with the source of people's expectations about victimization—the myths and fantasies about crime that are played out in the media every day. Crime victims are invariably surprised by their experience because almost everything they have learned about victimization is a lie. They are totally unprepared for the reality.

In Chapter 2 we move to the crime itself, describing its immediate impact on the victim and exploring the meaning of the violation of self. Every victim experiences a crisis reaction through which he or she must come to recover from the victimization. We outline the three stages of the typical reaction in Chapter 3, explaining how the victim can best be supported at each stage. One of the most important parts of the work of recovery is the victim's search for a reason, an explanation for why the crime happened. This process, and the self-blame that often accompanies it, are discussed in Chapter 4.

The reactions of other people, including loved ones and strangers such as the police, can have a strong influence on the victim's recovery. The victim's feelings of guilt and shame, a sense of being stigmatized by the victimization, are often strengthened by the insensitivity of others. Chapter 5 deals with these reactions and the reasons for them. In Chapter 6 we explain the workings of the criminal-justice system and the attitudes and values that victims often encounter in their dealings with the police and the courts.

The last chapter contains information about how to get help—resources for emotional support, medical care, legal assistance, crime-victim compensation, and other victim needs. It also includes strategies for making the institutions that deliver these services more responsive. Three appendices contain a discussion of nationwide crime statistics, designed to help the victim put his or her experience into perspective; a guide to the structure of the criminal-justice system; a dictionary of legal terms; and a list of specific resources for many of the most common victim needs.

This book is also intended for the loved ones of crime victims, the family and friends who often become caught in their own strong feelings about the crime. Victims need the understanding and support of those who know and care about them. Often these people can make the difference between full recovery and lingering disability. Specific suggestions are given in each chapter to guide these loved ones so that they, too, can understand their reactions and make themselves available to give support at each step of the healing process.

Many professionals will find this book useful in their work. Police officers, prosecutors, court officials, nurses and doctors, social workers, counselors, and those who work in victim-assistance centers will recognize many of the problems we explore. The institutions that are supposed to serve victims are sometimes unresponsive, but there are many people in them who want to supply what the victim needs. This book will help those who care about victims to focus more clearly on their needs and to avoid inflicting the additional pain that victims have often suffered from bureaucracies in the past.

In a sense, this book is for every person who has heard footsteps in the night and been afraid. We are all victims of crime because we are all afraid of victimization. The information in this book can set us free: free from unrealistic expectations, free from fear of the unknown, free from the need to blame the victim, free to offer help. It can cut through the victim's terrible sense of isolation. It can help us to recognize exactly what it is that we fear, to acknowledge our own vulnerability, and to affirm the strength and intelligence of those who have been victimized.

This book is not a scholarly analysis, although it has been illuminated by many disciplines and is firmly grounded in social and psychological theory. We began our work with a rough formulation from crisis-intervention study about the effects of victimization on the victims of personal crime. By talking with a number of victims, we have confirmed and refined our formulation. Our results are suggestive rather than definitive. The book is frankly subjective in that we have made no attempt to stifle the influence of our own experiences and outlooks in the shaping of the material.

We have learned that the victim's perception is central and valid and, in the best sense, nonnegotiable. The crime victims themselves are the real experts of this book. Those with whom we have talked have been remarkably resilient people, able to come through the worst experiences very well. In doing the book, we have discovered that most people have great reserves of strength from which to draw in times of crisis. We have also been reminded that for every wound there is a healing process.

PREFACE TO THE SECOND EDITION

Much has changed in the six years since the first edition of *The Crime Victim's Book* was published in 1979. The victim's movement has burgeoned into a major social force, stimulating both an increased awareness of victims' needs and a significant change in public policy with respect to victims' rights. We are delighted to see these long overdue changes, and this Second Edition has been revised and updated to reflect recent advances in victim services and in victim-rights legislation.

But the core of the book remains the same because the experience of being a crime victim has not changed. Every victim must still confront the awful reality of his or her deliberate violation by another human being. And while many improvements have been achieved in the victim support system, much work is yet to be done. Social change is always a slow process—one that is especially resisted by bureaucratic institutions such as the criminal-justice system. Progress has been made, but many problems persist.

Our own perspective has been altered by the distance of six years' time, and we see things in *The Crime Victim's Book* that we didn't notice before. We see the class bias in our discussion of the victim's experience, for example. The victims we describe here are people like us—middle-class, educated, relatively affluent, with high expectations for places like hospitals and courtrooms. These people were raised to believe that the police officer is your friend. Many victims of crime, especially the ethnic-minority poor, have had very different experiences with the police and the courts and the other institutions that deal with victims—and so their expectations are very different. We thought at first to correct this bias in the Second Edition by adding their perspective to our discussion, but we soon realized that we had no basis on which to do that: no experience of our own and no empiric data from the work of others. We realized, in short, that *nobody knows* except the victims themselves what it is like to be poor and the victim of a personal crime. So the best we can do is to acknowledge our bias and to note that it is shared by too much of the victim research we know.

A second thing we have noticed about *The Crime Victim's Book* is how little we said in the first edition about the complicated issue of crimes that occur within families and among people who know each other. The past six years have seen a great increase in public awareness of these crimes and a growing advocacy movement for its victims. As family-violence research continues and matures, the differences between stranger-to-stranger crime and crime between nonstrangers may emerge more clearly. At the same time, we believe that all such crimes share a critical element: the intention to violate is always present, however it may be rationalized by the offender.

The issue of intentionality, upon which our view of personal crime as a violation of self depends, has provoked much comment and discussion since the publication of the first edition. Many thoughtful critics have questioned whether each and every crime against a person is indeed motivated by the intention to harm. We appreciate this opportunity to clarify our thinking.

There are three ways to look at any personal crime: from the perspective of the victim, from the perspective of the offender, and from the perspective of a third-party observer. From the victim's point of view, any destructive act committed by another person is seen as intentional. You can't help feeling that it was done on purpose when it's done to you. In an automobile accident, for example, in which a person is killed, the surviving family will feel that the driver of the other car caused the accident on purpose and ought to be blamed and punished. This is irrational, perhaps, but there it is. From the victim's perspective, life is full of interpersonal, destructive acts which are experienced as an insult to the ego and elicit the range of responses—fear, anger, guilt, etc.—we have outlined in this book.

The criminal offender has a very different perspective on things. Offenders always disown intentionality. They never take personal responsibility for what they do to their victims. Most commonly, the offender says, in effect, "I'm doing this, but it's not my fault." Offenders see themselves as victims, too—victims of poverty or of bad parents or of a racist society. They will even blame the victim for what they do. A robber who shoots the man he first threatens only to rob may say afterwards, "He made me do it. I could see in his eyes that he was going to jump me." From the point of view of the offender, the crime is never an act of intentional personal violation.

Among third-party observers, both points of view are expressed, although an individual tends to see crime consistently from one perspective or the other. Some of those in society invariably see the act of personal crime as an intentional harming of the innocent victim. Others tend to see it as invariably an act without personal responsibility in which the criminal is as victimized as his or her prey. (This ability of people to see crime from both perspectives helps to account for the fact that both extremes of the political spectrum can espouse the cause of crime victims' rights.)

This book sees personal crime from the perspective of the victim. What we have written here is intended to be helpful to those who have suffered at the hands of the offender. Part of our helpfulness is to assume the point of view of the victim, to see the crime as an intentional and destructive violation of the self.

Beyond the empathy and understanding needed to foster the healing of individual crime victims, there are broad social and public policy efforts underway to assist victims in many ways. An agenda for the future has emerged. A new feature of this Second Edition is an appendix which includes major excerpts from the recommendations of two important task forces: The President's Task Force on Victims of Crime and the American Psychological Association Task Force on the Victims of Crime and Violence.

The revision reflects the comments and suggestions of many readers who have been in touch with us since the publication of the first edition. We have been especially moved by the letters from crime victims who have been helped by the information and support they have found in these pages. We hope that victims, their families and friends, and all of the professionals who deal with victims in their work will find even more help in this new, revised edition.

MORTON BARD
DAWN SANGREY
April 1985

The Crime Victim's Book

Second Edition

1

I Never Thought It Could Happen to Me

I never thought it could happen to me. I was very comfortable living on this street. I figured it was safe here—my friends are here and this is my home. And you just don't think that someone is going to come in like that and take your things. It may happen on some other street, but not in my house, not on my street.

—Burglary victim

People are fascinated by crime. The newspapers are full of the suffering inflicted by one human being on another—murder and mayhem cover the front pages like some contagion. Nowhere is the fascination more clear than in the popularity of what the television networks call their "action-adventure" programs. Night after night in colors that are brighter than life the drama unfolds: Criminals do terrible things, and the forces of justice pursue them. We seem transfixed by these violent images.

And yet the victims of actual crimes are invariably taken by surprise. No matter how preoccupied a person has been with crime, no matter how fearful, the raw experience of victimization is still a shock. Each crime victim says it, in one way or another: "I never thought it could happen to me."

3

Some of the surprise is inevitable. Every personal crime, from pocketpicking to murder, catches the victim off guard. You just can't be on your guard all the time. People need to perceive themselves as invulnerable so that they can function. We need to believe that the world is safe. Every day we renew this faith in a thousand unconscious expectations: The sun will come up; the water in the tap is safe to drink; the cars speeding past will stay in the proper lanes; the stranger who walks behind us is harmless. No one can live in a continual state of seige—and so the attack, when it comes, is always unexpected.

But the shock of being victimized goes deeper. When a crime victim says: "I never thought it could happen to me," he or she also means: "This isn't what I expected." Despite years of reading about crime, hours of watching cops and robbers on television, victims and their loved ones are not prepared for the reality.[1] The crime itself and especially the events after the crime are full of nasty surprises. The media do not help us to understand what being a crime victim means.

Expectations and Realities

Crime news and crime drama attract huge audiences because they tap the undercurrent of an unresolved anxiety. Symbolically the crime-show rape, the arson on the eleven o'clock news, and the late movie murder are the same—they are all unpredictable, uncontrollable, life-threatening events. Sensational crimes epitomize a central human fear. Something bad is going to happen to me, and I won't be able to stop it. What holds us in front of the violent images is a wish to control the threat, to understand it, and thus to be safe.

Issues of fear and control are embedded in all violent themes. Skyjacking fascinates because people are afraid of flying—despite the airlines' considerable efforts to make air travel a pleasant experience. Murder mysteries have been popular for centuries in one form or another; we all have a profound fear of sudden, violent death. In the same way, crime has become prime-time television entertainment because so many people are afraid of being victimized.

The fear itself is appropriate enough. People are naturally afraid of crime. Victimization is a fearful experience. But while the news and entertainment media are clearly preoccupied with crime, they do not encourage us to confront our anxiety directly. They focus our attention instead on certain external details of the crime experience, creating a distraction that feeds the fear and keeps us from dealing with the reality.

Victimization continues to be a nasty surprise partly because we don't think about crime victims when we think about crime. The way crime is treated in both news and drama encourages us to identify with the other actors—the criminals and the police. People condemn the criminal, of course, but they are also intrigued. Americans have always been fascinated with good guys and bad guys. We have a long tradition of romantic outlaws, and our ambivalence about criminals runs deep.

The heroes and villains on the screen have an extraordinary power—the ability to kill—often symbolized by the guns they carry. The ordinary viewer (even if he or she owns a gun) is powerless by comparison. These characters don't have to struggle ineffectively with their problems as the rest of us do. They have magical instruments for conflict resolution—just press the trigger and the problem goes away.[2] Both criminals and police officers can go behind the scenes, into the secret places in the community—the darkened bars, the brothels, the courtrooms, the jails. They are the insiders, the ones who know what's really going on. Most of them are loners; they have no families to tie them down. Their nights are charged with excitement, filled with adventure. They don't have to keep their tempers or mind their manners. Nobody tells them what to do. By identifying with these extraordinary people, the viewer expresses the wish to be special, powerful, invulnerable.

A crime victim is quite unexciting by comparison. The crime-story victim rarely holds the center of the stage because victims are neither glamorous nor powerful. The victim is a loser, an ineffective cipher in the power game. So crime victims are virtually ignored, clearly categorized as the least interesting people in the drama.

Much of the media treatment of actual crime is also devoted to the exploits of criminals and police. We live in a culture that makes television specials and best-selling books out of mass murder. Criminals get the widest possible coverage for the grisly details of their stories.[3] Victims are generally relegated to a sentimental paragraph or two, a faded high-school snapshot on the inside page. The names of the criminals become household words, but nobody remembers who the victims were.

Presenting crime in this way allows us to ignore the victim's experience. It's almost as if the victim has become invisible. Occasionally we are treated to a quick, lurid glimpse of the battered body or a brief interview with the victim's relatives, but beyond these sensational tidbits, the media generally leave the victim alone. Focusing on the victim would interject a cold note of reality: Crime means that innocent people get hurt—people like us.

When a person is actually victimized in a personal crime, he or she finds that no one is very interested. People have been conditioned to think about and react to crime by focusing on two things: what the criminal did and how the police are going to catch him. In a striking number of cases, they do exactly that when confronted by a real victim. If your house is burglarized, you will probably be asked, "What did he take?" It is unlikely that anyone will want to know how you are feeling. Victims themselves do it. A man who had been beaten and robbed talked with his son for an hour about the crime; the entire conversation was devoted to the police investigation of the case.

It is natural to avoid painful subjects, and so it is easy to follow the media's example. But the victims of real personal crime invariably suffer when their experience is ignored. They feel left out, abandoned by their loved ones and the professionals who are supposed to serve them. They may try to hide their own feelings and reactions, only to have them surface in strange ways. The reality of any crime includes a victim who has been hurt—and not necessarily physically. When we neglect this reality, we injure the victim further.

Crime victims are often surprised by the depth and severity of their emotional reaction to victimization. When we think about the effects of crime on people, we tend to focus on external events such as physical injury and property loss. The media especially foster our sense that crime is physically violent. News coverage ignores hundreds of purse snatchings, burglaries, and other "minor" crimes in favor of the relatively few murders. Television has become a *circus maximus* where police officers, criminals, sheriffs, outlaws, gangsters, and other professional combatants spend their hour wreaking havoc on each other and a variety of innocents. Crime is practically defined in the media as a sensational, physically violent, external event—an event whose effects are obvious and bloody.

The exaggerated prominence given to physically violent crimes fosters a central misconception about the injuries that crime victims can suffer. The actual victims of real personal crime often suffer grievous and painful injuries that are not physical. They may lose their capacity to trust people, for example; they may be overwhelmed with guilt and shame; their relations with their loved ones may suffer serious disruption. These invisible wounds are rarely part of the media portrait of crime, and people tend to underestimate their significance. A victim who has not been physically harmed may find that his or her friends consider the crime a minor incident, no matter how the victim feels about it. They think they know what serious crime is—they've seen enough of it on television.

Few victims are prepared for the aftermath of victimization, the ways that a crime can echo and reverberate against the rest of the victim's life. The media present crime and its effects in highly structured segments—four column inches of print, thirty minutes of air time. Crime stories have a beginning, middle, and end. In dramatizations, the ending is usually happy since the main purpose of these programs is to entertain. Sorrow is overcome, broken bones are mended, criminals are captured and put behind bars—all in the space of sixty minutes. Everything works out all right.

These happy endings and formalized structures prepare us for a similar tidiness in reality. We have been reassured, falsely, that the wounds inflicted by crime are time-limited and easily healed. But the injuries of actual crime victims are rarely mended so easily or quickly. It often takes weeks or months for a victim to regain emotional equilibrium. The effects of the victimization are felt in many ways over an extended period of time. Normal recoveries are uneven—lapses into helplessness or fear can be expected long after the crime.

Television crime shows can also contribute to victim frustration by raising the victim's hope that the crime will be solved and the criminal brought to justice. An overwhelming majority of the crimes committed in TV dramas are solved, customarily within the hour. Typically, the television detective begins working on the case immediately after the crime is committed. He or she does not stop to fill out reports, work on other cases, go to court, have dinner with the family, or take some suits to the cleaners. And the TV detective almost always gets "his man."

The reality is very different. Most real crimes are never solved. And while everybody realizes that some criminals get away, a victim often feels cheated and angry if no arrest is made. Victims can't help feeling that their drama ought to work out the way the stories on television do.

If, on the other hand, a suspect is arrested and the case does go to trial, the victim is likely to suffer another disillusionment. Most people have never been inside a real criminal courtroom, but a great number have watched dramatizations of courtroom scenes. Perry Mason argued his cases with dignity and passion in a wood-paneled hall filled with silent, admiring spectators. From such television and movie images, many victims develop high expectations about court procedures—and their experience in an actual courtroom is often disappointing and disturbing. Stand-up comics and at least one situation comedy in a recent television season may make light of the disorder in the legal process by suggesting that it is simply hilarious, but a crime victim seeking justice from the courts is more likely to be enraged than amused.

Confronting the Victim's Experience

People can adjust to reality when they know what to expect. Experiences that meet our expectations are easier to handle, even if they are difficult and painful. But whenever experience fails to meet expectation, a person's adaptation is complicated. Most of us have had little or no opportunity to understand the reality of crime victimization. We have been misled and confused by the media. And so we are unprepared when the criminal strikes.

But the crime victim's experience need not be a mystery. Victims of personal crime, their loved ones, and the professionals who serve them can come to understand what happens to victims. The rest of this book is designed to foster that understanding. It provides a detailed description of the victim's experience during and after the crime. It explains how victims feel and how they and their loved ones are likely to react. It details the problems that can arise and tells how to get help if they do. When victims and those who care for them understand these things, they may still be surprised, but they will also know what to expect.

It *can* happen to you or to someone you love. Everyone is vulnerable to personal crime. But if you can confront that reality, you can also learn what happens and how to help.

NOTES

1. The relationship among actual criminal events, the perception of these events, and the presentation in the media of both actual and fictional crimes are many and complex. It has been demonstrated, for example, that people who watch a lot of television are more afraid of crime than those who watch less (reference to come). The 1984 Report of the Attorney General's Task Force on Family Violence recommends a reduction in the amount of violence shown on television and in the movies. "The Task Force heard continually from both victims and professionals that violence is most often learned behavior and that these behavior patterns are frequently passed from one generation to the next. As the research on the subject is published, the evidence is becoming overwhelming that just as witnessing violence in the home may contribute to normal adults and children learning and acting out violent behavior, violence on TV and the movies may contribute to the same result." (p.110)

2. The average number of violent acts per hour of prime-time television has remained about the same in the past 10 years, but the weapons used have become increasingly more sophisticated. Whereas in earlier years a single gunman with a simple handgun was the rule, nowadays we have terrorist bands armed with bombs and the A-Team, who carry M-60 machine guns and an incredible array of other military-style weapons. See "Why TV Won't Let Up On Violence" by Sally Bedell Smith, the *New York Times*, January 13, 1985, section 2, p. 1.

3. In the past, criminals elevated to celebrity status by their sensational crimes have also occasionally commanded large sums of money for the media rights to their stories, but legislation has recently been enacted to discourage this particular irony. Section 1402 of the

Federal Victims of Crime Act of 1984 provides that a federal judge may order all "literary profits" of convicted federal criminals paid into a Crime Victims Fund for victim compensation and other victim services. Similar statutes have been enacted, as of January 31, 1985, in 32 states; typically these laws provide that all monies derived by a criminal from his or her notoriety be paid into an account for the benefit of victims of crime, often specifically the victims of the particular criminal.

2

Violation: The Invisible Wound

You feel stripped naked. You feel as if someone has exposed you totally. . . . You're powerless. . . . You're powerless. *Violation* is an adult way to explain that, but it isn't an adult response. It's reminiscent of the kind of helplessness that goes back to early childhood. And I think that's what makes it so crucially painful. Because you can't fight back.

—Victim of a purse snatching

Every crime against a person is an act of violation. Some criminals are physically violent: muggers, rapists, murderers.[1] Some threaten bodily harm. Others break into victims' homes and take their possessions. But whatever the mode of attack, the victims suffer a common underlying injury: the violation of self. They are wounded in the very essence of themselves, the center from which every person integrates life.

Victims of personal crime often express their sense of having been attacked in a sacred, inner place. Don Jackson is a young architect

11

who lives in a high-rise building in Chicago.* He was surprised by
a pair of robbers in the elevator of his apartment building as he was
on his way to work. They threatened him with a knife, took his
money, and fled. Don returned to his apartment, called the police,
and then got in the shower and washed himself carefully all over.
He had taken his usual morning shower only an hour earlier, but he
felt dirtied by the crime, as if the thieves had contaminated him in
some way, although they had not even touched him physically. The
violation of self can be experienced as a desecration of the person.

It is an invisible wound, and so it is often overlooked. Physical
violence is external and dramatic, but emotional injury can be at
least as painful. After the police had come and gone, Don called a
friend to tell her about the crime. They talked about how it happened
and about what had been stolen. Then his friend said, "Well, at least
you weren't hurt." Don was silent but he felt misunderstood, almost
rebuffed. He wanted to say, "Yes I was. Yes I am."

The part that has been hurt is the private inner space that defines
our being. The self is as real as a person's hand or heart, but it isn't
physical. It has no anatomical site. It can be conceptualized as invisible, but within—some call it the soul; others, the spirit; others,
the ego. The self encompasses everything that a person means when
he or she says "I."

The growth and change, adjustment and readjustment that produce an individual self are incredibly complex and quite miraculous.
Becoming one's own person is a lifelong creative process—and this
process *is* the person. As each of us develops, we shape our selves
from all of our experience—the people we know, the things we think
about, all of our fears and hopes and dreams. The self is the part that
makes each of us a unique individual.

Personal possessions can take on symbolic significance as expressions of self. The way a person dresses, his or her car, home, and
furnishings are all outward manifestations of inner identify. We sur-
round ourselves with extensions of ourselves that have emotional
value because they express who we are. Logically, then, the theft or
destruction of a person's possessions can be experienced as a violation of self.

---

*All of the examples in this book are taken from the actual experiences of victims. We have
changed their names and other identifying details to preserve their privacy.

People tend to think in dollar amounts when they measure the loss from theft. But the value of property is much more complex. Karen Ashby has lived in New York City since she was first married, forty years ago. She used to say she lived a charmed life because she'd never been robbed. But last winter she was coming out of the theater and her little black evening purse was snatched from under her arm. Mrs. Ashby is barely five feet tall and she was afraid, but she ran after the thief shouting, "Give that back. It's mine." It's mine. It belongs to me. She treasured that purse for its associations: It was a gift from her husband; she had carried it to parties and special events for years; she lent it to her daughter for her first prom. There wasn't any money in the purse, but it had significance because it represented a part of her life. She felt as if the thief had snatched a piece of her.

Crime victims are also threatened in another dimension because the violation reverberates in their relationships with other people and out into their sense of the world as a whole. Every person is an interweaving of three dynamic strands: physical body, self, and relationships. Anything that affects one part of a person also affects the other parts—everything *is* related to everything else. So a criminal act of violation is never an isolated event that can be contained in one part of the victim's life. It spills over, affecting everything in the victim's experience.

After Mrs. Ashby's purse was snatched, she became nervous whenever she was out after dark. She started involuntarily at the sound of running footsteps. Her husband tried to reason with her. "Look," he said, "you don't have to worry. I'm here. I can protect you." But he was unable to reassure her, and her fear became a problem between them. They began to quarrel about things like whether they should take a cab to a neighborhood movie.

In more serious crimes, the disruption can go on for years. Kevin Johnson was murdered in a sudden confrontation with a stranger five years ago. Kevin is dead, but he left three generations of family, the survivor-victims of the killing. They are still struggling to put their lives back together. Kevin's brother explained the long-term effects of the crime:

It's a terrible thing. I don't think anybody recovers from it. There are too many complications that happen after. How do you bring up children without a father? What do you tell them about his death? They go to school—my little niece in school last week, the teacher said two parents must come to this meeting. She came home and she was shaking. She said to her mother, "You have to tell the teacher. I couldn't tell her."

If I ever met [the murderer] I would say, "You didn't just kill one person. Do you realize what you've done to this family?" Because it's not just one person; he really killed six people. My mother has never gotten over it, to this day. My father has become a very nervous man. And my parents are distant from each other now. Somehow they can't comfort each other.

We had a very open house—I mean as far as we could always discuss things. My parents always talked very openly with us. Even a job change, my father would talk to us about it. That was how it was. But now, my father won't even let us say Kevin's name. When this happened, discussion went right down the drain. Because everybody went into themselves.

Because the violation of self is invisible, it's hard to put your finger on what's wrong here. The people in this family get up, go to work, send their children to school, come home, eat dinner—in this sense, they are functioning. But something essential has gone out of their lives. Each member feels estranged, off balance, as if some central ordering principle has been lost. The dynamic interaction within the family group has broken down. Their sense of being right with each other and the world is gone.

Sources of Centering

Many victims of personal crime experience this loss of equilibrium. The world is suddenly out of whack. Things don't work the way they used to. Victims have been deprived of their sense of personal control; they feel as helpless as small children. In normal development, people grow from totally dependent newborns into adults who can manage their own lives and handle the normal stresses of day-to-day living. Two stages of this growth are especially important because they are so threatened by the violation of self: the development of trust and the development of autonomy.

Newborn infants gradually learn that their bodies, their environment, and the people in it can be counted on to meet their needs. The certainty and continuity of care is the baby's first experience of a benign and manageable world. We develop a feeling in these early days that is essential for our further growth: the sense that the world is a reasonably predictable place. Psychologist Erik H. Erikson calls this feeling "basic trust."[2] It fosters a sense of invulnerability in a familiar and essentially harmless environment.

The criminal act of violation compromises the victim's sense of trust. It is a clear demonstration that the environment is not predictable and that it can be harmful. Everyone realizes these facts intellectually, of course, but people tend to carry on their lives as if the world were basically a trustworthy place. We could not function at all if we did not make this assumption on some level. If the world were entirely dangerous, the only way to be safe would be to stay in bed with the covers over your head.

Because crime is an interpersonal event, the victim's feeling of security in the world of other people is seriously upset. The crime victim has been deliberately violated by another person. The victim's injury is not an accident; it is the direct result of the conscious, malicious intention of another human being. Some people can't be trusted—again, we all know that, but the victim is confronted with human malevolence in a very graphic way.

The other essential component of a person's equilibrium is the sense of autonomy.[3] As infants we are all quite literally dependent on others for life. A person starts out in life as a sponge, soaking up experiences from the environment, other people, and his or her own self that blend together to make an emerging personality. The developing child gradually learns to master the world—to walk and talk, to fight for toys and share them, to read and fill out job applications, to work and to love.

The ability to take charge of one's own life is the central qualification for adulthood. Getting there, developing from a baby into an adult, is a difficult and perilous transition. It takes a long time. It is a hard-fought battle for most people, and a source of great ambivalence—it's so nice to be taken care of, but it's also nice to be out from under someone else's thumb.

Adults need to be able to say, "I can stand on my own two feet. I know what I am doing with my life. *This* is who I am." Threats to autonomy are felt deeply and painfully in the self, and in a personal crime the victim invariably experiences this threat.[4] Whether the offender is a burglar or a rapist, a pickpocket or a robber, the message to the victim is the same: "You are *not* your own person. Right now you belong to me. I'm taking over, and there is nothing you can do about it." For some moment of time, however brief, the victim is powerless.

In crimes against personal property, the threat to autonomy may be somewhat muted. The victim whose purse is snatched loses control over her life for only a split second. The violation is a signal that her mastery of the world can be limited, her freedom circumscribed by the need to take precautions. It is a subtle threat.

Crimes that involve personal confrontation threaten autonomy much more directly. In any face-to-face encounter with a criminal the victim is painfully aware that his or her survival is on the line. Whether the threat is stated or implied, the loss of autonomy is absolute—the victim surrenders control on pain of death.

Together, trust and autonomy—the conviction that the world is manageable and that you can manage it—give a person a sense of psychological balance. When the self is in this state of equilibrium, everything "works." Things flow along and feel good. This quality of self is most noticeable when it is absent, when things are out of balance. Psychiatrist Karl Menninger has remarked that many of the terms we use to describe a person in emotional trouble come from the metaphor of equilibrium. "The man who feels himself 'falling apart' or 'going to pieces' has some vague sense of the unity and integrity of his personality. He *feels* rather than *knows* this [equilibrium] to be a normal or ideal characteristic of his life. By 'being upset' or 'unbalanced' or 'going to pieces,' he describes by implication an awareness of an equilibrium which we may well call 'the vital balance'."[5]

Every person lives in a kind of steady, moving state, adjusting to changes within the self and in the outside world all the time. The balance is continually shifting. Most people live from one stress to the next; their equilibrium is always being upset in little ways—a family quarrel, a bad report card, a bout with the flu, an unexpected bill. People who live fulfilling lives have learned to roll with the punches, adjusting to these everyday shifts in the order of things. They are able to change in the needed ways so that they regain their equilibrium at more or less comfortable intervals.

Each person has his or her own level of stress tolerance. Something that severely upsets one person may feel quite unimportant to another. But for every person there is a point of stress beyond which the self cannot make the necessary accommodation easily and quickly. Then things get out of hand. When we lose our ability to regain our balance, our lives become seriously disrupted. Being the victim of a personal crime is extremely stressful, well beyond the tolerance level for most, if not all, people. The violation of self undermines the fundamental sources of centering and sends the victim into an emotional tailspin. It takes time and energy and support for victims to regain their balance.[6]

Crimes against People: The Continuum

Personal crimes, crimes that violate the victim, span a broad continuum from pocket picking and burglary at one extreme to rape and murder at the other.[7] Although the injury to the self intensifies as the crime becomes more serious, the degree of violation experienced by an individual victim finally depends on the meaning of the crime in that person's life. What seems a minor incident to one victim may be a personal catastrophe for another. But crimes against people can be differentiated according to the degree of violation inherent in the crime. Rape, for example, is universally experienced as a more serious violation than burglary.

Criminal law distinguishes attempted crimes from those that are completed; attempts are usually classified as lesser offenses. But from

TABLE 2-1
Crimes Against People

POCKET PICKING PURSE SNATCHING	AUTO THEFT	BURGLARY	ROBBERY	ROBBERY WITH ASSAULT	SEXUAL ASSAULT	HOMICIDE
Violation of extension of self: property		Violation of extension of self: home	Violation of extension of self: personal possessions	Violation of extension of self: personal possessions	Violation of extension of self: clothing	Ultimate violation of self—the destruction of the person
Loss of trust		Loss of trust	Loss of trust	Loss of trust	Loss of trust	
Threat to autonomy (control)		Threat to autonomy (control)	Loss of autonomy (control)	Loss of autonomy (control)	Loss of autonomy (control)	
			Threat to survival	Threat to survival	Threat to survival	
				Physical injury to the external self	Physical injury to the external self	
					Violation of internal self	

the victim's point of view, an attempt can be just as violating. The destructive intention of the criminal is as apparent in an unsuccessful crime as in a successful one, and the intention alone is still threatening. The violation may not be as severe, but the impact of an attempted crime is hardly inconsequential.

POCKET PICKING AND PURSE SNATCHING

In pocket picking and purse snatching, the target of the criminal is some extension of the victim's self—the money, the credit cards, the wallet. The victim loses these symbols of self and experiences the violation of trust and autonomy that is at the center of every personal crime. A person expects to be able to walk down the street without having his or her property stolen. When a wallet or purse is taken, the victim suffers a rude reminder of vulnerability. Usually these crimes involve only momentary contact, but they are still personal affronts.

AUTO THEFT

The place of auto theft on the continuum depends upon the significance of the car in the victim's life. For some people their car is a more important extension of self than their home. Where alternative transportation is not available, the loss of an automobile becomes a major disruption, and its impact is intensified by the victim's sense of being stranded. One couple whose car was stolen found that all of their normal routines were affected.

> We really loved that car, you know. It was our first car, the one we got right after we were married, and it had taken us everywhere—to school, to work, on our vacations, everywhere. And then suddenly it was gone. We had to ask people to take us to the grocery store. We had to walk to the laundromat with all our piles of laundry. And whenever we went out anywhere, we had to go with other people and we had to do what they wanted to do. Not that they didn't ask us what we wanted to do, but somebody else always had the last word, and that wears on you after a while. There was no way to get to one of my jobs without a car, so I was getting rides from friends, but I would have quit that job if they hadn't found the car.

BURGLARY

Burglary also involves extensions of the self, but it is more grievous than purse snatching because the offender has violated the home of the victim. Most people feel their homes to be places of refuge and safety, shelters from the dangerous outside. We breathe easier behind our own familiar doors. And our homes are our nests, filled with the people and the things we love. The burglar intrudes on this security and privacy. Burglars quite literally threaten us where we live.

Burglary victims often feel this intrusion much more deeply than the property loss they suffer. In one case the burglars went through all of the personal papers in the house. The father of the family couldn't get over his rage about this invasion of their privacy: "I feel like they *know* about me. They picked through my whole life. When I saw the papers thrown all over, I thought: 'Who's been rummaging around in my life?' " Another victim of burglary was more touched by the loss of her sanctuary: "You think of your house as impregnable, you know, and you find that it isn't like that at all. Somebody can easily get in if they want to."

ROBBERY

Pocket picking, purse snatching, auto theft, and burglary are crimes of stealth. These violations are not accompanied by overt threats of physical violence. In robbery, however, another element is added to the violation.[8] The offender threatens the victim with physical harm. The victim encounters the robber face to face; a person who is robbed is immediately aware of a total loss of control. Robbers confront their victims with an explicit threat: "Your money or your life." The loss of autonomy is complete. If a weapon is involved, this loss is even more acute.

ROBBERY WITH ASSAULT

In robbery with assault the threat is carried out: The victim is physically attacked.[9] Victims of assault experience the terrible fear of losing their lives and the humiliation of being unable to defend themselves. Their bodies are injured so they also carry a painful physical reminder of their loss of autonomy and the deep violation of their trust. These emotional wounds are mirrored in their physical wounds, the concrete evidence that they could not take care of themselves.

SEXUAL ASSAULT

Sexual assault involves further intensification—the privacy of the victim's inner body is violated. "In the crime of rape, the victim is not only deprived of autonomy and control, experiencing manipulation and often injury to the 'envelope' of the self, but also intrusion of inner space, the most sacred and most private repository of the self. It does not matter which bodily orifice is breached. Symbolically they are much the same and have, so far as the victim is concerned, the asexual significance that forceful access has been provided to the innermost source of the ego."[10]

Rape victims suffer the penultimate violation. Short of being killed, there is no greater insult to the self. Extensions of the self are violated—the victim's clothing is disarrayed, perhaps torn. The external self, the physical body, is handled and injured. And the site of the inner self, the interior body space, is also violated. Victims of rape rarely talk about this inner violation. It is simply too painful. But many of them do mention what they have seen so clearly on the rapist's face. "I knew he was going to kill me. I saw it in his eyes."

The rapist uses sexual acts to humiliate and degrade the victim, wrenching these acts out of their usual meaning as expressions of desire and love. The objective in rape is to violate, not to gratify or be sexually gratified. But people are so accustomed to thinking of sex as gratifying that many cannot separate any sexual act from positive feelings. Some grisly jokes result from this confusion: "Why didn't she just lie back and enjoy it?" But force is the antithesis of pleasure.

Rape victims commonly suffer from terrible self-doubt because they cannot separate their feelings about sex from the violence done to them. Rape often goes unreported to the police because the victim is so ashamed. In cases in which the victim is a man—a growing problem among sex crimes—the victim's shame may be tinged with the fear of being regarded as a homosexual. Both men and women victims are often afraid that they will be accused of seducing the rapist, in spite of the fact that seduction or anything else even remotely sexy was entirely absent from their brutal experience.

The crime of rape has become a powerful metaphor for the violation that victims of other crimes experience. One man who had been robbed and beaten in his apartment said that he understood what it must be like to be raped. "If a woman talked to me about being raped, she'd never believe it if I said it to her, but I know what it's like. My home was taken over; my body was taken over; I was violated; I mean I was literally raped. It's an incredible feeling of impotence, when your body is in somebody else's total control, and you're the slave. It's an incredible outrage."

HOMICIDE

Homicide is the ultimate violation, the destruction of the self. The homicide victim's life is abruptly and violently terminated. Those who are left, the loved ones of the dead person and anyone who witnessed the death, have also been violated. These survivor-victims are confronted with their own mortality, with proof positive that they may, at any moment and quite without warning, be deprived of their lives. This shock will have deep and powerful repercussions.

The death of a loved one is always difficult to handle. When death is sudden, the survivors must also cope with the surprise of an unexpected loss. In homicide, there is an additional, cruel dimension: The victim has been deliberately destroyed in a willful and malicious act. The members of Kevin Johnson's family describe this aspect of their loss as central to their inability to recover from his murder.

> My mother said, "If he had been sick or hit by a car, then maybe I could accept it. But they stole him from me." And I felt that she hit it right on the head. Because it's not so much that he's dead—it's how he died. Someone took him, with no more thought than if they were taking a pack of cigarettes. If a person dies of a heart attack, or whatever, you grieve, but in time it heals. You remember the good things. But here the last thing you remember is that he was killed by someone who didn't even know him.

Preexisting Relationships: When Victim and Offender Know One Another

Most reported personal crimes are stranger-to-stranger encounters. The offender is usually not a person whom the victim knows,[11] and for some this gives the crime a terrible impersonality, underscoring its arbitrary and random nature. How can a person who doesn't even know you want to hurt you?

There are also, of course, personal crimes in which the victim and the offender are known to one another. Assault, sexual assault, and murder can occur within the family, for example. Most child abusers are either related to or already known by the child victim. Sometimes neighbors and coworkers and school classmates steal from one another. All of these crimes raise painful questions. They present special problems for the victim and also for the criminal-justice system. Such crimes are psychologically and legally complex in ways that have only begun in recent years to receive the special study they merit.[12]

While it is beyond the scope of this work to analyze the complexities of personal crimes in which the offender and the victim know each other, much of what we say here is relevant to these crimes. It is especially important to note that even where there has been a preexisting relationship, the objective of the offender does not change. A man who beats his wife may tell himself that he is only chastening her, just as a child molester may truly believe in the loving goodness of the act. But the basic motivation of such behaviors is to violate the integrating self, however else they may be justified.

Special Vulnerabilities: Special Victims

Certain people have vulnerabilities which affect them more intensely when they are victims of crime. Because they occupy a special place in society, their experience of the violation of self has a different character, and they often suffer additional complications. Among these special victims are the physically and mentally handicapped, the elderly, children, and homosexuals.

People who are blind or confined to a wheelchair or deaf, for example, are especially unable to defend themselves against the criminal's attack because they can neither flee nor fight. A retarded individual is especially vulnerable to manipulation and trickery. The defenses employed by the physically and mentally intact are not available to these special victims. Their vulnerability increases their sense of violation when they are the victims of crime.

Among the very old and the very young, a similar powerlessness prevails. The elderly who have failing physical powers feel the threat of a blow or of being knocked down more acutely than a stronger, younger person does. Old bones break so easily and mend so slowly. The knowledge of their limitations greatly increases the fear of the elderly, as well. In contrast, the very young may be at risk because they know no fear. Children are special victims when their innocence and inexperience exposes them to exploitation. They are also more easily victimized by physical and sexual abuse.

The special vulnerabilities of each of these groups arouses a heightened compassion when they are victimized. Crimes against them are seen as especially atrocious, and these victims often elicit passionate interest and support from law enforcement personnel and others who have the opportunity to help them after the crime.

Homosexuals are especially vulnerable to crime because of their stigmatized status. Those who exploit the gay and lesbian population may see them as "fair game" since many homosexuals keep their sexual preference secret. There is also a pattern of abuse whose object seems to be the relief of unconscious conflict in the offender. Homosexuals can arouse a rage which is expressed in harassment, taunts, threats, assault, and even homicide—and all may be in the service of destroying that which the violator suspects in himself. If there is some secret concern about one's own masculinity, for example, what better way to purge it than by harming a person who embodies the feared characteristic? Unhappily, gays or lesbians who are so victimized have little reason to expect support from the larger community or the criminal-justice system, and the absence of such support can increase their sense of isolation and deepen the violation they experience.

Community and Chaos

The violation of personal crime disrupts the lives of individual victims by destroying their personal sense of order and control. It also disrupts the standard of order in the community, and so each crime is a social violation as well as a personal one.

Order in the community depends upon the internal equilibrium of each individual in that community. Each person contributes to the life of the family, the neighborhood, and the nation so that these larger human systems work. People establish and manage their homes, care for their children, and produce and exchange goods and services within the shelter of a dynamic and essentially balanced social order.

The social equilibrium is maintained through social custom—a vast invisible network that holds us together and largely determines the way that we treat each other. Relatively few of these expectations and values have been formalized into laws. They are, for the most part, quite informal, even unconscious.[13] The fact that we expect parents to take care of their children, for example, is so much a part of our daily lives that we don't even think about it. Much of our daily behavior is governed by conventions that have the force of social law.

Social order works in much the same way as biological order does. In the human body, individual cells, tissues, and organs function together according to biological law to maintain the equilibrium of a healthy organism. This orderly process keeps us going physically just as the customs of our community keep us going socially.

Both the community and the body are threatened with disorder when the laws of the systems are broken. Biological disorder can take many forms—from a digestive upset to a massive infection. Social disorder occurs whenever the harmony of the community is upset. Child abuse is one example; war is another. In most cases, the system is able to right the balance, restoring order and reestablishing its integrity. But some disorders are so destructive that they threaten the system with breakdown; some upsets are so severe that the balance cannot be restored and the life of the system is threatened.

One of the most destructive biological disorders is a group of diseases called cancer. These more than 350 disorders have one thing in common—wild, uncontrolled cellular growth. Physical malignancy is a profound threat to the lawful order of the body. Cancer destroys the complex and elegant interlocking of body systems that work together to sustain life. The fundamental organization of the body may fragment under the impact of malignant attack. Indeed, the most basic biological drive—self-preservation—can be compromised.

The threat of cancer can serve as an analogy for the threat of criminal violation.[14] The community may be seen as a complex and elegant interlocking of systems that sustains the life of the body politic. Law-abiding individuals are like the healthy cells of the physical body; they make up the tissue of society in an orderly social process. The violating criminal can be regarded as a social malignancy. The many varieties of personal crime share one thing in common—they are the acts of destructive people who are beyond social control. Social malignancy is a profound threat to the lawful order of the community and can threaten the very life of a society.

What the criminal does—whether it is stealing property or harming another person physically—is frightening. But what a criminal *means* is even more frightening. Because they are violent predators, criminals are the embodiment of chaos. They stand against all we struggle for, personally and socially, in our efforts to maintain some order in our lives. At the core of the criminal's behavior is the desire, perhaps unconscious but surely powerful, to take over, mess over, "rip off" another *person*. A personal crime is an interpersonal encounter in which the rules that order such encounters have been suspended.

If, for example, a vandal breaks the stained-glass windows of a church or paints swastikas on a synagogue, the object of the violence is more than the physical property. The intention is to violate the people for whom these objects are sacred. The harm intended and done is to the inner self of those whose symbols have been desecrated. Such acts of violation invariably succeed. If a person wishes to hurt Jews grievously, what better way than to paint swastikas? It is an indirect but extremely effective assault.

The behavior of the violating criminal is highly symbolic even when it seems, at first glance, to be motivated by something as material and concrete as taking possession of another person's color television set. The things that a thief takes have monetary value, but they also have personal meaning; they belong to and stand for the person who owns them. Acquisitiveness may be one factor that motivates a thief—it is probably the usual conscious factor—but destructiveness is another. The theft is invariably a violation of a person.

The destructive intention of the predatory criminal makes sense of behavior that otherwise seems crazy. It explains why a burglar will sometimes spend a long time tearing up the place, opening every drawer and closet, ripping things apart and spilling them everywhere. Excessive property destruction is usually explained by saying that the burglar was searching for valuables, but most burglars know where the valuables are. And many of them still take the time to leave a mess.

An extreme example of this wish to defile the victim is the burglar who urinates or defecates in the living areas of the victim's home. One burglar even explained his act of defecation in a note: "You left me with shit. I leave you with shit."[15] The same impulse to violate explains the mugger who assaults his victim after the victim has handed over the money, and the rapist who batters his victim long after she has assured him that she will submit. We call such violence "senseless," but in fact it makes perfect sense.

The social malignancy of personal crime, like the biological malignancy of cancer, assumes many forms. But at the heart of each instance is the same terror: the fear of a force that is out of control. Most people are terribly afraid of both cancer and crime. Both are essentially mysterious. All kinds of explanations are offered, but nobody really knows why a cell goes berserk and becomes malignant, or why a person becomes a criminal, intent on the violation of others. These events are the epitome of chaos. The absence of any clear explanation leaves enormous room for psychological disorder and alarm.

Cancer and crime are also terrifying because our defenses against them are so minimal. No one wants to feel helpless in the face of a threat, but we all know that in spite of whatever preventative measures we take, we may still get cancer, still be the victim of a personal crime. In both cases, the system has turned against itself: The cancer is one of our own cells gone wild; the criminal is a fellow human being with malignant intention. Any cell can become a cancer, just as any person may turn out to be a criminal.

Although we speak about prevention—crime prevention, cancer prevention—the term is really a misnomer. Not smoking does not guarantee freedom from lung cancer; staying out of dark alleys does not guarantee freedom from sexual assault. We can certainly take reasonable precautions and use the limited information we have to reduce our risk, but that's all we can do. Talking about prevention in relation to either cancer or crime is a kind of wishful thinking and may even be a disservice from the point of view of the innocent victims of these malignancies. A more appropriate and realistic term would be something like "risk reduction." There is much we can do to reduce our risk, but nothing we can do will *guarantee* our safety.

Home of the Brave

The idea of the violated self can be enormously helpful to victims and their loved ones as a metaphor that explains the emotional upset they experience. Yet practically no one talks about fear of crime or the suffering of crime victims in these terms. Why is such a useful notion so universally ignored?

In a culture that is essentially materialistic, such as ours, most people are not very comfortable with abstractions. Americans understand physical, concrete things very well. They can relate to the loss of property or to physical injury—our bodies and our things consume most of our attention. But when the self, a nonphysical entity, experiences damage that cannot be seen or measured or bandaged, many of us are at a loss. We respond to such injury with suspicion, like the police officer who remarked of a rape victim, "There isn't a mark on her." If we can't see it, we have trouble believing it.

The self is an abstraction, and so it is mysterious. Many crime victims are disturbed because there seems to be no reason for their pain. The physical wounds have healed, the insurance has taken care of the property loss, and still they feel hurt. It is difficult for people to deal with the invisible wound precisely because it is so intangible.

Americans like to think of themselves as movers and shakers, people who get things done, problem-solvers who can take on the world with their rational and technological skills. This tends to give us the illusion that we can do anything, an illusion that is threatened by problems that resist solution. One doctor who works with cancer patients described the difficulty that people have in accepting and helping his patients: "Given the current cultural myth about our supposedly high degree of technological control, and our inordinately high premium on rationalistic self-control, any powerful evidence to the contrary—that we are more insignificant and vulnerable than we pretend to be—becomes horrifying."[16] The same sense of horror is often aroused by criminal victimization.

Americans also tend to resist the fact that people sometimes need help. This is, after all, the Home of the Brave. We admire independence and self-reliance. The pilgrims and the pioneers were rugged individuals; they could take care of themselves. A crime victim is a dependent person—he or she is in trouble, in need of help. Victims are likely to be seen in our culture as weaklings and failures, especially if they express their needs emotionally. There is little tolerance for tears in our society, even when they are clearly appropriate; keeping a stiff upper lip is the rule. Psychologist Martha Wolfenstein suggests that "perhaps in America, particularly, where emotional control is highly valued, and the possibility of experiencing depression or despair tends to be denied, the distress of the . . . victim . . . is likely to be underestimated."[17]

The implications of criminal violation are so terrifying that we are all tempted to skip over what the criminal has done to the victim. It's like closing the door on a monster or stepping back from the edge of a precipice. We move almost instinctively away from the victim's experience and think instead about criminals—their backgrounds, their motives, their capture, their punishment. Thinking about the criminal puts some intellectual distance between us and the crime. It gives us a sense that we are doing something about it. And so, for as long as people have tried to deal with crime, they have focused deliberately, almost stubbornly, on the criminal. As a result, we have not looked for very long at the victim or at the feelings that criminal acts of violation arouse in all of us.

It matters a great deal, of course, why criminals do what they do. But from the victim's point of view, the criminal's motives are really quite irrelevant. Whatever the reason, the victim must deal with the result. Victims are standing on the ledge, staring the monster in the eye. For however brief a moment, the victim has been brought face to face with the terrifying truth that none of us is ever completely in control. A crime victim knows exactly what it feels like to be threatened and helpless.

Psychic injury—damage to the self—can be a fearful thing. It is as real as physical injury. And the invisible wound will heal, over time, as a physical wound does. But it cannot be ignored without risking further damage.

NOTES

1. The precise names and legal definitions of the various personal crimes vary from jurisdiction to jurisdiction because law enforcement is largely a function of state and local agencies. The names we use are defined in the glossary in appendix B at the end of this book. Our usage generally follows that of the SEARCH Group, Inc. *Dictionary of Criminal Justice Data Terminology*, Second Edition (Washington, D.C.: Government Printing Office, 1981).
2. Erik H. Erikson, *Childhood and Society*, 2d ed. (New York: W. W. Norton and Company, 1963), p. 247.
3. The word *autonomy*, as it is used in this discussion, includes what recent theories beginning with the work of Julian Rotter have called "locus of control."
4. For the child or the adolescent, who is still engaged in the struggle to achieve autonomy, criminal victimization is particularly grievous because it can interfere with the important work of establishing an autonomous self.

5. Karl Menninger, Martin Mayman, and Paul Pruyser, *The Vital Balance: The Life Process in Mental Health and Illness* (New York: The Viking Press, 1963), pp. 80-81.

6. The psychological crisis precipitated by criminal victimization is discussed in detail in the next chapter.

7. This discussion of the continuum of personal crimes is modeled after Morton Bard and Katherine Ellison, "Crisis Intervention and Investigation of Forcible Rape," *Police Chief* 41, (1974): 68-73.

8. Robbery and burglary are commonly confused. Robbery can be defined as "the unlawful taking or attempted taking of property that is in the immediate possession of another, by force or threat of force." Burglary can be defined as "unlawful entry of any fixed structure ... with or without force, with intent to commit a felony, or a larceny." In robbery the victim is present; in burglary, he or she is not. Both definitions from SEARCH Group, Inc. *Dictionary of Criminal Justice Data Terminology*, Second Edition.

9. The crime of assault encompasses a very broad range of offenses—all unlawful physical attacks including threats and attempts—so that it covers everything from a minor verbal threat to a physical beating that brings the victim close to death. Almost half of reported assaults occur between people who know each other. Since our discussion here is focused on stranger-to-stranger encounters in which there is an element of surprise, we have omitted "pure" assault from the continuum. What most people fear is the physical threat that accompanies robbery and sexual assault. More information about assault may be found on p. 174 in Appendix A: Crimes Against People.

10. Bard and Ellison, "Crisis Intervention," p. 70.

11. It is widely believed that crimes by relatives and close acquaintances are underreported in criminal-justice statistics, so that the proportion of crimes committed by strangers may be somewhat overstated while the number of crimes committed by nonstrangers may be somewhat understated. According to the 1980 National Crime Survey, 72 percent of rape cases, 83 percent of robberies, and 59 percent of assaults involved a criminal who was a stranger to the victim (*Criminal Victimization in the United States, 1980*, p. 45). The one exception in most jurisdictions is homicide. In 1982, 22 percent of the murders reported to the police involved relatives or lovers as both offender and victim, and in only 43 percent of reported murder cases were the victims either strangers or of unknown relationship to the offender (*Crime in the United States: 1983 Uniform Crime Reports*, p. 11).

12. See, for example, Maurice R. Green, ed., *Violence and the Family*, American Association for the Advancement of Science Selected Symposia Series (Boulder, Colorado: Waterview Press, 1980); Barbara Smith, *Nonstranger Violence: The Criminal Courts Respond* (Washington, D.C.: National Institute of Justice, 1983); and John J. Spinetta and David Ringler, "The Child-Abusing Parent: A Psychological Review," *Psychological Bulletin* 77 (1972): 296-304.

13. This means that the police do not really keep the peace in a society; the people do. Police are often blamed when the social order breaks down, especially if there is a sudden increase in violence. But maintaining the social equilibrium depends upon the cooperation of all of the people in a community, and once the equilibrium has been upset, there is little or nothing the police can do to reestablish it.

14. This analogy between cancer and crime is developed in more detail in "Action Research and the Question of Social Malignancy," a paper delivered by Dr. Morton Bard in acceptance of the Kurt Lewin Award, The New York State Psychological Association Annual Convention, New York City, April 24, 1982.

15. Martin Symonds, "The Rape Victim: Psychological Patterns of Response," *The American Journal of Psychoanalysis* 36 (1976): 28-29.

16. Donald R. Pellman, "Learning to Live with Dying," quote by Dr. Charles Garfield, *New York Times Magazine*, 5 December 1976, p. 71.

17. Martha Wolfenstein, *Disaster: A Psychological Essay* (Glencoe, Illinois: The Free Press, 1957), pp. 83-84. This remarkable analysis is useful in our context because, although Wolfenstein's study is confined to victims of such disasters as tornadoes and wartime bombings, these victims are in a state of crisis that is similar to the one provoked by a personal crime.

3

Things Fall Apart: Victims in Crisis

Things fall apart; the centre cannot hold;
Mere anarchy is loosed upon the world,
The blood-dimmed tide is loosed, and everywhere
The ceremony of innocence is drowned . . .
—William Butler Yeats
"The Second Coming"

A lot of the feeling was shock. It was a brutal experience.
It was something that doesn't happen, you know, I mean
you hope it doesn't happen to you. I felt at times elated
because I had escaped death, since I thought I was going
to be killed. It seemed like nothing was important any
more.

—Robbery victim

Being the victim of a personal crime is extremely stressful. The
violating criminal strikes without warning. An elderly man is mugged
on his way to the supermarket. A couple comes home from a weekend
holiday to find their apartment in shambles, burglarized. A woman
goes out to get the mail and is raped. These people are going along,

32

minding their own business, when suddenly the world becomes chaotic.

The criminal's choice of victim is usually arbitrary, determined by chance factors that are beyond the victim's perception and out of his or her control. The street happens to be empty. A woman happens to resemble another woman whom the rapist knows and hates. From an innocent victim's point of view, the crime doesn't make any sense. The criminal seems to have come out of the blue.

There is no foolproof way for a victim to predict what a criminal will do. Cathy Nunzio was awakened early one morning by the sound of a burglar in the next room. She lay in her bed, terrified. "I had no idea who he was or what he would do to me. I would never break into somebody's house, and I thought: This person is not like me. He might do anything." Most people have little or no experience with personal threat. Confronted by an actual criminal, they are at a loss. Nothing in the typical victim's previous experience has prepared him or her to assess such a frightening situation.

This intense stress often precipitates a crisis reaction in the victim.[1] The sudden, arbitrary, unpredictable violation of self leaves victims feeling so shattered that they cannot continue to function the way they did before the crime. Things fall apart, and victims are unable to pull themselves back together right away. Psychiatrist Gerald Caplan of Harvard University, who has written extensively about crisis intervention, describes the crisis situation this way: "The essential factor influencing the occurrence of crisis is an imbalance between the difficulty and importance of the problem and the resources immediately available to deal with it."[2]

People in crisis situations have remarkably similar reactions. Unpredictable stress that threatens the self is very difficult to manage. Since victims have no advance warning, they are unable to anticipate the effects of the stress and gather their resources to withstand them. The strategies a person has used in the past to deal with difficulty may fail him or her completely, and this failure will increase the stress geometrically, short-circuiting the victim's self-confidence and further undermining the ability to cope.

Crime victims in crisis can be expected to suffer from a wide range of difficulties. They may become physically ill. Their ability to think, to feel, to act, and to relate to others may be seriously compromised for some time after the crime. Each individual responds in his or her own way, but every victim experiences some disruption.

Dealing with Crisis

The severity of the victim's crisis is in direct proportion to the degree of violation of self. This depends first of all on the nature of the violation and its meaning to the victim. Thus the physical violence of an assault usually precipitates a stronger crisis reaction than the less intense violation of a purse snatching. When property is taken, its emotional value is more important than its monetary value. A person who is robbed of an object that has great sentimental meaning will suffer a deeper sense of violation than one from whom expensive but insignificant things are taken.

The capacity of each person to deal with stress fluctuates over time. The force of a particular stressful event depends on the victim's previous experience, the symbolic significance of the stress, and the other circumstances in the victim's life at that moment. A rape victim whose husband had died of cancer a year before the rape described herself as relatively unaffected by the crime. She said the rape did not upset her as much as it otherwise would have because she knew it wasn't the worst thing that could happen to her. The rape seemed less significant than her earlier tragedy.

A third and crucial element that influences the progress of a crisis reaction is the kind of help the victim receives in the moments and days immediately after the crime. Many people seem to think that maturity or strength of character or good mental health should prevent a person from falling apart in a crisis situation. This is simply not the case. Any person who is subject to enough stress will be thrown into a state of crisis, and criminal violation of the self is more than enough stress for most people. Crime victims in crisis aren't weak or immature. They are having a natural and appropriate response to a serious threat.

The family and friends of the victim can be extremely helpful during the crisis if they understand and accept the victim's reactions. On the other hand, those who come in contact with victims after the crime—including loved ones and also strangers such as the police and the nurses in the hospital emergency room—can add to the victims' distress by being critical of their reactions and failing to meet their needs.[3]

People in crisis are off balance, and they often do strange things that trouble them and their loved ones. Seeing the victim's experience as a crisis can help everyone involved work through the difficult periods more easily. It helps to remember that the victim's feelings and behavior *always* make sense. They may not be understandable or acceptable or functional, but they make sense from a psychological point of view.

The crime victim's experience can never be reduced to a formula. Violation disrupts the self in as many ways as there are victims. At the same time, most victims experience at least some of the feelings and behavior associated with a crisis reaction—and people's reactions to crisis have a pattern. Most victims will recognize themselves in some of the descriptions here. The typical crisis reaction can serve as a broad outline on which victims can overlay their own unique experiences.

The Crisis Reaction

A crisis reaction develops in three stages—from initial disorganization of the self through a period of struggle to the eventual readjustment of the self. The reaction is as necessary to the recovery of the victim as is the period of healing after a physical wound. Each progressive step is an essential part of the emotional repair process.

The lines of demarcation between the stages often shift and become blurred during the recovery process. Victims of crisis rarely progress from one stage to the next in a straight line. They slip back to prior stages, move ahead, slip back again, until gradually and unevenly they move out of one phase of the reaction and into the next. Relapses are particularly common during the second stage, but eventually these recoil patterns will occur with less frequency until finally, in a good recovery, they will diminish altogether.[4]

IMPACT

Immediately after the crime, during the impact phase of the crisis reaction, the victim falls apart inside. His or her sense of personal intactness and integrity has been shattered. The self responds to violation by becoming disorganized. Victims often feel as if they are in shock.

Some victims become numb and disoriented. They move about aimlessly or feel physically immobilized. Physiological disturbances such as the inability to sleep or to eat are common. Disbelief is a frequent reaction: "This just can't be happening to me."

When burglary victims first walk into their homes after the crime, they often experience a curious delayed reaction. One woman explained, "As soon as I came in, I knew something was wrong, but I couldn't figure out what it was. Everything was out of place. I walked through the living room, and then it hit me: We've been robbed." Another victim went through a similar series of disbelieving reactions. She found the door to her house unlocked and wondered why she had left it that way; then she came into the kitchen, noticed that all the lights were on, and felt angry at her children (she keeps telling those kids to put out the lights); finally, she saw that the television was gone, and the impact of the crime struck her. She was so disoriented that she had to sit down and catch her breath.

The impact phase is often marked by feelings of vulnerability and helplessness. Victims are sometimes filled with a profound sense of loneliness, a feeling that they are alone and bereft. They may become quite childlike and dependent, unable to make even the simplest decisions. Psychologist Martha Wolfenstein explains this reaction as a reversion to an earlier stage of development:

A feeling of being abandoned probably plays a major part in the emotional distress of a disastrous experience. This feeling has its roots in early childhood. The small child becomes anxious when mother is away because he is helpless to satisfy his own needs and is in danger of being overwhelmed by distressing feelings which he cannot himself alleviate.... The sense of helplessness in the impact of a disastrous event throws the individual back to the childhood position. All his vital needs are threatened with frustration and his acquired capacity to take care of himself is set aside by an overpowering force.[5]

The victim may seek reassurance and direction from others during the impact stage. He or she may seem uncertain and ask for advice. "I can't handle this," the victim is saying. "Help me. Tell me what to do." Immediately after a crime there are usually many things that need to be taken care of—someone has to contact the police and deal with them; calls must be made to insurance and credit-card companies; whatever mess the criminal has left has to be cleaned up; the victim may be asked to identify a suspect. All of these external demands can make the victim feel swamped.

The initial impact reaction may be expressed several hours or even days after the crime. Victims may seem to be all right and then suddenly become disorganized. People who are asked for help at this point sometimes feel that the victim should already have recovered; they may become moralistic and judgmental, denying the victim's appeal for aid. They seem to be saying, "You're an adult. Act like one." Even if it is not expressed in words, this attitude adds immeasurably to the victim's distress. The victim needs to have some structure provided in a suddenly chaotic world, some help in restoring order. The need for this support is temporary; it will diminish over time if it is satisfied. But if the help does not come, the victim's need for direction can become fixed; he or she may continue to seek reassurance and be unable to move to the next stage of recovery.

A much more helpful response is for the other person to regard the victim's request as natural and to fill the need. Most people are reluctant to tell others what to do; nobody wants to be a busybody. But in the period right after a devastating stressful experience, the victim may ask—in words or actions—to be given some direction and support. Cathy Nunzio could hardly gather enough strength to get out of bed after the burglar left her apartment. She never saw the intruder, but she trembled visibly for several hours. As soon as she got up, she called a neighbor who contacted the police and then stayed with her for the rest of the night. They sat together for a while, drinking coffee and talking. After the police left, they straightened up the apartment. They got a hammer and some nails so that Cathy could nail shut the window through which the burglar had come. Cathy's friend did more to foster her recovery than all the insurance money can buy. This is not a time to mind your own business.

Neither is it a time for intrusion. The victim's autonomy has already been violated by the criminal; a "helpful" person who tries to second-guess the victim, imposing what the helper thinks the victim wants, can add to the sense of violation. Some people who think of themselves as good helpers indulge in which might be called "the rescue fantasy." They imagine that they can save the victim by insisting that he or she do what *they* think is best. This kind of ego-tripping is very far from true helpfulness. It is as if the helper is saying, "See how wonderful I am because I am helping you."

The rescue fantasy is a common pitfall among even the professionally trained. It has several dangers. Helpers who see themselves as rescuers derive important ego benefits from the victim's dependency. They may unwittingly encourage the victim to continue to lean on them long after their support is no longer needed. And, of course, the helper may be wrong about what the victim needs. By imposing their own interpretation on the victim's experience, these well-intentioned people can add to the victim's difficulties instead of relieving them.

Really helping a person in trouble requires extraordinary sensitivity and discipline. People who really want to help must focus on the victim, listen carefully for the victim's expression of his or her needs and then respond to that expression—without imposing their own suggestions or judgments or perceptions. The ideal helper is one who is able to create a climate in which victims will be able to ask for and get whatever help they want.

Meredith Richards was raped by a man who climbed into a basement window of her house one afternoon when she was alone. After the rape he stayed, talking with her, for almost an hour. When he finally left, she called the police. She kept herself steady and rational through the police interview, just as she had been while the rapist was talking to her. As the police were leaving the house, a friend drove by on her way home from work. She saw the police car and stopped to find out if anything was wrong. Coming up the walk, she saw Meredith with the police in the doorway. Her face was so white that her friend was immediately concerned. "Are you all right?" she asked. Meredith burst into tears. Her friend was the first person to ask that crucial question.

Victims sometimes seem confused during the impact stage; they may have trouble recalling the details of the crime. A victim may be unable to think clearly or to talk coherently. This is a natural, temporary reaction. Again, if other people become impatient or angry, they will only make it worse. The most supportive listener will encourage victims to express themselves, and the listener will refrain from making any critical comments. Even an offhand remark ("I can't believe you don't remember what the mugger looked like!") can be perceived as an insult by the victim.

A crime victim's entire structure of defenses becomes weakened under the stress of violation, leaving him or her unusually accessible to the influence of others. This characteristic response makes the behavior of other people unusually powerful in the period right after the crime. The victim's accessibility can be a danger or an asset, depending on how others act.

Consider, for example, a man who has been robbed and severely beaten. He is shattered physically and emotionally, really clobbered. His most admired friend visits him in the hospital and asks, "Why in the world were you carrying all that money?" Inherent in the questions is an accusation, which is hardly what the victim needs. It adds a further burden, increasing the emotional pain by suggesting that the crime was partly the victim's fault.

Under ordinary circumstances, the victim might be able to protect himself from this accusation. He could say, "Look. I was coming from the bank, which is only two blocks from my house. I had to cash my paycheck; I needed the money for the weekend. What was I supposed to do—fly home?" But since he is in crisis, the victim has lost his ability to defend himself. His friend's untimely demand that he account for himself will leave him feeling even more helpless than before.

The friend's insensitivity has another, even more destructive, effect. It destroys the victim's trust in him at the very moment when the victim most needs to confirm it. This compounds the victim's violation of trust, increasing his sense of isolation and despair. When the victim's defenses are down, almost anyone who is in touch with him can produce additional disorder, especially if the other person is a loved one.

The same situation could have produced a positive experience. Instead of accusing the victim, the friend might have said, "You must feel terrible. I'm so sorry you've been hurt. What can I do to help?" Such a response would have engendered greater trust between the two than ever before. It would have acted as an antidote to the victim's violation of trust, healing his wounds and renewing his faith in the basic trustworthiness of other people. Because the victim is especially vulnerable during the impact phase, such thoughtfulness on the part of others has a much greater impact than it would under less stressful circumstances.

One way or another victims will reconstruct their defenses. None of us can function very long without them. If a victim does not get proper support during the impact phase, his or her defenses may come back together in a dysfunctional way that will cause considerable difficulty later. One woman became permanently suspicious and fearful after she was mugged. Several years later she sought help; through long sessions of psychological counseling, she was finally able to regain her sense of trust. A broken bone will knit by itself if it is left untended, but the bone may then have to be broken again and reset long after the injury. Victims may reconstruct their defenses in a way that will later require them to be torn down and rebuilt through the counseling process.

Cathy Nunzio's experience with her neighbor is a good example of how important early support can be. Cathy asked for and got the help she needed right after the crime happened. She recovered her equilibrium in a short time, and now the burglary is just a blurred memory. Another victim who, like Cathy, was awakened by the noises of a burglar in her apartment, was not so furtunate. She had no one to turn to, and she has continued to suffer from fear.

I still have nightmares about intruders. I think I hooked some of my biggest fears onto that experience. I didn't have anybody to talk to about it at the time, so I wasn't able to get it out of my system. I really didn't have people that I trusted enough to tell about my feelings then. I couldn't tell my family, so it was sort of bottled up. And I'm still carrying it around with me. It was traumatic for me to wake up and find somebody in my room. And now, if I hear a noise, I immediately think that's what's going on. I have to get up and look so that I know there's no one there.

Adequate help in the beginning can encourage functional reconstruction of the defenses so that later psychological intervention is less likely to be necessary. If another person—a friend or relative, a police officer or a nurse—is able to move in quickly and with authority, he or she can do a great deal to reduce the effects of the crisis. Minutes of skillful support by any sensitive person immediately after the crime can be worth more than hours of professional counseling later.

RECOIL

In the second phase, the recoil stage of the crisis reaction, victims begin to struggle to adapt to the violation and to reintegrate their fragmented selves. The work of recovery requires the victim to deal with a number of distressing emotions including fear, anger, sadness, self-pity, and guilt. These feelings are sometimes contradictory, and they may be so intense and painful that the victim cannot face them all at once. Victims often go through a series of defensive maneuvers to buy time so that they can admit their feelings in tolerable doses.

Thus the second phase involves two kinds of activity: Sometimes the victim will be able to feel and work on the painful emotions aroused by the experience; at other times he or she will defend against the feelings by denying them. This process has been described as a "waxing and waning of tension" and has been compared to the natural pattern of sleeping and waking.[6] After victims have struggled with the crisis for a while, they become tired and put their troubles aside so that they can rest.

Family and friends can be most helpful in this phase by being nurturing and comforting, allowing the victim to find his or her own recuperative rhythm, and thus supporting the struggle. Gerald Caplan suggests that the best help is active: "The sufferer will be given opportunities for rest from his wrestling with his problem; but he will also be stimulated and encouraged to 'wake up' after his rest periods and return again to his consideration of the problem."[7] Again, the helper needs to pay close attention to the victim's own expression of needs.

It has become fashionable among certain self-help philosophies to view denial as a kind of stubborn weakness of will, a self-destructive indulgence. In fact, some denial is an essential part of the healing process in a crisis situation. It allows the victim to develop a gradual immunity to the onslaught of feelings that would be overwhelming if they had to be faced all at once. And both denying and facing feelings can be active processes that will use up the victim's energy and absorb his or her attention during this period.

Defending against the feelings may take a hyperactive form; some victims throw themselves into their work or some other structured activity. They become very "busy," bustling with projects and plans that are totally unrelated to the crime. For others, the crime itself may provide activity through which they can distract themselves. Contacting agencies, filling out forms, phoning the police for information about the progress of the investigation, and so on may help victims to protect themselves from the feelings the crime has aroused.

Many victims go through a period of direct denial—they feel emotionally detached, unable to respond with much feeling to anything. This temporary suspension of emotional capability can be an extension of the shock of the impact stage. To prevent themselves from being pulled under by their upsetting feelings, victims may insulate themselves from their feelings altogether. Sometimes hyperactivity and emotional deadness work together in denial, especially among Americans, who are culturally predisposed to value getting things done as an antidote for feeling helpless.[8] The victim may feel as if he or she needs to seal off the feelings so that they will not interfere with getting back to normal at work and in social situations.

Between these periods of denial, victims begin to deal with their feelings about the crime. The work of facing these emotions includes remembering the events of the crime and permitting oneself to reexperience the feelings that have been aroused by the violation. Some victims "play back" the crime repeatedly in their imaginations. They may want to talk about it endlessly, reviewing the events in minute detail. Victims often dream about the crime.

Residents of Chowchilla, California, were plunged into a crisis in July, 1976, when twenty-six children from the community were kidnapped in their school bus. These victims had an unusual opportunity to relive the crime. After the children had been safely returned to their homes, a local television station arranged a rerun of the news tapes covering the kidnapping, and more than 500 people crowded into the auditorium to watch. The mother of one of the victims explained her interest in the rerun: "It brought back things we've got to get out in the open; Andrea's been holding it back and we can't let that well up inside her."[9]

It may be painful for people who love the victim to support his or her need to relive the events of the crime. But this mother's intuition is right; repressing emotions can be harmful. A man whose daughter was murdered found no one among his family and friends who could bear to hear about his feelings. Everyone kept telling him how strong he was. "I didn't even want anybody to ask if I was all right. When somebody asked, I said, "Sure. I'm fine.' I wanted somebody to *know* I wasn't all right. I didn't want to have to confess it." As victims become able to talk about their feelings, they need a sympathetic, interested audience.

Fear is one of the most difficult emotions with which victims must come to terms. Reliving the experience sometime after the crime, the victim may be able to feel the intensity of the terror for the first time. Often the victim can only allow the full force of the emotion sometime after the immediate threat is gone. The fear of helplessness is always elicited to some degree by the violation of self. Beyond that, some victims have also been actually threatened or physically injured. They may bear wounds as evidence of their injury, visible reminders of their fear. Physical wounds can arouse shame and guilt as well; victims often feel that they should have been able to prevent the injury.

Many victims are afraid that they will see the criminal again. A man whose wallet had been picked was obsessed for days afterward with the thought that any stranger he passed on the street could be the pickpocket. A woman who had been raped began to "see" the rapist every time she went out alone. She felt compelled to sleep with all the lights on because she was so afraid he would come back.

Victims often experience special fears about specific details of the crime, phobic reactions to particular places or times of day or kinds of people. An elderly woman who had been robbed in the elevator of her apartment building became unable to ride in any elevator after the crime. Another victim who was assaulted late one night near his home began to stay inside after dark. A man whose overcoat was stolen while he was eating in his favorite restaurant vowed that he would never go in the place again. Phobic reactions often have a magical quality, as if avoiding certain places or kinds of people could act as a talisman, protecting the victim from future harm. These fears may seem irrational to the victim, but they can also be quite compelling.

Sometimes a phobic reaction brings some latent fear to the surface. Racist feelings are common in cases where the criminal is of one race and the victim of another. If the criminal is black, for example, and the victim is white, the victim may become afraid of all black people. The society is racist, and everyone in it is affected by racism. No one is free of its taint, though many people struggle to overcome it. Victims who have tried to maintain unprejudiced attitudes toward people of other races can be deeply troubled when their racism surfaces in a phobic reaction. A woman whose apartment had been burglarized was asked to describe the person she imagined the burglar to be.

> I just assumed he was a young, black man. It never occurred to me that he might be a Puerto Rican, for example. I also think that maybe I didn't dwell on it because I am very conscious of my prejudices. I think they're pretty mild compared to many people's, and I think I deliberately didn't want to put labels on this guy, so I didn't think about it too much. I really didn't want to say, "Oh, this was just some ... whatever ... some ... nigger (uncomfortable laughter) breaking into my place." I'm aware of those feelings and that's what people think, immediately. The whole business about he committed a crime, so he must be black. That kind of prejudice makes me angry so I think I was fighting it unconsciously.

The best way to handle fear is to allow the victim to express it. Given adequate ventilation, these feelings will eventually diminish along with the other intense emotions aroused by the crime. But other people are sometimes so threatened by the victim's fear that they can't listen. The victim's efforts to release the fear by talking about it may terrify the listeners so much that they will cut the victim off to protect themselves. The other person may say, "Let's not talk about it anymore. If you don't think about it, you'll forget it." This is the worst kind of advice because it encourages the fear to go underground, where it can really cause trouble.

Another common, and sometimes overwhelming, feeling after the crime is an intense anger toward the criminal. Feelings of rage can be especially difficult because victims usually have no realistic means to vent their anger on the criminal. Most victims never see the criminal again.[10] Even if the offender is apprehended and successfully prosecuted, the legal proceedings will take months. The absence of the criminal creates an emotional vacuum; the victim has no way to confront the person who has made him or her so angry.

One way to release these feelings is through fantasy. Fantasies and dreams about revenge are not uncommon, especially among victims who have suffered physical violence. The imagined retribution may be quite graphic and violent; in some cases it will seem shocking to the victim. One rape victim had a recurrent fantasy that she would use a huge pair of scissors to castrate the rapist, a vision that horrified her even as it satisfied her need to express her rage.

Len Baron is a professional musician who lives in Los Angeles. Last winter he was robbed by two men. They came to his apartment after his show, pretending to be friends of another performer Len knew, pulled a gun, tied him up, and rifled the place. Len is a large, explosive man, and he is so furious about the robbery that he shakes whenever he talks about it.

> The outrage is so uncontrollable and justifiably so. You can't ask a human being to be more than a human being. I had fantasies for weeks afterward of running into them on the street and their not seeing me and just killing them. . . . Grabbing one of them from behind and choking him or punching him in the balls and making him helpless and kicking, smashing his head in. Just incredible fantasy. The cops said to me, "If by chance you

ever see this guy anywhere on the street, follow him until you see a cop and tell the cop that this guy once held you up and that he carries a gun. Don't go near him yourself." My feeling was, if there wasn't a cop around, I'd just go after him.

The wish for revenge is natural, and its expression in fantasy can be helpful. When victims allow themselves to imagine vengeance, their fantasies provide an important outlet for their frustrated anger and help to dispel it.

Some victims express their anger in another way, by turning it on people other than the criminal whom they blame for their violation in some way. Victims who find it difficult to express anger may turn the anger inward and blame themselves instead. The need to blame somebody is part of a larger adaptation which each victim works through during the crisis. Crime victims have an almost universal need to construct a reason for their violation, to find an answer to the question "Why me?" A great deal of time and energy will be devoted to this task during the recoil stage. It is so central to the healing process that we have considered it separately, in the next chapter.

When the victim's anger is directed toward people who are trying to help, the helpers may feel bewildered. They may also become defensive and return anger for anger, a natural but unfortunate response. Thus victims can cut themselves off from an important source of comfort in their attempt to deal with anger. If the people who become the objects of the victim's wrath can understand that the victim needs to get mad at somebody, they may be able to absorb the anger more easily.

It's actually a kind of backhanded compliment. The victim is most likely to become angry with people who are close to him or her—those who can be counted on to care about the victim even after the rage has been discharged. The most helpful response is to acknowledge the anger without taking it personally, to say, "I hear you. You are really angry." This gives the victim a chance to blow off steam.

Among the most distressing aspects of the recoil phase are the great shifts in mood that victims often experience as the second phase progresses. One day they will feel very much on top of things;

the next day they are almost overcome again by feelings of help-lessness and anxiety. These mood swings are a normal part of the victim's recovery work, but they can be very discouraging and fright-ening. Victims sometimes feel as if they are never going to really recover from their experience.

Friends and loved ones can help the victim not to panic on the downswing if they can provide some stability and reassurance during the bad days. When victims become discouraged and feel that they'll never make it, the last thing they need is another person who reflects that fear by sharing it. Someone who is emotionally distant enough to remind the victim that he or she has been coping pretty well can be very supportive.

A different reaction—both more rare and more serious—is found in the crime victim who is unable to get beyond the symptoms of the impact stage or who makes what seems to be a normal recovery and then is suddenly thrown back to earlier acute symptoms. All crime victims experience uneven progress through the stages of recovery, but some suffer acute or chronic reactions for a very long time after. These extreme cases are now seen as suffering from Post-traumatic Stress Syndrome, the same anxiety disorder that has af-fected some returning war veterans.[11]

Crime victims who suffer Post-traumatic Stress Disorder reexper-ience the events surrounding the crime over and over again. They may be tormented by intrusive memories of the crime or by per-sistent dreaming about it or by suddenly acting or feeling as if the crime were happening again. Some of these victims have a sense of being cut off from themselves or from their loved ones. Others feel cut off from the world as their interest in activities that once were important to them seems to disappear. Symptoms such as disturb-ances of sleep and difficulty in concentration remain acute or sud-denly recur sometime after the crime. The victim may need to continue to avoid activities or situations that recall the crime. When reminded of the crime by day-to-day events, he or she may continue to suffer from sudden intensifications of fear, anger, or anxiety. If a crime victim suffers from such symptoms for a long period without getting much relief or if symptoms such as these suddenly appear some time after the crime, the victim needs professional help.

REORGANIZATION

In the normal course of a crisis reaction, the recoil phase will eventually give way to the final phase—reorganization. The violated self becomes reorganized over time as the victim assimilates the painful experience. Feelings of fear and rage diminish in intensity, and the victim begins to have emotional energy left over to invest in other experiences. The victim's level of activity becomes more even and balanced as the need to deny the victimization ebbs. Victims think less about the crime and become less interested in talking about it, but when it does come up, the conversation is less emotionally tinged and much less upsetting. Gradually victims are able to put the experience into perspective and commit their energies to other things.

The more serious the violation, the longer a full reorganization will take. It is impossible to give accurate time frames for various crimes because individuals vary so much, but the full recovery often takes longer than people expect. The victim of a rape, for example, can be expected to be in some stage of crisis for the better part of a year, even with the best help. Delayed recovery is normal.

Some time after the crime, victims may be reminded of their violation by some outside event. They may see a person who looks like the criminal or read about a crime that is similar to their own experience. Such a reminder can evoke some of the earlier pain, an echo of the crisis reaction, but the episode is usually short-lived and relatively muted.

Victims never entirely forget the crime. Their suffering lessens, but other effects of the experience remain as part of the self. Their view of themselves and of the world will be permanently altered in some way, depending on the severity of the crime and the degree of its impact. The violation of self can hardly be called a positive experience, but it does present an opportunity for change. One of two things will happen: Either victims become reordered, reborn, put back together so that they are stronger than before, or their experiences during the crisis will promote further disorder with long-term negative consequences.

A great deal depends on the kind of help the victim receives. The victim of a personal crime has been violated by another person. If the victim's recovery is supported by other people, their help provides a kind of counterbalance to the violation, reassuring the victim of the essential trustworthiness of most people. The victim who receives appropriate help from family and friends, for example, will come out of the crisis with a heightened appreciation for them and a greater ability to seek their help again. Weathering a crisis can be a strengthening experience for victims and those who love them.

Putting the Crisis in Perspective

Ellen Saunders is nineteen, a junior at one of the colleges in the Boston area. She lives at school during the week, spends weekends with her boyfriend in another state almost a hundred miles away, and also has two part-time jobs. Last spring during exam week, Ellen's car was stolen. Her crisis reaction is a classic example.

> I never lend the car to anybody, but I lent it to my friend Sara because it was her last night in town and it was her birthday and she wanted to go see her boyfriend. I had an exam to take the next morning, and I was all burned out, so I went to bed early. At three o'clock in the morning somebody came pounding on the door to say there was a phone call for me on the second floor. Sara was calling from Cambridge and she was hysterical. She said the car was gone, the car was gone. [Ellen called the police to report the theft. She also called her boyfriend. Then she went back to bed. The next morning, she began to experience the full impact of her loss.]
>
> I had been writing this term paper all week. The bibliography was in the car and some of the books were in the car and some of the first draft of the paper was in the car, so that was like: Well, what do I do now? I was just . . . I was just completely drained. I flipped out. I mean I really did. I wasn't going around screaming and yelling and crying or anything, but *I couldn't do anything.* I was just sitting there, watching television and talking to people.
>
> More and more people were finding out about it, and some of them were being really supportive. But there were some real jerks around who were saying things like: "You'll never get it back so don't even think

about it. My car got stolen in Cambridge and I never got it back." Or: "My friend's car got stolen and he never saw it again."... I couldn't write my paper because I was just too blah, so I went in and talked to my professor. And he said, "Don't worry about it. You can have a week or two-week extension if that's what you need." So I didn't do anything much the day after it happened. I worked on my paper a little bit.

When I went down to dinner that night, Sara was there. So I came in and sat next to her, and she said, "You can only sit here if you don't talk about the car. Because I've been hearing about this all day, and I just don't want to hear about it anymore." I couldn't believe she had said that to me. Everybody at the table got embarrassed. They were all looking away, trying to pretend it hadn't happened. I just sat there and ate my dinner without saying a word and went back upstairs to my room.

I felt fragile. I remember thinking, "I haven't got time for this. I have to start work next week." I felt very vulnerable physically. I was really kind of numb and exhausted physically as well as emotionally. I didn't want to have to deal with anybody. I felt like saying, "Don't push me too far about anything because I will just shut you off and ignore you." Like when Sara said that at the dinner table, I wanted to say, "*Please* don't say things like that to me. I'm too tired for that." I wanted to be cuddled and to hide my head.

I decided that I was going to go out and look for the car. And I was really serious about it. I was going to start where it had been parked and look around there and then go look in some other prime spots in the city. I wanted to go and find the car and hide in the back seat so I could hit the guy who stole it over the head with a baseball bat when he came back. And it was so weird for me because I am always getting after my boyfriend when he wants to settle something by fighting. I couldn't believe that I really wanted to do that. But I did. I wanted to take the top of the guy's head off.

I woke up the next morning and I was still just physically exhausted, didn't want to be by myself at all but didn't want to really talk to anybody. I wanted to go sit with somebody and watch television. The whole time I was calling the police and they were reassuring me, but I think they were just trying to make me feel better. So I wrote the paper and turned it in. I called up my boyfriend and said I was going to stay and look for the car. And he said, "Come home." He finally talked me into coming home because it was a crazy idea and I just would have driven myself nuts.

I thought about it a lot for the first couple of weeks and then gradually less and less. The day before the police found it, I hadn't said anything about the car for maybe five or six days, and the day before they found it, I said, "I think the car is really gone." And then the police called up and I flipped out! We went and got it, and for three weeks after that I kept the car in the parking lot at home. I locked it all the time. The first time I took it to work, I probably looked out the window to be sure it was there half a dozen times during the day. It's really just since the end of the summer that I've been comfortable leaving it parked on the street somewhere. I'm still paranoid, but not as bad as I was. It was terrible.

And I didn't hear from Sara all summer. I really, honestly, felt worse for her than I did for me at first. But then she took off and she didn't call or write or anything all summer. After the car was found, I wrote to a friend of ours whose address I did have and told him to tell her. And I know she found out about it because I saw somebody at school who had seen her. But I still haven't heard from her about it. And that really makes me angry.

About four months later we were in Boston for the weekend, staying with some friends. We parked the car [illegally] on the corner when we came in that night, and when I got up in the morning, I went out to get something out of the car and it was gone. And I just went berserk. I called the station and found out it had just been towed away. When I hung up the phone, I was just sitting there shaking.

This may seem to be much ado about nothing. How can anyone carry on so about having a car stolen? But that's the point. Personal violation is *personal*; its emotional impact is very individual. Ellen's life was so disrupted by the theft that she was plunged into a crisis. Her car is a clear and strong extension of her self, a symbol of her mobility and the means by which she is able to carry on the activities that matter most in her life. It functions as a kind of portable home, and so it was full of things that were important to her the day it was stolen.

The reactions of Ellen's friends are also typical, some of them helpful and some of them destructive. The professor who extended her paper deadline was clearly attuned to the level of difficulty she was experiencing. Her boyfriend was able to interject a note of common sense at a crucial point. But Ellen's relationship with her friend Sara may never be the same. The car has been returned, but the distance the theft has created between these two young women remains. On balance, Ellen is making a good recovery, working her way out of the crisis and gradually reorganizing her self.

NOTES

1. The term *crisis* is used in ordinary conversation to refer to a wide variety of decisive, emotionally significant, or distressing events. In medicine, *crisis* refers to the turning point in a disease or fever, after which the patient either recovers or dies. In this book we use the word *crisis* to refer to a very specific set of circumstances: a sudden, arbitrary, unpredictable event that is threatening to the self and produces significant disruption in the emotions and behavior of the threatened person. This definition is more narrow than that of many sociologists and psychologists, some of whom have taken the term *crisis* out of its original contexts in crisis intervention theory and applied it broadside to all sorts of stressful situations. Chronic alcoholism, for example, is *not* a crisis by our definition.

2. Gerald Caplan, *Principles of Preventive Psychiatry* (New York: Basic Books, 1964), p. 39. The work of Erich Lindemann is usually cited as the first significant contribution to crisis intervention theory [see, for example, "Symptomatology and Management of Acute Grief," *American Journal of Psychiatry* 101 (1944): 141-148]. Caplan's *Principles of Preventive Psychiatry* is widely held to be authoritative.

3. Chapter 5 explores some of the reasons why other people can be so insensitive to the needs of victims.

4. The phases of a crisis reaction are given different names in various studies. Our terminology is related to that used in two reports of the rape trauma syndrome. Ann W. Burgess and Lynda L. Holmstrom, "Rape Trauma Syndrome," *American Journal of Psychiatry*, 131 (1974), and Sandra Sutherland Fox and Donald J. Scherl, "Crisis Intervention with Rape Victims," *Social Work*, January, 1972.

5. Wolfenstein, *Disaster*, p. 57.

6. Caplan, *Principles of Preventive Psychiatry*, p. 46.

7. Ibid, p. 46.

8. For a discussion of the particularly American quality of this combination of defenses, see Wolfenstein, *Disaster*, pp. 107-112.

9. *New York Times*, 28 July 1976.

10. The Federal Bureau of Investigation publishes "clearance rates" for eight Index Crimes each year. These rates show the percentage of each of these crimes for which an offender is arrested and charged with a criminal offense (not, please note, convicted). In 1983, the clearance rates were 76% for murder, 52% for forcible rape, 26% for robbery, 61% for aggravated assault, 19% for larceny theft (which includes pocket picking and purse snatching), 15% for burglary, 15% for motor vehicle theft, and 17% for arson (*Crime in the United States: 1983 Uniform Crime Reports*, p. 159).

11. Diagnostic criteria for Post-traumatic Stress Disorder may be found in the American Psychiatric Association's *Diagnostic and Statistical Manual of Mental Disorders*, Third Edition (Washington, D.C.: APA, 1980).

4

Why Me? The Search for a Reason

I think if you grow up the way I did—in very middle-class circumstances—no matter what you read it's very hard to believe someone wants to do anything bad to *you*. Especially since you're a good person and go to all the right concerts and read all the right books. You don't deserve it.
—Victim of a pocket picking

People have been trying to understand and control evil since the beginning of time. One view traces the origin of religion to primal human fear. Throughout history we have developed beliefs to explain the forces that harm us and have devised rituals to neutralize those forces. Ancient or primitive religious ceremonies of expiation often include rites in which a person or animal is killed as a means of influencing aversive events.[1] The bargain is a simple one. The gods get the victim; the group gets some sense of control over the threatening evil.

In other cultures and at other times in the development of American culture, the suffering of innocent people has been explained in terms of some superhuman force. Whether the gods are seen as just or simply as very powerful, these explanations have the benefit of giving people a sense of control because they establish a reason for the victims' fate. But in the secular world of modern crime victims, their experience is rarely invested with this kind of significance. Victimization has the same quality of undeserved pain, but there is no underlying tradition that explains the suffering. And the lack of an explanation is just as intolerable for the personal crime victim in a modern urban setting as it is for a primitive. When something bad happens, people need to establish a reason so they can feel that the threatening events in their lives make sense.[2]

Putting the Pieces Back Together

If the world doesn't make sense, people can't do anything with confidence. Victims of personal crime need to find some way of pulling themselves together. They go through a mental process to reorganize and understand the world that has become chaotic. This process helps to reintegrate the violated self, reducing the dissonance caused by its fragmentation.

A victim wants to be able to say, "I understand this thing, and I am no longer frightened by it." To repair the damage done by the violation of self, it is natural for the crime victim to attempt to attribute his or her victimization to something. The victim develops an explanation for the crime in the form of a belief about why it happened.

Attribution is so common and so important in dealing with life events, especially those that arouse conflicts in people, that it has become a central concern in social psychology. Feelings of personal control have been found to have positive psychological effects, and feelings of helplessness can be devastating. If people cannot predict what is going to happen in a stressful situation, they feel increased fear and are less able to cope with the situation. These findings help to explain why crime victims are so eager to determine a reason for their victimization.

The explanation that a crime victim establishes depends in part on the victim's personality. The conviction can be either self-blaming or blaming of someone or something outside of the self. The victim may feel that the crime is essentially his or her own fault. Some people believe that they deserve whatever they get. Attributions of personal blame may involve things that the victim has done or neglected to do, "sins" of commission or omission. Alternatively, victims may place the blame outside of themselves, feeling that the action or inaction of someone else caused the crime.

The victim's attribution underlies the obvious answer to the question of cause. Clearly the violating criminal is the cause of the crime, but this is not a satisfactory explanation by itself. There is no question that the criminal is a harmful force; everybody knows that criminals are out there. But the question still is: Why me and not you? Attribution is a mechanism for defending against the arbitrariness of the victimization.

Cancer victims have a similar need to explain their disease by attributing it to someone or something. Most people are aware of the fact that there are cancer-producing agents in the world, but cancer victims still need to explain why *they* got cancer. In one study of cancer victims, more than half of them spontaneously offered attributions for their illnesses in interviews.[3] The criminal, like the cancer, is given. Victims still need to account for the fact that the criminal violated *them*.

Identifying a cause, however rational or irrational, gives people a sense of order and predictability in their lives. People do not want to believe that things happen randomly; they want to believe that they happen *because*. Theoretically, a crime victim might answer the question "Why me?" by saying, "It's no one's fault. Criminals strike arbitrarily and mysteriously. There is no way to account for this attack. The criminal may strike again tomorrow. There is nothing I can do." But this sort of explanation is intolerable. Order is dependent upon anchoring the experience in an attribution.

I Am Responsible

Self-blaming attributions take many forms. Victims often point to something they did before the crime that made it possible for the criminal to succeed: The unlocked window invited the burglar; the wallet in an outside pocket encouraged the pickpocket; the short skirt incited the rapist.

The victim seems almost eager to take the responsibility. George Baker's apartment was burglarized soon after he moved in. He expressed his attribution about the burglary this way:

> Well, I became concerned about my kind of blasé attitude toward this thing—that it wouldn't happen, that kind of attitude. I was not careful enough because I had in fact left the window open. . . . I hadn't bothered to put the locks on the windows. That was something I didn't think it was necessary to do right away. My guess is that [the unlocked window] was a pretty open invitation to this guy. I think my lack of caution had a lot to do with the fact that my apartment was burglarized, and I take responsibility for that.

Another victim, a woman whose purse was snatched while she waited for a bus, explained the crime by saying that she realized the neighborhood might be dangerous but she didn't have the money to pay for a taxi. "I took a chance and I got caught. I feel responsible in that I did something I knew I shouldn't have done."

Attributions such as these may have some base in reality, but they are often carried beyond reality. If a person leaves the window unlocked, the opportunity for a burglary is clearly presented. Most burglars would rather steal from an apartment that is easy to get into. But a simple cause-and-effect explanation is not warranted in such circumstances because chance also plays a part. The open window does not explain why the burglar chose that particular building in the first place. A closed window is certainly no guarantee that the burglary will be prevented. The wish to save taxi fare is hardly a blame-worthy impulse. But people like to make causality as simple as possible: A happened before B, therefore A is the entire cause of B. Victims often see their own behavior as the deciding factor because then they feel that they're back in control.

Self-blaming victims sometimes associate the crime with some previous and seemingly unrelated bad behavior. Victims who feel guilty about something they have done may connect that guilt with the crime. A robbery victim who had a quarrel with his wife the morning of the crime decided that the robber punished him. The criminal can be seen as the arm of some higher moral force that metes out justice. A rape victim who is single and sexually active offered this attribution: "When I went off the pill, I was so arrogant that I said, 'Now I'll get raped.' And I was. So now I don't go off the pill." Victims are sometimes not consciously aware of attributions that are related to feelings of guilt.

Attributing the crime to one's own previous bad behavior may reflect the thinking of a highly moral person, one who believes strongly in right and wrong. Self-blame comes easily to a person who has a highly developed conscience, one who is quick to feel guilty and very anxious to do the right thing. Self-blaming victims may also be people who feel as if their lives should always be under their control. They may feel that they are responsible for whatever happens to them and that they should have been able to prevent the crime. Since they didn't, they're culpable.

Blaming oneself is bound to be pervasive in a society that values individual effort and personal reward. Most Americans are encouraged to take personal credit for their achievements. We also tend to feel responsible for our shortcomings, failures, and personal suffering. In such a society, it is not at all surprising that many people explain their victimization in egocentric terms.

The self-blaming attribution may be self-punishing, but at least it restores a sense of order to the world. Some victims see their experience as a kind of expensive education. Believing that they know the cause of the crime and that the cause is in themselves, they resolve to correct their behavior so that they can avoid being victims in the future. Such planning is useful in reordering the fragmented self because it allows the victim to feel that he or she has regained control. Indeed, there is current thinking which indicates that for some victims self-blame is a necessary condition for good recovery.[4] These victims may or may not feel guilty and self-condemning, but they do feel more in control.

A person who has been victimized may become obsessed with preventive measures after the crime. Some burglary victims invest in elaborate new locks or alarm systems. Many people who have been assaulted on the street change their patterns of travel; they may walk several blocks out of their way to avoid the street where the crime occurred. Some people buy guns or sign up for self-defense courses because they want to feel more confident about facing another criminal. Other victims just think or talk about taking preventive measures.

The victim's loved ones are often tempted to belittle these efforts. They may feel such gestures are futile—locking the barn door after the horse is gone. But the impulse to take action to prevent another crime is positive. If the victim recognizes some error in his or her behavior that made the crime more possible, it is certainly worthwhile to correct the error. Whatever victims can do to feel more safe will be emotionally reparative. The fact that victims feel able to *do something* will also restore some of their lost autonomy.

Sometimes the victim's efforts to prevent future crimes seem excessive to others, and sometimes they are excessive. It is important for the victim to maintain realistic expectations; no matter what a person does to prevent crime, chance will still play a role and revictimization is always possible. But so long as the victim's preventive efforts are active and reasonable, they should be encouraged.

There is a danger in blaming oneself, however. When victims feel guilty and act guilty, other people may get the idea that they *are* guilty, that they really had some complicity in the crime. This misperception can add to the victim's sense of violation, especially if the guilt is not wholly conscious. It can also deprive the victim of sympathy and comfort if others feel that he or she is not entitled to their concern.

Especially harmful are people who like to play at being the "shrink," those who assume that they can understand the victim's unconscious motives. Myrna Field moved to Detroit from a small town in upper Michigan. She was the victim of two robberies within a year of the move. One of her new acquaintances subjected her to amateur analysis.

> Someone told me a couple of weeks after the first experience that I was a victim in the sense that I was like one of those people who is a *victim*, that's my role in life or something. I think it was a really nasty thing to say.... In fact, I saw him after the second experience and he said the same thing. And I told him I thought what he was doing was trying to

explain to himself that this would never happen to him. But at the same time, when he first said that, I believed that it must be so, somehow, because when the second thing happened, I remember feeling afterwards: Why do these things happen to me?

If other people mirror the victim's self-blame, his or her guilt will be reinforced.

An additional complication can arise in the self-blaming victim's dealings with police officers and prosecutors. Some of those who work in criminal justice have become expert in sensing a person who feels guilty. They may misread the signal and decide that the victim has some responsibility for the crime when, in fact, the guilt is the result of having been forced to surrender responsibility. This misunderstanding is especially likely in rape cases, since many people are predisposed to view the rape victim with suspicion. It can prevent the crime from being accurately perceived and adequately prosecuted.

The complicity that comes from helplessness is extraordinarily painful. Victims cannot defend themselves. In crimes of stealth, there is no confrontation—the crime is discovered only when it is past and cannot be undone. When criminals confront their victims directly, the victims submit because survival seems, rightly, more important than self-assertion. The fact is an innocent victim cannot help being victimized.

It is difficult for police officers and prosecutors to identify with the victim's helplessness. They are responsible for the prevention of crime and for the capture and punishment of criminals. Achieving their professional goals involves active and successful resistance to crime. They cannot feel helpless against the criminal if they are to do their jobs. Sympathizing with the victim's position requires them to accept the fact that a criminal has had the upper hand. No matter how much they understand this possibility intellectually, criminal-justice professionals still must find it emotionally threatening. It is sometimes easier for them to assume that the victim must be guilty.

They Are Responsible

The alternative to blaming oneself is to blame someone else. A victim in search of an attribution may decide that others are at fault.

People who are linked to the events surrounding the crime are often
believed by the victim to be responsible in some causal way. The
landlord who employs a careless doorman may be blamed for a
burglary, for example. Or people may blame the police for not being
present on a deserted street.

Other-blaming attributions may take the form of a more general
condemnation of the forces the victim holds responsible for what
he or she sees as the weakening of traditional institutions: the high
divorce rate, neglectful parents, the failures of the church, the indifference of modern medicine, and so on. Many people feel as if
there has been a steady decline in moral values since the 1950s, a
loss that they attribute to such factors as the war in Vietnam, the
permissiveness of the sixties and early seventies, or increased cor-
ruption in government highlighted by the Watergate scandal. Such
broad attributions may be expressed or believed by victims who
place the cause of the crime outside of themselves.

Violence and destructiveness are so foreign to the immediate experience of most victims that they are genuinely puzzled by personal
crime. If the victim's attribution focuses on other people, he or she
may articulate a number of possible forces that could have been the
cause. One victim of urban vandalism was shocked when a group of
teenagers rampaged through his neighborhood after a rock concert.
He tried to cover all the bases when he was asked about the reason
for the crime:

> Well, traditionally, I guess you blame the parents. Apparently these kids
> have not been made to understand that when one is in someone else's
> area or environment, they should act accordingly, like they're in their
> own. . . . I would say [the cause lies] in the home, but I don't think you
> can just lay it there. I mean, also the root could be in just the difference
> between suburb and city. There's a certain amount of electricity in the
> city, especially for young people. It's all alive, you know? That might
> have something to do with it. I wonder if the educational system stresses
> [respect for property]? Or maybe it's just the way society works. I mean,
> you see constant property abuse and people abuse in areas like movies
> and TV. I mean, this is a violent country. . . . I think it's from several
> areas, the whole spectrum of things.

Such an attribution can leave the victim feeling rather hopeless; one hardly knows where to begin to correct such widespread social problems.

Attributing the crime to someone else allows victims less sense of personal control than they feel if they blame themselves; many people feel they have less power over outside forces than over themselves. But blaming others has the advantage of allowing the victim to feel righteous anger: "Isn't it awful that they let these terrible things happen to me?" Blaming others also makes it possible for the victim to feel entitled to sympathy and support.

At the same time, and somewhat paradoxically, victims who project the blame outward may be seen by other people as less deserving of help. A belligerent, other-blaming victim seems stronger than a penitent, self-blaming one. The other-blaming victim may even be seen as threatening and find that he or she has alienated people who might have helped. Police officers confronted by a victim who asks accusing questions about police procedures can easily become defensive and wary. After the robbers who tied up Len Baron left his apartment, he worked his feet loose and hopped to the phone to call the police. Ten minutes later they arrived at the door and were greeted by an enraged victim who attacked them before they could even untie him. "Where the hell were you?" he screamed. Several days later, Len called the responding officers to find out about his case, but they never returned his call.

Blaming others is usually less punishing for the victim than self-blame. But blaming others can also provoke further difficulties, especially if the person blamed is a loved one, because the victim may lose that person's support. Whether the other-blaming attribution is expressed or just believed, the loved one will feel a loss of trust and faith that can have long-term repercussions in the relationship. If the victim feels as if his or her spouse is responsible for the crime, for example, that attribution may precipitate a personal crisis in the marriage.

We do not mean to suggest that the victim can or should be expected to consider the relative merits of alternative forms of attribution. Attribution is not a rational, decision-making process. It is a mechanism that is activated consciously or unconsciously by the victim's need to explain the crime and so repair the damaged self.

Victims are usually aware at some point after the crime that they have established an explanation for it, although the attribution may not be expressed to others if the victim feels it to be irrational or shameful. The reason for a particular victim believing a particular attribution is always complex and individual.

The Illusion of Control

Attribution studies have found that people who believe they are in control gain all the benefits of the belief—personal comfort and strength to withstand pain and cope with the crisis—*whether or not the person is actually in control.*[5] The illusion of control is just as good as true control for the purposes of short-term repair, and so it is helpful to support victims in whatever attributions they make. It can be harmful (and it is surely insensitive) for other people to insist that the victim be rational during the impact stage of the crisis. The best support is provided by those who are able to listen, hearing out the victim's notions about the reason for the crime and supporting the need to make them.

Friends and loved ones are sometimes tempted to argue with the victim about the attribution. Victims who blame themselves seem to be adding the pain of guilt to the pain of violation. The impulse to protest is natural: "Stop it. You're being much too hard on yourself." People who are directly accused of blame by the victim will feel the need to protect themselves. Loved ones also develop their own attributions to defend against their own distress. Everyone is upset by the crime, and sometimes victims and their families have terrible quarrels in which opposing theories about why the crime happened become entrenched positions.

It is useful to distinguish between supporting the victim's feelings and agreeing with his or her perceptions. The feeling that the victim is expressing when he or she makes an attribution is the wish to get back into control. The other person can reflect and support that feeling ("You're really upset about this. That's a natural reaction.") without being drawn into a discussion of the validity of the attribution. Victims need to find a reason in whatever way they can, and those who want to help them should support that effort as reparative.

Loved ones who are involved with the victim in the crisis period can also be aware of the dangers inherent in attribution. If the victim is alienating others or creating the impression that he or she really is guilty, another person can sometimes act to prevent these difficulties. The accused husband can remember that the victim needs to blame somebody and try not to take the accusation personally. The responding officer can be aware of the victim's need to attribute and take that into consideration in his or her own perception if the victim seems guilty. Victims cannot be expected to take these precautions—they're too involved in trying to find a reason.

The Attributions of Loved Ones

The important people in the victim's life—family and close friends—also need to explain the crime because they identify with and are threatened by the victim's pain. Their attribution may take the form of self-blame or of blaming others, depending on the situation and the personality of the loved one. The other person's need to attribute has the same source as the victim's: It is a way to restore order to a disordered universe. It is intolerable to feel that there is nothing you can do to prevent loved ones from being hurt. This is especially true if the victim is seen as a person in need of special protection—a child or an elderly parent, for example. Those who love the vulnerable ones may feel that they have failed them in some way because they have not kept them safe.

If another person is actually present during the crime, feelings of self-blame may be very strong. A husband who is forced to stand by while robbers take his wife's purse, for example, may be almost overwhelmed by feelings of shame and rage. Similarly, if the victim is attacked at home while other family members are absent, they are likely to berate themselves for leaving the victim alone. No one can be around twenty-four hours a day to protect loved ones, but others in the family may still feel that they played a role in the crime just because they were absent.

"If only" is a common phrase on the lips of those whose loved ones are victims of personal crime. "If only I had met him after school. . . . If only I hadn't gone to my bridge club that night. . . . If only I had phoned to see if she was all right." It is quite possible that the presence of another person would not have prevented the crime—even possible that the presence of another person would have aggravated the situation in some way. But the friends and family of the victim wish they could have prevented the crime, and sometimes they blame themselves in order to make sense of it all.

The loved one may also blame someone else. A third party or some more general force is sometimes seen as the cause of the crime. But sometimes the loved one blames the victim. Feeling the need to attribute the crime to something, feeling the victim's pain, and perhaps feeling guilty because he or she didn't stop the criminal, the loved one may turn on the victim. Sometimes this attribution is expressed directly, even angrily; then it is likely to increase the victim's sense of isolation and guilt. If a boy is mugged in the schoolyard and then his parents scold him, he is going to feel even more confused and hurt. Yet the parents' need to defend against their own pain in this way may be very strong.

Blaming the victim may take a more subtle form. The other person may ask "helpful" questions that indicate that the victim is at fault: "Why didn't you . . . ?" "Don't you think you could have . . . ?" The other person may give the victim advice: "The thing to do is simply not walk down that street after dark." This sort of questioning or advice may be quite innocent and well-meaning, but it is clearly not helpful to the victim because it cuts him or her off from the other person. How can the victim get comfort from a person who suggests, however indirectly, that the victim is responsible for the crime?

Victims sometimes respond to these accusations with anger, creating a spiral of bad feeling between them and their loved ones. These upsets in the relationship occur at the very time when the victim most needs help from those who care about him or her. If the victim is unaware of the loved one's conviction that the victim is at fault, it may still contaminate their relationship because it can become an undeclared tension between them. Thus the unfinished business surrounding the crime may be perpetuated for months or even years after the event.

The significant others in the victim's life have not themselves been directly victimized, and it seems reasonable to hope that some of them will be able to order their priorities and make an effort to put the victim's needs first. If one person cannot manage this, perhaps another can. Loved ones who feel a strong urge to blame the victim would do well to withdraw temporarily and urge the support of others who are not so emotionally entangled.

Adding Insult to Injury

Victim-blaming is a very common occurrence in the aftermath of a personal crime. It provides a ready-made answer to the question "Why me?" It's a cruel answer, and it is almost always unwarranted by the facts, but it can be terribly seductive. Practically everyone has been exposed to enough popularized psychology to know about concepts such as unconscious motivation. Under the influence of their need to attribute, both victims and their loved ones are ripe to decide that the victim has been somehow unwittingly responsible for his or her own injury. Victims who accept the blame may be further violated by their confusion and guilt as they struggle to uncover the alleged unconscious impulses that made them arrange for the crime to happen.

The trouble with victim-blaming applied on a broad and general scale is that it denies the sudden, arbitrary, unpredictable nature of a personal crime. Suppose that two men are drunk and quarreling. One of them dares the other to shoot him. If his companion pulls out a gun and murders the one who dared him, the murder victim

might be said to be somewhat responsible for the crime. Such behavior on the part of the victim is characterized in some victimology
research as "victim precipitation" of the crime. But the overwhelming majority of personal crimes do not happen this way. There is no
study that shows that crime victims are, by and large, responsible
for the crimes that befall them.[6] Such a formulation is judgmental—its
purpose seems to be to fault victims and thus to judge them unworthy. As such, wholesale victim-blaming is essentially moralistic.

It is a central conviction of this book that the contrary is true:
Most crime victims do not cause crimes to happen. For the most part
victims are not motivated by unconscious destructive wishes that
are acted out in their participation in the crime. Almost all victims
of personal crime are genuine victims of a catastrophic life experience. We believe, in short, that most victims didn't do it.

But blaming the victim is so common that it is useful to follow
the unconscious-motivation theory out to its logical conclusion. According to psychoanalytic theory, masochism requires pain in a close
relationship; masochists need to be hurt by those they love because
in their development they have experienced a perversion of sense—a
masochist believes that to be hurt is to be loved. In most personal
crimes, this formulation simply does not fit because the criminal and
the victim are strangers. They have never seen each other before,
and they will never see each other again. It is impossible for them
to have a masochistic relationship.

Even if one broadens the possible motivation of the crime victim
to some general construct such as "all unconscious self-destructive
impulses," the victim still cannot be blamed for most personal crimes.
Unconscious motivation is used to explain behavior in which the
person's life plan and continuing relationships are involved. People
with unconscious needs to hurt themselves might, for example,
choose a job with a punishing boss or a marriage with an unfaithful
partner. But unconscious motivation is ordinarily not operating in
sudden, unpredictable events such as a personal crime. The victim-
blaming theory gives the unconscious mind more power than it has;
it assumes that people can have unconscious control over chance
events.

The relationship between a criminal and a victim is much more like the relationship between a cancer and its victim than it is like the relationship of sado-masochistic lovers. Heavy smokers do not smoke because of their anticipation, conscious or otherwise, of the exquisite pain of lung cancer. People smoke because it gives them pleasure. They may believe they can avoid getting cancer, despite considerable evidence to the contrary. Or they may be choosing the lesser of two evils, preferring the risk of cancer to the pain of withdrawing from cigarettes. Making this kind of choice, taking this kind of chance, is very far from choosing to smoke because one wishes unconsciously to be subject to the pain of cancer.

Similarly, a man who takes a walk after dark in his neighborhood and is mugged is almost certainly not asking for the mugging. The victim may be unaware of the danger. He may simply refuse to be afraid in his own home territory. He may have needed to buy a quart of milk for breakfast. Criminals, like cancers, are basically mysterious, unpredictable agents of harm. People with unconscious desires to hurt themselves arrange for something more predictable and certain.

Blaming the victim ignores the enormous complexity of the decisions involved in keeping oneself safe from harm. It says, in effect, that everyone could be safe all the time if they simply wished to be and were healthy enough to arrange their lives accordingly. This is nonsense. It ignores the whole function of accident and chance in our lives. It says that if a man is walking along a street and he is suddenly struck by a flowerpot from the twelfth-story balcony, that person unconsciously placed himself in the way of the pot!

When something bad happens, it is not usually the fault of the injured person. Crime victims are not guilty until proven innocent. There are chance events in life. People do what they can to reduce the harmful effects of chance in their lives, but no one can eliminate them completely. It is possible to lessen the probability of one's being a victim of personal crime, but it is simply not possible to reduce that probability to zero. This is a painful and disturbing fact of human life. The victim-blamers, who choose to deny the chance factor, are acting out of an understandable need to find a reason for the crime. But they have chosen a punishing answer.

The Complications of Altruism

It is sometimes said that criminals are themselves victims, victims of a social system that forces them to commit crimes.[7] Attributing the criminal's behavior to some demanding necessity is a thoughtful alternative to saying that all criminals are bad people. A person who tries to understand the broader significance of human events, who is not quick to hate, who wants to see both sides of a question may find that simply condemning the criminal is distasteful.

Victims of personal crime often think about what motivated the criminal to violate them. One woman who had been robbed at gunpoint expressed this compassionate view: "I think criminals are products of their families and their environment. And I think they must have been brutalized as children and become psychopathic or whatever the term is . . . sociopathic . . . for a person who acts out his powerlessness and feelings of aggression onto, you know, innocent people." A burglary victim tried to give the burglar a "good" motive: "I guess I'd rather think that the guy was doing it to feed his kids than just to make himself some extra money." Such expressions testify to the wish to understand the criminal. They may also help to make the crime seem less frightening in retrospect.

But this kind of thinking can introduce an additional complication in the recovery of a crime victim. When victims feel that the criminal had some justification, it may be extremely difficult for them to allow themselves to feel angry. If the criminal is, in the victim's imagination, a person who acts out of desperation—an addict who had to have the money for a fix or a black person who has suffered intolerable racist torment or a parent who can't get a job—then the victim may be caught in his or her own altruism. The victim may ask, "How can I be angry at the poor criminal?"

Attributing the criminal's behavior to some social malaise can pull the crime victim down into a spiral of helpless depression. The victim may feel: "The criminal couldn't help it. I couldn't help it. The society is to blame. There is nothing any of us can do about the injustices in society. We are all helpless." Such feelings can be very destructive to the victim's recovery. They are sometimes a cover for unresolved anger, and it would probably be better for the victim if the anger could be expressed directly.

Some victims who think about the reasons for the criminal's behavior are just trying to make sense of what happened. No one knows what motivates a criminal, but speculations about the personal and social pressures that produce criminal behavior can help us feel more in control. Victims who are able to resolve their crisis may come to accept what has happened to them as the sad but inevitable evidence of human imperfection.

Who Is to Blame Really?

People who have been directly affected by the crisis of personal crime will experience a clear and powerful need to make an attribution about the crime. And even people who have never known a personal crime victim want to find reasons for crime because it produces such anxiety.[8] This desire to attribute crime to something is quite apart from our interest as individuals or as a society in reducing crime. The need to find a reason will be satisfied by any plausible answer, whether or not it is true and whether or not it allows for the formulation of preventive measures.

Obviously, however, unless people find some right answers, unless the attributions they make are true, whatever they do to prevent crime either personally or socially will not be effective. If, for example, punishing criminals is not a deterrent, our society can punish criminals from now until doomsday and still not find any relief from crime. But people who believe that punishing criminals will reduce crime, or that moving to the suburbs will protect them from mugging, can find short-term relief by constructing this belief and acting on it. All of which is to say that there is no necessary connection between getting relief from the need to make an attribution and getting relief from the real threat of crime.

As a matter of fact, if the attributions chosen are not the right ones, people can use up a lot of energy supporting programs and taking various defensive actions only to find nothing happens to the crime rate. The need to attribute must and will be satisfied by the individual crime victim, but it is also useful to consider what is known about the real reasons for victimization. Unfortunately a great deal of misunderstanding about the causes of crime has been encouraged by the academic community, the police, departments of justice, and public officials at all levels. The truth is that no one knows very much about why crime happens, and so we have been able to do very little about it.

People do things that make them more likely candidates for crime victimization. Leaving the keys in an unlocked car in a high-crime area increases the probability that the car will be stolen. But the situation is far more complex than a simple cause-and-effect relationship. If a person parks his or her car in a low-crime area, locks it, and takes the keys, the car may still be stolen. The very best anybody can do is to decrease the statistical probability. There is no way that anyone can guarantee that he or she will never be a victim of crime, at least as long as there are criminals in the world.

How, then, does one account for the fact that some people are repeatedly victimized by personal crime, and others never are? There is a probability factor; it isn't just pure chance, but most theories that have been constructed to explain the probability end up blaming the victim in some way. There are several alternatives.

First of all, lack of knowledge is a determining factor for many victims of personal crime. Some victims take risks out of ignorance. Many people do not realize, for example, that some locks can be easily picked; in their naïveté, they may fail to replace vulnerable locks in a new apartment. Just because these people are uninformed, they may be victims of a burglary. Their lack of knowledge does not mean that they have an unconscious wish to be victimized; it simply means that they need to be educated about locks.

Criminals are incredibly sensitive to cues in the environment and from other people that permit them to target an unwary victim. They have a nose for a likely "hit." A professional burglar can spot that vulnerable lock in a seemingly casual walk up three or four flights in an apartment building, just as a professional pickpocket can spot tourists who lack the knowledge to protect themselves. People who live in cities develop the defensive mechanisms they need to reduce the probability of their being victimized, and they can usually spot a newcomer who is an easy mark. The city dweller may even make friendly suggestions to strangers to help them become more careful, such as urging a woman in the subway to hold on to her purse straps instead of just leaving the purse lying loose in her lap.

There is a wealth of information around from all kinds of sources that attempt to educate people so that they will not become victims of crime. But some people have not been exposed to such defensive ways of thinking, and they are statistically more likely to be victims. Not because they are self-destructive or even because they are stupid, but simply because they are ignorant. They lack information.

A second possibility is that people who become crime victims increase their probability of being victimized because of some conscious choice they have made. This might be called playing the percentages. Each person has to make decisions all the time about the kinds of risks he or she will take in life. Some people decide, for example, that they simply refuse to lock themselves into their own homes. Turning their nests into prisons or armed camps may be so uncomfortable that they would rather take the risk of being burglarized than take what seem to be extreme measures to avoid that possibility.

Every individual has his or her own personal sense of where this line should be drawn, but every person draws it. There is no way to be absolutely sure you won't be burglarized. At the extreme limit of protective deterrence, you might hire an armed guard to live in the house twenty-four hours a day. Most people choose to limit their protective measures to some lesser alternative. One woman, for example, draws the line just short of the Fox police lock, a device that includes a strong steel bar that rests against the door on the inside and fits into a slot on the floor so that it braces against the door. She just refuses to have one of those things in her front hall. There is a legitimate choice factor involved in such decisions. When people are aware of the risks and aware of their own feelings about the kinds of measures they can take to cut the risks, they can make a rational decision about how to play the percentages.

Any person can devote only so much time, energy, and money to protection from criminals. Beyond that, there is a real revulsion in many people to the feeling that they must always be careful, always be suspicious, always lock up their possessions. The last years of the late Howard Hughes were a kind of dreadful parody of the extent to which fear can become a self-destructive obsession. People who are continually worried about locks and alarms and self-defense cannot be very happy people.

Mary Connolly made a number of changes in her life after she was the victim of a mugging. She takes more precautions now, and she feels as if the mugger has continued to influence her decisions in a disturbing way.

> I was not aware of the world the way I am now. I don't carry a handbag anymore. I carry a few dollars in my pocket—enough to give but not too much to lose. I hide my jewelry if I ride the subway. I've become wise and wary in a very oppressive way. You almost feel that you're punishing yourself rather than that the world is taking care of these people who should be punished.

There is a point where not trusting other people begins to erode the quality of one's life.

There is a third possibility, a third factor that may explain a crime. Perhaps the victim's personality is involved. If criminals can detect the qualities in people that make them more likely to be vulnerable to victimization, one might logically consider isolating those qualities and teaching people who have them to change. Much of the writing about crime prevention takes this basic strategy. However, qualities that may alert the criminal to a prospective victim are often exactly the qualities that most people value in an individual. Openness, willingness to trust, and the desire to believe the best about a stranger, for example, are ordinarily considered to be virtues. People who have these qualities are also likely to signal the criminal that they would make a good victim.

This is a dilemma that strikes at the heart of our social system. If people hope for a better world, they need to teach their children to be good people—kind, loving, thoughtful, caring of others. Yet this kind of goodness is really quite dysfunctional in a predatory environment, and while it may be desirable in an abstract sense, in day-to-day living in areas in which criminal victimization is likely, it is a real disservice to train children this way. They are, simply, more likely to be hurt if they trust people.

Victim-blamers say, in effect, that there is something wrong with victims. It seems more likely that there is something right with many of them. The good person is the logical target of the predator. The lion hunts the gazelle, the lovely one. If a parent manages to raise a child who is not spontaneously suspicious of others, who is willing to believe the best of people, who is polite to strangers, who is not antisocially aggressive, that child is likely to be maladaptive in a hostile environment. His or her good qualities may alert the predator and make the child a candidate for victimization.

Parents seem to have a rather bitter choice. They can raise good children who may become victims, or they can raise hostile children who will adapt well in a predatory society. How can we be both appropriately defensive in a world that includes criminals and actively supportive of the human qualities we most highly value?

Related to this dilemma is the fact that many people are victimized by personal crime when their defenses are down because they are in trouble or they are having a good time. Crowds at a carnival are ideal groups in which to find pickpocket victims, for example, because people are happy and relaxed, off their guard. People are often victimized while they are on vacation for the same reason. Conversely, a funeral provides a good opportunity for a burglar to get into the home of the family of the deceased because everybody will be away and also because they are likely to be preoccupied with their grief and therefore to take fewer precautions than they normally would. There are burglars who work the circuit of the bereaved by reading the obituary pages each week. People are especially vulnerable when they are distracted by joy or by distress.

There are no easy answers to the questions raised by criminal victimization. It is useful to be aware of the need to attribute and to recognize the added problems that attribution can engender. When we can acknowledge the fact that human life is a risky business, we are in a better position to calculate the risks we want to take. Parents can try to raise children who are trusting and good but who also have a tolerable level of suspicion and caution when it is appropriate. All of us can learn to respond to cues in the environment and to be on our guard selectively when it is necessary. This is what city people call "street sense." Approaching this realistic outlook is certainly a great challenge, but it seems the only alternative if we are to keep the social fabric together while we try to find some more successful ways of coping with the flaws in it.

NOTES

1. In some traditions the victim in these rituals is a blameless one who assumes the faults of the entire community and then is symbolically or actually destroyed. One of the earliest recorded examples of this practice is the new year's celebration of the ancient Mesopotamians, who saw their king was temporarily divested of his power and subjected to ritual humiliation as an expiation for the sins of his people. In Jewish tradition, the sacrificial victim is found in Hebrew rituals celebrated in ancient times during Yom Kippur. In these ceremonies, two goats were used as a sacrifice to atone for the transgressions of the Children of Israel. One of them, called the scapegoat, was set loose in the wilderness after the sins of the tribe had been confessed over its head (see Leviticus 16:21-22). The Christian concept of the crucifixion of Christ as an expiation for the sins of all people is a direct descendent of this tradition; one innocent is singled out to bear the sins of the whole world (see Hebrews 9:13-14).

2. The need to gain some control, symbolic or real, over the things that threaten is so strong that there is virtually no culture in which it does not play an important role. Psychologist Abraham Maslow, in devising his hierarchy of human needs, placed safety second only to physical well-being among the primary needs of individuals [*Motivation and Personality*, 2d ed. (New York: Harper and Row, 1970), pp. 39-43.] If people do not feel a certain measure of personal safety, their functioning is seriously compromised.

3. Morton Bard and Ruth B. Dyk, "The Psychodynamic Significance of Beliefs Regarding the Cause of Serious Illness," *Psychoanalytic Review* 43 (1956): 146-162.

4. See, for example, R. Janoff-Bulman, "Characteriological Versus Behavioral Self-Blame: Inquiries into Depression and Rape," *Journal of Personality and Social Psychology* 37 (1979): 1798-1809 and D.T. Miller and C.A. Porter, "Self-Blame in Victims of Violence," *Journal of Social Issues* 39 (1983): 139-151.

5. Ellen I. Langer, "The Illusion of Control," *Journal of Personality and Social Psychology* 32 (1975): 311-328.

6. Researchers have used a number of different definitions of victim precipitation; studies in this area present all sorts of methodological problems. See Robert A. Silverman, "Victim Precipitation: An Examination of the Concept," in I. Drapkin and E. Viano, eds., *Victimology: A New Focus* vol. 1 (Lexington, Mass.: D.C. Heath, 1974) and Richard F. Sparks, *Research on Victims of Crime: Accomplishments, Issues, and New Directions* (Rockville, Md.: National Institute of Mental Health, Center for Studies of Crime and Delinquency, 1982).

7. Criminal behavior is the result of complex and varying sets of personal and social factors. A great deal of research has been devoted to determining what these factors are, but the results of these studies are inconclusive. Poverty is generally acknowledged to be related to criminal

behavior, for example, but no one knows why some poor people become criminals and others do not.

8. Fear of crime affects many people, including some who have never been victims of a crime. Public opinion polls show that people express fear of crime in general while at the same time indicating that they feel safe in their own neighborhood and believe that their neighborhood is less dangerous than others. The National Crime Survey Reactions to Crime project found that women and the elderly generally express more fear of crime than do people in other groups, despite the fact that women and the elderly are not among the most-victimized population groups. These fears were explained by the content of communications about crime, which tend to emphasize female victims and elderly victims. The Reactions to Crime project also found that people who have not been personally victimized may be very strongly affected when they hear about the victimization of others, especially relatives, friends, or neighbors. (*Report to the Nation on Crime and Justice: The Data*, Bureau of Justice Statistics, 1983, p. 18)

5

The Mark: Feelings of Guilt and Shame

I just hate to think of myself as a victim. It's like when I
lost my job—I hadn't done anything wrong, but it was so
embarrassing to have to tell people that I had lost my job.
And when this happened, I felt the same way. It was like
a guilty secret. I didn't want to talk about it.

—Robbery victim

In the criminal's jargon, the person who is victimized is sometimes
called the *mark*.[1] The word carries a bit of a sneer; it suggests contempt for people who make good targets because they are so trusting
and naïve. It also implies that the criminal is smarter than the victim—that criminals are successful because they are more clever
rather than simply because they are more ruthless. The mark is a
sucker, a patsy, a fool—not quite smart enough to take the proper
precautions.

Crime victims are commonly seen as losers and failures: They have
been defeated by the criminal, who has outwitted them; they have
failed in their efforts to protect themselves. This judgment is probably
made in one way or another by most of the people who come in

76

contact with the victim after the crime. Some feeling of contempt for the victim is shared by practically everyone in our society. It certainly helps to account for the way victims are treated within the criminal-justice system and in the society at large.

In effect, victims of personal crime are stigmatized by their victimization. They are marked by others as different, flawed. Sociologist Erving Goffman describes the mechanism of social stigma: "An individual who might have been received easily in ordinary social intercourse possesses a trait that can obtrude itself upon the attention and turn those of us whom he meets away from him, breaking the claim that his other attributes have on us. He possesses a stigma, an undesired differentness. . . ."[2] The rest of us, who consider ourselves "normal," label the stigmatized person, often without being fully aware that we are doing so. We separate ourselves from victims as if they were beneath us.

Most professionals who see crime victims in their work are dealing with people who are strangers to them, a circumstance that makes stigmatizing the victim relatively easy. When you don't know very much about someone, it is easier to see that person as different from yourself. But the impulse to label the victim can be so strong that it will overcome the bonds of a deep friendship. A woman who has been raped, for example, may find that her friends are uneasy around her. The close friend of one rape victim struggled for some time after the crime to release herself and her friend from the power of the stigma:

> I remember feeling badly for a long time that I would look at her and I would think, you know, that's the woman I know who was raped . . . and I was really feeling bad about this preying on my mind and I couldn't, you know, forget it. I felt it was a real injustice to her that she had to carry this burden. . . . There is still that certain aura of being, ah, I think of it as tarnished. You're not quite whole and pure anymore and people remember that. And it's so unjust. . . . But I found those feelings in myself.

The Negative Identity

The fact that crime victims are stigmatized by their victimization adds a whole other dimension to their struggle to recover from the effects of their experience. In addition to facing the personal crisis precipitated by the criminal's violation, victims must also deal with their new, negative identity: the label "crime victim/loser." The sense of violation and the need to find a reason for the crime are essentially internal, private experiences. But a person's identity comes in part from his or her relationships with others; identity is social as well as personal. After the crime, victims become concerned about what other people think of them, about how the victimization has changed them in the eyes of others. And since the way we feel about ourselves is often influenced by what we think others feel about us, victims may accept and internalize negative judgments about themselves as a result of the crime.

Every victim of personal crime experiences some feelings of guilt and shame. These feelings are often complex and unfocused, especially during the impact phase. In the less serious violations, the victim's sense of being stigmatized is often expressed in a vague sense of embarrassment or uneasiness. When the victim has been physically injured, the wounded body is often felt to be shameful in some way. John Maxwell was hurt when he struggled briefly with a pickpocket who took his wallet. The next day John realized that his finger had been broken and dislocated in the encounter. He went to the hospital and had it set, but he felt as if he were carrying a badge of dishonor. "The biggest trouble I had was . . . it's funny, but I felt ashamed about the cast. I have a feeling that it had to do with the violation of the thing."

Rape victims commonly suffer from feelings that their bodies have been defiled. One woman remembers the ride to the hospital vividly because she had such a terrible wish to be able to get away from her own body. "I felt so contaminated. I didn't want to touch any part of me or have any part of me touch any other part."

Guilt comes from a sense of having done something wrong.[3] The guilty feeling may be motivated in part by the victim's need to find a reason for the crime, as we saw in the last chapter. Self-blame allows victims to reorder the world because it explains why it makes sense for them to suffer.

Some victims experience a kind of generalized guilt by association. Criminals emanate from dark places—alleys, corners, dim streets in the night. Anything having to do with crime becomes associated in people's feelings with dirtiness, ugliness, evil. These diffuse negative feelings may be shared by victims, who feel contaminated by their unwitting involvement in this nasty business.

Feelings of shame come from a sense of having been a failure. Many victims have a persistent conviction that they should have been able to do something to prevent the crime from turning out so badly. Victims may be ashamed of their inability to remain in control of the situation, even if they can also see that this expectation is unrealistic.[4] It would be foolish, for example, for an unarmed person to try to disarm a gunman, but people who have been held up by armed robbers often express shame because they did not try to defend themselves.

Barbara Preiser was attacked by a purse-snatcher one rainy evening as she was walking near her home. She tried to resist the attacker, but she still felt ashamed because she was unsuccessful.

> I have a friend who was confronted by a robber. She went into a karate crouch and made a loud noise. And the robber said, "Oh my God, no!" and ran in the other direction. And she didn't know karate. I didn't have the presence of mind to do anything really effective. I shouted, "Don't you dare!" and hit at him with my open umbrella, a very ineffective weapon. Having presence of mind is very different.

Barbara's expectation that she should have been able to remain cool seems unfair, but the hero fantasy often colors a victim's judgment of his or her performance under stress.

The relationship between shame and trust has been explored by sociologist Helen Merrell Lynd, who explains that personal feelings of shame are related to violations of trust, especially a loss of one's trust in a benevolent and orderly world:

> What we have thought we could count on in ourselves, and what we have thought to be the boundaries and contours of the world, turn out suddenly not to be the "real" outlines of ourselves or of the world, or those that others accept. We have become strangers in a world where we thought we were at home. We experience anxiety in becoming aware that we cannot trust our answers to the questions: Who am I? Where do I belong?[5]

The crime victim, who has suffered a grievous violation of trust, is especially vulnerable to the anxiety that Lynd describes.

Feelings of shame and guilt seem to vary with the degree of physical injury experienced by the victim. The social meaning of a physical wound is quite different from its significance to the self. Victims who suffer bodily injury experience a more intense violation of self than those who escape physical harm, but the social effect of physical injury is usually positive. Victims who sustain physical wounds are obviously, visibly injured in a way that everyone can recognize. They can be helped—their hurt bodies can be bandaged and soothed. Physical wounds also represent tangible evidence of the victim's blamelessness because the wounds suggest resistance, even if the criminal came up from behind and was never seen. A physically injured victim is less likely to feel ashamed and less likely to provoke blaming feelings in others.

On the other hand, victims who are not harmed physically are considered fortunate, and while their sense of violation of self may be less strong, they are more vulnerable to negative social criticism. Uninjured victims are more likely to worry about their submission to the criminal, to feel as if they complied in the crime in some way. Since their emotional injuries are invisible, they may feel unjustified in seeking sympathy and embarrassed by their neediness. Other people are less likely to know how to help them and more likely to project their guilt over this frustration onto the victim who is physically intact. Thus, on balance, the victim who is not harmed physically is probably more vulnerable to the backwash of shame and guilt.

Self-Defense: The Hero Fantasy

Victims commonly express their feelings of guilt and shame by wishing that they had defended themselves more vigorously against the criminal's attack. It's as if every victim has a scolding parent inside who says, "Why didn't you stick up for yourself?" Victims of the personal property crimes—burglary, auto theft, pocket picking, and purse snatching—tend to dwell on their stupidity and negligence in failing to take proper precautions. People who have been physically threatened or injured by a criminal are likely to focus on fantasies about self-defense.

Victims who have been robbed at gunpoint, for example, often express the wish that they had had a gun when the criminal approached them. Women who have submitted to a rapist may have fantasies later in which they attack and overcome their assailant. One rape victim was surprised right outside her front door; she clenched her house keys in her hand during the assault. Later she expressed the wish that she had put out the rapist's eyes with them. Self-recrimination is usually the dominant theme of these wishful fantasies. Their main purpose seems to be to discharge the guilt that the victim feels, and they are usually adaptive.

But it is important for crime victims and others to distinguish between imagination and reality in thinking about self-defense. The wish to avoid the stigma of victimization is both primitive and powerful. It is the theme of a rather disturbing film called *Death Wish* in which the protagonist acts out the fantasy of many crime victims. The hero is a man whose family has been brutalized by street criminals; his wife was murdered and his daughter raped. He responds by taking vigilante revenge, arming himself and taking long walks in deserted parks at night to provoke muggers, whom he shoots and kills when they try to attack him.

Death Wish enjoyed quite a popular run when it first opened in 1974. But when it was subsequently scheduled to be seen on national television, Brian Garfield, the author of the novel on which the film was based, asked the network not to air the film. He said that he believes the film is dangerous because it has inspired several people to commit actual vigilante crimes.[6] Vengeful fantasies about hurting the criminal can be useful and healthy as a form of emotional repair after the crime. Whether a person can or should actually resist a threatening criminal is quite another matter.

Both crime victims and people who have never been victimized tend to assume that defending yourself is the ideal course of action.

Many people admire the victim who resists; he or she is seen as brave and honorable, heroic. Crime victims who defend themselves successfully are the American Dream come true—a potential loser, an underdog, ends up being a winner. This attitude helps to explain the popularity of the movie *Death Wish* and also the widespread approval expressed for victims such as Bernhard Goetz, the New York City man who reacted to the alleged verbal harassment of four teenagers on the subway by pulling out his gun and shooting them. Submission is viewed in our culture as cowardly, and we tend to feel contemptuous of the victim who does not fight back. Some victims probably resist precisely because they are afraid of being labeled cowards.

If the reality of self-defense in a confrontation with a criminal can be separated from all the emotion that surrounds it, a very simple fact emerges: Resistance is a risky business. Recent research affirms what one instinctively knows about the outcome in such confrontations: Crime victims who use physical force in their own defense are more likely to be seriously injured.[7] Even a police officer with a gun is trained to submit to an armed attacker if the officer has been surprised. Your chances of getting out of the situation without being seriously hurt are better if you don't put up a fight.

But, since so many victims kick themselves later because they didn't try to be heroes, it may be useful to consider whether resistance can realistically be seen even as a possible option for most people. One of the hardest things for a normal, reasonable person to do is to injure another person deliberately. The social prohibitions against hurting others are very strong. They are inculcated early and deeply rooted. In a person who has a normal moral upbringing, these prohibitions become part of the self; they function pretty independently of the particular circumstances in which the person may find himself or herself. That is, of course, the way they are supposed to function: People can't go around killing each other and hold the society together for very long.

There are, however, a growing number of self-defense advocates who purport to be able to teach a person to suspend these prohibitions temporarily. Short courses in self-defense that hold the promise of turning potential victims into heroes are being offered. For the most part these courses are extremely dangerous because they give only the illusion of protection. A few hours of self-defense training is unlikely to increase most people's chances of being able to defend themselves. A normally socialized person just cannot suspend the lifelong value of not harming another person, not even when life is threatened.

Typical of the self-defense books is one which outlines a number of defensive strategies for women who are in immediate, life-threatening danger in a rape situation.[8] Among other things, the book suggests that the potential victim lovingly caress the face of the rapist in a seductive ploy to get her hands on his head, and then put her thumbs in his eyes and push them out. From what we know of human behavior, it is unlikely that a normal woman would be able to do that. And if the woman *did* succeed in blinding the rapist, she would have to deal with her feelings about inflicting such horrible damage on another human being.

The trouble with advice of this sort is that it can make a victim doubt himself or herself after the crime. One rape victim who believed she had an opportunity to hurt the rapist made a conscious decision not to do so. Afterwards she asked herself whether she had done the right thing.

> If you get raped, they say it's your own fault, and I think I went through that. Not in terms of society but in terms of my view of myself. There were things I could have done that I didn't feel free to do. My boyfriend did this whole thing about "Why didn't you go for his eyes?" I don't know how I could live with that. No matter what he did to me, I don't know how I could live knowing that I had done that to him. But it's a hard thing to bear. And you know this gets to be, I guess, very existentialist. You have to make your decisions on the basis of what's going on at the time. But, boy, do you think it over and think it over afterwards. The nights I have thought through attacks—when you're literally fighting it out by moving in bed. It's a bad period to go through. You have to fight back some place... But we can't fight with them. They're too destructive.

A criminal is a person who has deliberately embarked on a course of predatory violence—a person who has suspended the social prohibitions against hurting others. Criminals are able to do what they do because they are not under the normal moral constraints. These constraints tend to function in an all-or-nothing fashion; once they have been suspended, the criminal may move from one level of violation to another with relative ease. A burglar who breaks into a house and surprises a woman in bed may rape her. A robber who is disappointed by a small "take" may shoot the victim. In most cases criminals and victims are not peers in this regard. The criminal is much more likely to be able to hurt or kill the victim than the victim is to hurt or kill the criminal. Victims who suffer from the hero fantasy may act on the illusion that they can defend themselves and may thereby suffer grievous injury or death.

Barbara Preiser recognized this crucial difference between her attacker and herself.

> If someone is going to risk whatever it takes to snatch my purse, he is going to be successful because I'm not going to risk whatever may be at stake to defend it. Since they've made that decision, they may also decide to hurt you. My feeling is that this stranger might have killed me. Or broken something. Or how about a good scar? When the rules are down, you don't know what they are. But I haven't made that decision to hurt someone.

Another victim put it slightly differently: "If somebody is going to be a criminal, you just never know what they might do. I mean, somebody who does that is crazy to begin with."

People who allow themselves to be critical of a crime victim's behavior reveal an understandable anxiety about their own vulnerability, but the criticism is neither fair nor helpful. Every act of crime is a unique instance, and no one should presume to know exactly what is right in each situation. Self-defense training can be offered as an alternative, a way of increasing a person's options. But when it becomes attack advocacy, this training has the potential to induce enormous guilt. It is not helpful for others to advocate fighting back *or* submitting *or* any other single "right" behavior. The victim is the only person in a position to know what could or should have been done. And the victim's survival is the bottom line. A police officer who has been trained to help rape victims says it all when he tells them, "If you survived, whatever you did was the right thing."

Very few people can predict with certainty what they will do in any stressful situation—let alone a confrontation with a criminal. Under the stress of a sudden threat, a victim's behavior is highly spontaneous. Even a person who anticipates the possibility of being victimized is likely to behave in surprising ways. Nancy Tornbury teaches chemistry in Albuquerque. She was assigned to a new school in a high-crime neighborhood. She discussed with her husband, who is a police officer, exactly how best to deal with the possibility that she might be threatened traveling to and from her new job. They decided that purse snatching was the most likely crime and made elaborate preparations to minimize the losses involved.

Nancy decided to carry a purse that had no value to her. She reasoned that if and when an attempt was made to snatch it, she would feel free to just let it go. She put all of her valuables in her inside pockets every day before she set out for work. She and her husband even rehearsed the purse snatching so that she would feel reasonably comfortable about the execution of their defensive plan.

As the couple had anticipated, an attempt was made to snatch Nancy's purse. Two young men came up to her as she was on her way out of a downtown parking lot. They walked past her, and then one of them turned and grabbed the worthless purse. She refused to let it go. She had never screamed before in her life; now she heard herself screaming and screaming. The would-be felons scuffled with her briefly and knocked her down before they fled empty-handed. She never did surrender her empty purse, in spite of all her rehearsing.

It is nonsense to ask a crime victim: "Why didn't you resist?" It is equally unfair to say: "You should have submitted." No one can predict what a person will do when suddenly confronted by a criminal. Victims do the best they can, and no one is in a position to judge their behavior. It is almost inevitable that the victim will feel some guilt, but it is also useful for everyone involved to remember that recrimination and regret can only inflict further damage.

Alienation, Depression, and Denial

Negative feelings about the self are difficult to communicate, especially in a culture that values winners with bright, optimistic smiles.

A crime victim who is feeling ashamed and guilty may find it extremely difficult to share these feelings with others. The inability to
talk about negative feelings can, in turn, make them seem even more
important, setting up a cycle of anxiety in which the victim is increasingly preoccupied with emotions he or she cannot confess. The
victim may feel isolated and alienated from others. One young man
described the feeling this way: "Ever since this happened, I feel
different from other people. It's almost like I don't belong . . . somehow
as if I'm not a part of the human race anymore. It's me and them,
and I'm the one on the outside."

Feelings of guilt and shame are often expressed in sadness or
dejection. Self-blaming victims may have an unconscious need to
punish themselves and in extreme cases become so depressed that
they are unable to function. Most victims do not go to this extreme,
but many experience some feelings of sadness in an effort to discharge their negative feelings about themselves. They feel wishy-
washy and blue, unable to concentrate, moody, preoccupied with
themselves. They pick at their food and worry about their health.

Victims who feel guilty and ashamed may also relieve these feelings
through various forms of denial. Many personal crimes are never
reported to the police. In some cases nonreporting probably reflects
the victim's reluctance to be identified with the stigma attached to
victimization. A victim may also express disinterest in the crime,
refuse to talk about it, behave as if it never happened, and so on.

Fantasies about revenge and recriminations about not defending
oneself can also be seen as forms of denial. The victim replays the
episode with a different outcome in imagination, and the pain of
remembered submission is muted.

Occasionally a victim becomes preoccupied in an obsessive way
with self-recrimination, even to the point in a few cases of acting
out the revenge fantasy. This is apparently true of Bernhard Goetz,
who had been the victim of an aggravated assault in the subway four
years before he became a celebrity by shooting the youths who
allegedly harassed him—again, in the subway. After his previous victimization, Mr. Goetz had applied for (and been denied) a permit to
carry a handgun like the one he used in the shooting. He had also
been active in crime prevention efforts in his New York City neigh-

borhood. Not only was his gun loaded, but Goetz himself was primed by his painful past experience. The fantasy of revenge for a grievous victimization is not uncommon. What is uncommon is carrying the fantasy out in actual behavior.

Fortunately, most crime victims do not act out their wishes for revenge in such an extreme fashion. And once in a while a victim is actually able to come away from a second attempt feeling better. An elderly professor who had his wallet lifted by a pair of pickpockets became preoccupied with careful plans to avoid a recurrence of the crime. When he was victimized initially, the two thieves used a common ploy. As the professor got up to leave the bus, one of the criminals preceded him down the aisle; the other fell in behind. When the bus stopped the one in front dropped a package and bent to pick it up; the one behind then pushed the professor into his stooped confederate, and in the resultant confusion the victim's wallet was lifted from his back pocket. The thieves were gone down the street before the professor even realized what had happened.

The victim's monetary loss was relatively small, but his emotional injury was significant. He felt so indignant about being violated that he became obsessively alert in public places and trained himself to be ready for any such future incident. And, as it happened, another attempt was made to lift his wallet under the same circumstances. Again, there were two "dips" working together, one of whom created confusion at the bus door. This time the professor clamped his hand firmly on his wallet as he was jostled from behind. The thieves got off the bus empty-handed, and the professor was finally relieved of his lingering bad feelings.

Guilt and shame are common, normal reactions to the violation of self that occurs in a personal crime. Earlier it was noted that victims sometimes act as if they *are* guilty, which can be confusing to police officers and court officials, who may suspect complicity on the victim's part. A sensitive friend or relative should keep an eye out for this kind of confusion. Those who are close to the victim can also help if they are tolerant of the victim's need to express negative self-evaluations. If the loved one can just listen, without becoming argumentative or alarmed, the victim will often discharge these feelings and move beyond them.

It is tempting, but not usually helpful, to argue with a victim who feels guilty. One victim of auto theft kept insisting that he was a stupid jerk to leave the car door unlocked. His friends wisely avoided being drawn into a discussion of his intelligence. A sympathetic, noncommital remark—"I can understand how you might feel that way"—is much more supportive. If victims seem to be denying their experience, it is probably best to tolerate their behavior. People need to rest after emotional turmoil, and denial is one way to get some distance from the victimization.

Sometimes the victim's inability to talk about his or her experience expresses the wish to be comforted nonverbally. Like a small child who cannot explain fear and pain, the victim may want to be held and reassured without words. Silence doesn't always mean that the person is inaccessible to help. Loved ones can find other ways to let victims know that they are still valued. A victim who is feeling worthless may be comforted by some treat—a meal out, perhaps, or a small gift—something that says the person is special to family and friends.

The special care of loved ones can do a great deal to help a victim who is feeling guilty and ashamed. But the victim will also have to deal with the reactions of strangers, people outside the warm circle of family and friends. In a society that stigmatizes crime victims, these reactions can be difficult to handle.

Denying the Victim

People are usually stigmatized because something about them arouses strong feelings in others, feelings that are difficult to handle. The stigma creates distance; it allows the other person to say, "I'm not like that. It couldn't happen to me." Thus people of normal intelligence stigmatize the mentally retarded, the intact person stigmatizes the physically handicapped, white Americans stigmatize black Americans, and so on.

Similarly, nonvictims often feel that they and the crime victim are different in some crucial way. How else can nonvictims assure themselves that they will not be victimized? If victims can be seen as less competent, less strong, less smart, essentially less human than other people, a person who has not been victimized can feel immune to victimization. Seeing the victim as basically different, the other person can say, "It won't happen to me. I'm safe."

No one is invulnerable to personal crime, of course. Given the right set of circumstances, any person can become a crime victim. But most people need to deny that possibility. One form of denial is the feeling that somehow the victim just isn't like other people, including yourself. Stigmatized, victims lose their identity for others and become what writer Richard Brickner has called "a dream others are having about themselves."[9] The dream is the fantasy of invulnerability—the wish that you will never be the victim of a personal crime.

Most of us would like to believe that good is rewarded and evil is punished. Psychologist Melvin Lerner explains this wish as an expression of the human desire for a just world:

> It seems that most people care deeply about justice for themselves and others—not justice in the legal sense, but more basic notions of justice. We want to believe we live in a world where people get what they deserve or, rather, deserve what they get. We want to believe that good things happen to good people and serious suffering comes only to bad people....
>
> We do not want to believe that [incidents of undeserved suffering] can happen, but they do. At least we do not want to believe they can happen to people like ourselves—good decent people. If these things can happen, what's the use of struggling, planning, and working to build a secure future for one's self and family? No matter how strongly our belief in an essentially just world is threatened by such incidents, most of us must try to maintain it in order to continue facing the irritations and struggles of daily life. This is a belief we cannot afford to give up if we are to continue to function.[10]

The belief in a just world is regularly belied by reality: Innocent people are injured every day. To reconcile the contradiction, many people consciously or unconsciously decide that victims of misfortune are bad people. The illusion of a just world remains intact, but the innocent victim suffers a further victimization.

Thus the nightmarish fear that surrounds sexual assault helps to explain why rape victims until quite recently have been stigmatized with brutal consistency. Sociologists Kurt Weis and Sandra S. Borges found that rape victims have often been denied help after the crime.[11] The denial may be followed by some justification on the part of the denying person, some attempt to show that the victim only got what she really deserved. Weis and Borges point to the connection between this kind of reaction and the general stigma attached to losers in Western capitalist societies. They note that people who are in trouble in a competitive culture are often held to blame for their misfortune.

> Losers are not held in high regard; one avoids identifying with them. They are stigmatized for not winning in a competitive society. The general cultural dislike and disregard even extends to the point of blaming the victim for being victimized. In general victims are thought to have "asked for it" and deserved whatever they got.... Confronted with a case of severe injustice or victimization, the response is often denial followed by justification (My Lai, Vietnam: "It never happened—and what's more they deserved it!"). The reaction to an alleged rape is usually similar: It was not a real rape but a seduction, and if it *was* rape then the woman was already morally inferior.[12]

We try to account for the suffering by explaining that the victim deserves it.

The wish to believe that virtue will be rewarded persists despite overwhelming evidence to the contrary. It is sometimes experienced by a person in trouble as a kind of moral outrage: "I'm a good person. I do what I'm supposed to do. Why is this bad thing happening to me?" Belief in a just world also invites victim-blaming and victim denial on the part of those who have not been victimized. Attribution study has found that belief in a just world will cause people to perceive victims as deserving their fate and, perhaps, of having caused their victimization. It is common for those who witness tragedy to wonder, usually silently, what the victim has done to deserve this fate. The speculation serves to deny the possibility that the suffering is arbitrary and that the witness might be in the same boat tomorrow.

In fact, the world is not always a fair place. The social problems of our time are enormous and, for people of sensitivity and social

concern, enormously disturbing. We want to find answers for per-
sistent problems such as crime and poverty and racial injustice. But
these dilemmas have resisted solution: Urban renewal creates new
slums; busing precipitates race riots; sending young offenders to jail
turns them into hardened criminals; methadone is as addicting as
heroin. We thrash around trying to find ways out of these difficulties,
and the pain of recognizing them is compounded by frustration and
guilt when no one seems to be able to do anything.

Out of this struggle, people act to relieve their sense of failure by
finding someone to blame. Social problems that resist solution raise
the need for a culprit, a scapegoat, someone on whom to hang the
group's sins. The most logical scapegoat is the one who makes us
feel guilty—the victim.[13] When society's ineffectiveness in treating
the victim's problems becomes intolerable, many people fault the
one who made them aware of the problem in the first place. Thus
victim-blaming becomes more intense when efforts are made to relieve social problems and those efforts fail. The more people try—and
fail—to help, the more they need someone to blame.

Labeling the crime victim different—a loser, a sucker, a mark—is
only a small step away from blaming the victim for being involved
in the crime at all. It is almost effortless to move from the perception
that the victim is not like other people (especially you) to the judgment that what happened to the victim is his or her own fault. And
if victims can be seen as blameworthy, they may also be seen as
people who have lost their right to sympathy and help from others.
The rest of us can say to the victim, in effect, "You are responsible
for your own troubles *so I don't have to help you.*"

People in serious trouble are often further victimized by this defensive reaction on the part of those who might be expected to help
them. It seems that the less trouble a person is in, the easier it is to
get help. A small boy lost in a department store will get instant
attention and comfort from every adult within earshot; the little one
is really not in very much trouble and his problem is usually easy
to fix. But the victim of a serious personal crime suffers from a whole
series of painful and complicated problems, many of which resist
solution. A crime victim makes people feel helpless and uncomfortable. It is painful to witness suffering and to see your own vulnerability mirrored in it.

The victim's experience cuts too close to the things we fear the most—vulnerability, loss of control, mortality. In ancient times the messenger who brought bad news was sometimes punished or killed; today our reactions to the bearers of evil tidings may be less overt, but the punishing intention of stigmatization reflects a similar unwillingness to face the truth.

In a word, then, a crime victim can be threatening. Nonvictims defend themselves against the threat by blaming victims so that they can deny them. Victims are stigmatized; their personhood is denied and their legitimate needs ignored because nonvictims have trouble dealing with what the victim means to their own lives.

People have blamed their fellows for being victims since the beginning of human history. Stigmatizing the victim is hardly a modern invention. Over the centuries and from culture to culture, various rationalizations have been constructed to explain the practice. Blaming the victim has often been excused as the will of the gods or the expression of some natural law. In some early societies, people in trouble were avoided because it was believed that their misfortune was contagious, like the measles.[14] This superstition persists among sophisticated and educated people in our own time, people who avoid the crippled, the crazy, and others in pain because of some uneasy fear of contamination.

During the sixteenth century the Calvinists in England refined what we have since come to call the Protestant ethic—the belief that a person's success, especially in accumulating wealth and enjoying good fortune, is a sign of God's grace. The doctrine is easily extended to the logical opposite: Those who suffer must have displeased God in some way. Our Puritan forefathers were preoccupied with strength and weakness in a moral sense: The strong were good and survived; the weak were wicked and fell by the wayside.

Reactions to crime victims are often colored by this moral perspective, which is nicely summed up in the common expression: "There but for the grace of God, go I." Psychiatrist Martin Symonds expresses the same belief in modern secular terms: "If you act good, nothing bad will happen to you. Therefore, if something bad does happen to you, you weren't acting good. If you act right, nothing wrong will happen; something wrong happened, therefore you weren't acting right."[15]

Nobody Loves You When You're Down and Out

It is especially difficult for Americans to deal with the reality that good people can suffer serious misfortune. Innocent victims belie the American Dream, which is our national version of the just-world theory. In the American dream, all things are possible. Our systems of praise and blame seem to be grounded in the notion that people can do anything they really want to. The poor but talented person who works hard, strives mightily, and achieves success is an American hero—a winner.[16] Living in America can be especially gratifying if you are competent, successful, and lucky enough to avoid misfortune—but by the same token, it is especially hard to be seen as a loser in America.

People in our culture are socialized to feel personally hurt when they lose. They tend to see interpersonal transactions in competitive terms. Thus the interaction between the victim and the criminal can be perceived as a win-lose situation in which the victim is the loser. The victim is seen as helpless, incompetent, weak. This perception has a powerful impact on the treatment of crime victims in our society.

Several years ago there was a kidnapping case in which the plight of the innocent victim who is further victimized by being seen as a loser was played out with enormous irony. Patricia Hearst, the granddaughter of publishing magnate William Randolph Hearst, was forcibly abducted from her home by a small group of criminals, self-styled radical terrorists who called themselves the Symbionese Liberation Army. They imprisoned Ms. Hearst, raped her repeatedly, held her for ransom, threatened her life, and took her with them as they committed a series of robberies. Eventually the members of the kidnapping gang were either apprehended or killed, and Ms. Hearst was rescued by the authorities. She was then imprisoned and accused of having actively and willingly participated in the robberies committed by the gang. She was charged, found guilty, and served time in prison.

The attention given to the Hearst kidnapping is a telling example of how Americans are preoccupied with and confused by issues of personal power and individual worth. An extremely powerful family (the Hearsts have so much money we imagine they can do anything) was suddenly made helpless by a small group of criminals who threatened to kill their daughter. The abrupt reversal from great power to complete powerlessness engaged the American imagination for weeks, dominating the media and our conversation. And in the end, the jury's conviction of Ms. Hearst may well reflect their inability to believe that such a person could be made helpless by circumstances beyond her control. People like the Hearsts are supposed to be impervious.

Ms. Hearst was widely portrayed as if she were a spoiled kid playing terrorist. Many people seemed to feel that she should be held personally responsible for her transformation from a sheltered heiress to a glazed-eyed, gun-toting zombie. There was testimony at her trial by mental-health professionals who asserted that her participation in the robberies was caused by and evidence of the post-traumatic stress disorder brought about by her kidnapping and victimization. But this stress was almost entirely overlooked as an explanation for Patricia Hearst's behavior. People talked as if she were in control instead of under a threat to her life.

In less dramatic circumstances the need to deny our vulnerability finds expression in an idealized, middle-class lifestyle in which everything is neat and pretty. The meat in American supermarkets comes in a little plastic tray with a Saran-wrap cover—no hint of the slaughterhouse. The sick, the incompetent, the old, and the dying are put away—out of sight, out of mind. It becomes possible to believe that everybody is clean, attractive, well-groomed, healthy, smart, and invulnerable. Nothing ever happens that is ugly or out of control. A crime victim offends the aesthetic sense of this world, arousing a kind of revulsion instead of real compassion. The victim's vulnerability is felt as a lapse in good taste.

On an interpersonal and emotional level, this same lifestyle is informed by what Erik H. Erikson calls "the success ideology," the notion that it is possible (and desirable) to achieve a perfectly adjusted personality, free from internal conflict and invulnerable to change.[17] People who strive for this kind of success are likely to smile a lot and respond "Never better!" to the question, "How are you?"

The wish for such a personality, like the wish for an eternally youthful body, is essentially a way of denying human vulnerability. Conspicuous well-adjustedness is also the kind of interpersonal overachievement that tends to be quite competitive. Any person who falls short of the ideal—and the crime victim is one—is likely to be viewed with pity or contempt. Americans want to be successful; spontaneously and reflexively, we want to be winners. And so we stigmatize losers.

Complicity in the Ivory Tower

The academic community has not been immune to the prevailing ethic with regard to crime victims. Two distortions have been typical in the approach of these professionals to the victim: one is victim-blaming, the other is victim-denying.

Historically, the study of crime and crime victims has been the province of criminology, a subdiscipline of sociology. Kurt Weis once noted that most criminology is really what he called "victorology." Instead of raising broad questions about the society that both produces and suffers from crime, criminology has focused on the individual offender and his or her responsibility. It reflects "more interest in the winners (Latin: *victores*) than in the losers of criminal activities and [is preoccupied] with the criminal as an individual, mobilizing public and police forces to fight criminals rather than crime, and losing sight of the victims . . ."[18] Much of criminology, then, has been victim-denying in the same way that law enforcement has been: Traditionally, neither the criminologist nor the police officer has been very interested in the victim.

Victimology, a fairly new field within criminology, is devoted entirely to studying victims. In 1976, when the first issue of the international journal of victimology was published, the editor described the main preoccupation of the field:

Scholars have begun to see the victim not necessarily just as a passive object, as a neuter or innocent point of impact of crime into society, but as eventually playing an active role or possibly contributing in different measure to his/her own victimization. During the last thirty years, there has been a spurt of speculation, debate, and research on the victim, his role, the criminal-victim relationship, the concept of responsibility, the crime motive, and on behaviors that could be considered provocative. At the same time, certain types of crimes have been identified as being victimless. Thus the study of crime has acquired a more realistic and complete outlook.[19]

The needs or rights of victims were conspicuously absent from much of the early literature of victimology. The field was dominated by considerations of the victim's participation in and responsibility for the crime. In recent years, some shift of emphasis has occurred, but victimology is still not primarily concerned with victims' problems.

On the contrary, the work of many victimologists concludes that crime victims contribute to their own victimization, consciously or unconsciously, to one degree or another.[20] Some studies have focused, for example, on ways in which crime victims are legally and morally responsible for the crimes in which they are involved. Often this work is full of moral judgments and attributions of blame, including such statements as this, from the work of a respected and often-cited authority:

> In a way, the victim is always the cause of a crime.... All crimes necessarily have victims, and, necessarily, the existence of the victim or something material or immaterial that belongs to him make for crime and may actually produce a criminal effect. However, as so often happens, the victim not only creates the possibility of a crime but precipitates it. In other words, the victim may develop the direction of the offender's criminal conduct toward himself. Even if he is an innocent bystander, in certain cases his silent "bystanding" may make him not only a psychological accomplice but at the same time the one who establishes the criminal motive and encourages the criminal action. He may motivate the criminal unconsciously. Or he may motivate him consciously, disregarding the risk he is taking. Or he may feel that his provocation is justified. Or he may want to be victimized.[21]

The role of chance is virtually ignored in such analyses. The innocent victim who just happens to be in the wrong place at the wrong time does not seem to exist.

An even more extreme example of professional victim-blaming can be found in the work of certain psychiatrists who have made a specialty of looking at crime from a psychoanalytic perspective. David Abrahamsen, for example, in an analysis of a murder case, makes the following comment about victims:

> That the victim, through provocation and seduction, plays a large part in the execution of a violent crime must be brought to the attention of the public. To avoid becoming a victim of murder, assault, or rape will in the last analysis depend on how well the person is able to refrain from getting *emotionally involved* with someone who is potentially dangerous to one's life and welfare. Keeping one's distance from such a person requires much emotional insight about oneself as well as about others, and this is not easily obtained, since to a large extent we are governed by our unconscious feelings.... There is little doubt that many such victims could have avoided their fate had they been able from the beginning to scrutinize carefully their own motivations.[22]

According to this theory, victims of violence are driven by their unconscious motivations to arrange their own destruction. Again, no mention is made of the role of chance or of the many other factors that may pertain.

When crime victims were not being blamed by academics and mental-health professionals in the period before the mid 1970s, victims were largely being ignored. This book advances a model for victimization in which the crime is seen as a personal crisis for the victim; the central source of stress in that crisis is the violation of self. If one were to turn to research on stressful life events in the literature of the behavioral sciences before, say, 1975, he or she would find almost no data about crime victims. In an otherwise sensible and useful 1974 textbook for nursing students on crisis intervention, for example, the chapter "Situational Crises" lists six crises: premature birth, status and role change, experimentation with LSD, physical illness, divorce, and death.[23] Gerald Caplan, in his classic 1964 work on crisis intervention, reports on the crises of major surgery, natural disasters, industrial retirement, wartime separation, and the transition from high school to college, among others.[24] But almost nowhere is the crisis of crime victimization mentioned, despite the fact that being the victim of a crime is clearly one of the most common and most devastating personal catastrophes.

Social scientists are no more insensitive or lacking in compassion than other people. But neither are they immune to the threat of certain kinds of human vulnerability. When a crisis comes out of a natural event—a hurricane flattens the main street of a small town, or the young father of three preschoolers suddenly drops dead of a heart attack—it is unlikely that another person will feel responsible. Such events are sometimes called "acts of God"—they are clearly beyond human intervention. People who are not personally involved may feel sorry about such incidents, but they don't normally feel guilty about them.

The victim of a personal crime, on the other hand, can easily arouse stirrings of personal responsibility and feelings of guilt in others. We cannot help feeling that the crime could have been prevented. Many people who work in the social sciences are strongly motivated to understand social forces and remedy social ills. The plight of the crime victim can be especially painful for these people, and they may be inclined to feel somehow responsible for the victim's dilemma. Like the police officer, the social scientist may feel some sense of professional inadequacy when confronted with a crime victim.

It is not surprising, then, that the victims' advocacy movement which began to gather momentum in the 1970s was an indigenous movement empowered not by criminologists or victimologists but by crime victims themselves and by those who were helping them. Many of these first victim advocates were political activists from the women's movement. Fueled by their outrage against a society in which victims of rape were more often blamed than helped, these women established the rape crisis centers and 24-hour hot lines that became the models for helping victims in many areas. Recognizing the cruelty of the stigma that has burdened so many rape victims, their advocates organized protest events—speak-outs against rape, marches to take back the night. They also testified before lawmakers, brought suits, monitored the criminal-justice system, and used other skills and tactics developed during the civil-rights movement to bring about needed social and policy reform.

The political pressure applied by the advocates of rape victims resulted in the development of local mechanisms for giving assistance to these victims through the police or the prosecutor's office in many areas where no such help had existed before. As these programs became more widespread, their focus often broadened to other crime victims as well. Thus it was that the crime victims' movement began in the grassroots efforts of many victims and their advocates, beginning with the courageous rape victims who were able to say, "We will not be shamed any more."

Beyond Denial

Reading a newspaper story about a brutal murder, the average person will feel a mild, passing dismay about the victim—"tsk, tsk"—and a compelling urge to find out everything about the murderer. Typically we want to know all about the criminal—who he is, what he did, how he is being sought. Readers pour over the lurid details in search of protection—all of that information gives them an illusion that they know about and are in control of threatening persons like these. There is no positive emotional return from interest invested in the crime victim. On the contrary, victims make people face certain realities that they would rather avoid. Identifying with the person who lost control has the effect of intensifying feelings of vulnerability. Learning about the victim emphasizes the threat. For this reason, almost everybody is more interested in criminals than he or she is in victims.

The reality that the crime victim forces us to face is the fact that people are never totally in control of their lives. Most people need to feel in control in order to function comfortably and effectively. If reality has a disorganizing effect on people's lives and threatens their ability to function, they will naturally construct an illusion to keep their equilibrium. Most young people, for example, cannot quite believe that they are ever going to die.

Creating an illusion so that one can function might be called useful denial. It is useful for us to deny the fact that we are really not ever in total control of our lives. We need to deny it so we can go about our business and get things done—and most of the time our illusion of control seems to be reality. But when we are confronted by a crime victim, the cost of preserving the illusion is to deny the victim.

Acknowledging and identifying with a victim of personal crime is, thus, a difficult and threatening business—so much so that it is remarkable when it occurs. And it occurs more often all the time. Progress is being made in recognizing the victim primarily as a person in need—not a loser or a pariah or a mark, but another human being having a bad time. Police officers are being trained in crisis intervention so that they can be supportive to victims. Centers for rape victims are becoming common. The legislatures of 40 states have enacted some sort of crime-victim compensation. Seventeen states have a Victim Bill of Rights, giving victims more power in the criminal-justice system. Parallel activities have been taking place at policy-making levels in the field of mental health. The National Institute of Mental Health, the American Psychiatric Association, and the American Orthopsychiatric Association have recently established mechanisms for addressing the problems of crime victims. In 1984, the Board of Directors of the American Psychological Association received the report and recommendations of its Task Force on the Victims of Crime and Violence, which emphasized the need for improved service delivery and greater knowledge-building, with particular emphasis on psycholegal research.

Perhaps the single most important public policy statement in this surge of interest in and support for the victims of crime is the 1982 report of the President's Task Force on Victims of Crime. This extraordinary document includes this observation from the chairman of the Task Force:

> The important proposals contained here will not be clear unless you first confront the human reality of victimization. Few are willing to do so. Unless you are, however, you will not be able to understand. During our hearings we were told by one eloquent witness, "It is hard not to turn away from victims. Their pain is discomforting; their anger is sometimes embarrassing; their mutilations are upsetting." Victims are vital reminders of our own vulnerability. But one cannot turn away.
>
> You must know what it is like to have your life wrenched and broken, to realize that you will never really be the same. Then you must expe-

rience what it means to survive, only to be blamed and used and ignored by those you thought were there to help you. Only when you are willing to confront all these things will you understand what victimization means.[25]

NOTES

1. According to the *Dictionary of American Slang*, edited by Harold Wentworth and Stuart Berg Flexner (New York: T. Y. Crowell, 1967), the term *the mark* is "universally known," but used mainly in the subcultures of the underworld, the carnival, the circus, and among tramps.
2. Erving Goffman, *Stigma: Notes on the Management of Spoiled Identity* (Englewood Cliffs, N. J.: Prentice Hall, Inc., 1963), p. 5.
3. The distinction made here between guilt and shame is the same one drawn by Helen Merrell Lynd in *On Shame and the Search for Identity* (New York: Science Editions, Inc., 1961).
4. In Erikson's scheme of human development, shame is the opposite of autonomy. If growing children are successful in their attempts to master the environment, they develop self-confidence and become more autonomous. But children who are unable to master the tasks expected of them feel helpless and are filled with self-doubt and shame [Erik H. Erikson, *Childhood and Society*, 2d ed. (New York: W. W. Norton, 1963), pp. 251-254.] Because a personal crime is a significant violation of autonomy, it may call up an emotional echo of these issues.
5. Lynd, *On Shame*, p. 46.
6. C. Gerald Fraser, "ABC, CBS Stations Cancel Two Movies Regarded as Violent," *New York Times*, 4 November 1976. Ironically, during the week that we were revising this chapter, in February of 1985, our local television offered *Death Wish* on one of the networks as a featured movie of the week.
7. "Of all responses reported by victims to the National Crime Survey, physical force, trying to attract attention, and doing nothing to protect oneself or property resulted in the highest proportions of seriously injured victims (16%, 14%, and 12%, respectively). On the other hand, those who tried to talk themselves out of their predicament or took nonviolent evasive action were less likely to incur serious injury (both 6%)." (*Report to the Nation on Crime and Justice: The Data*, Bureau of Justice Statistics, U.S. Department of Justice, 1983, p. 23.) Richard Block and Wesley G. Skogan have found that while in general *nonforceful* resistance such as screaming or running away in the face of potential victimization by a stranger is a good tactic for the victim to use, "forceful and nonforceful resistance in the face of a knife or gun increases somewhat the probability of attack or injury over that for nonresistance." (*The Dynamics of Violence Between Strangers: Victim Resistance and Outcomes in Rape, Assault, and Robbery*, Evanston, IL: Center for Urban Affairs and Policy Research, Northwestern University, 1984, p. 73.)
8. Frederic Storaska, *How to Say No to a Rapist—and Survive* (New York: Random House, 1975), p. 97.
9. Richard P. Brickner, *My Second Twenty Years: An Unexpected Life* (New York: Basic Books, 1976), p. 153.
10. Melvin J. Lerner, "The Desire for Justice and Reactions to Victims," in J. Macaulay and L. Berkowitz, eds., *Altruism and Helping Behavior* (New York: Academic Press, 1970), p. 207.
11. Kurt Weis and Sandra S. Borges, "Victimology and Rape: The Case of the Legitimate Victim," *Issues in Criminology* 8 (1973).

12. Ibid., pp. 76-77.

13. William Ryan's *Blaming the Victim* (New York: Pantheon, 1971) is a penetrating analysis of how this phenomenon is expressed in the common belief that the poor are responsible for their poverty.

14. Bernard L. Bloom, "The 'Medical Model,' Miasma Theory, and Community Mental Health," *Community Mental Health Journal* 1 (1965): 335.

15. Martin Symonds, "Victims of Violence: Psychological Effects and Aftereffects," *The American Journal of Psychoanalysis* 35 (1975): 21.

16. The success of such a person is sometimes characterized as an example of "survival of the fittest," a phrase coined in the nineteenth century by social philosopher Herbert Spencer to describe his conviction that those who were the most privileged were also the most deserving. Spencer distorted Charles Darwin's theory of biological evolution to support his own theory of social evolution. Called "social Darwinism," it is essentially the notion that certain people are better suited than others to survive. Unrestricted economic competition and the neglect of individuals in need were two of the central hallmarks of this philosophy, which has since been used to justify various forms of racist and imperialist exploitation.

Social Darwinism suggests that people who suffer misfortune are naturally, biologically, inferior. The Nazis carried this idea to its logical extreme when they declared themselves a superior race and murdered six million Jews. Spencer's theory has long ago been discredited intellectually, but its offshoots persist, testifying to the seductiveness of an idea that allows people to deny the suffering of others. (Interestingly, most people who recognize the phrase "survival of the fittest" attribute it to Charles Darwin and believe it to be part of his theory.)

17. Erikson, *Childhood*, p. 274.

18. Weis and Borges, "Victimology and Rape," p. 75.

19. Emilio C. Viano, "Victimology, the Study of the Victim," *Victimology* 1 (1976): 1.

20. In his review of research on victims of crime in 1982, for example, Richard F. Sparks notes that "early studies of victims and victimization, and their lineal descendants, have served an important function by calling attention to the variety of ways in which victims may be involved in bringing about crimes committed against them . . ." (*Research on Victims of Crime: Accomplishments, Issues, and New Directions,* Center for Studies of Crime and Delinquency, National Institute of Mental Health, 1982, p. 37.) Sparks also notes the shift in emphasis that is occurring in victimology: "The early studies discussed above were, in one way or another, concerned with *causes* of crime and victimization. But what is often most important for policy purposes, it may be said, is the *consequences* of victimization rather than its causes: the extent of injury or loss suffered by victims and society generally and the extent to which existing or proposed programs of compensation, restitution, or special services can meet or are meeting these needs." (pp. 37-38)

21. Stephen Schafer, *The Victim and His Criminal* (New York: Random House, 1968), pp. 79-80.

22. David Abrahamsen, *The Murdering Mind* (New York: Harper and Row, 1973), p. 42.

23. Donna C. Aguilera and Janice M. Messick, *Crisis Intervention: Theory and Methodology* (St. Louis, Mo.: C. V. Mosby, 1974), p. xii.

24. Gerald Caplan, *Principles of Preventive Psychiatry* (New York: Basic Books, 1964), p. 37. See also the literature review by Larry L. Smith, "Crisis Intervention Theory and Practice," *Community Mental Health Review* 2 (1977).

25. President's Task Force on Victims of Crime, *Final Report*, 1982, p. vii.

6

The Justice Question: Victims, the Police, and the Courts

When any exposure to law touches your life, you become different. I felt very lonely and very much at sea with the whole business of pursuing justice. I felt more vulnerable in court than I had on the street. I felt weaker, I felt more helpless. I felt like an oddity who had no right to be there.
—Rape victim

Justice is one of those words—like *love* or *happiness*—that's hard to define. But everyone knows what it means. Justice has to do with getting what one deserves. It has to do with the hope that in the long run good people will be rewarded and bad people will be punished.[1] Among personal crime victims the belief in a just world is often translated into a wish for "satisfaction." Since they have been

103

aggrieved, it is natural for victims to expect—on some level—that their grievances will be avenged. Anyone who has been injured by another has a normal desire to get even. And in a competitive society, this desire can be honed to a fine edge: If you push me, I'll push you back, *and I deserve the chance to do it.*

For someone who has recently been a victim, *justice* may also mean getting special attention. The injured victim certainly deserves consideration: the solicitous interest of family and friends; prompt and courteous attention from the police; time off from work; help with the children; medical care; counseling; money to replace stolen property. Self-blaming victims may not expect these gestures because they feel too guilty to deserve them, but most other victims will feel as if they are entitled to compensation. Justice demands that things be put right again. Those who care about the victim are expected to help soothe the wounds and right the wrongs. It is perfectly natural—indeed it is healthy and appropriate—for the victim to want some special treatment.

Unfortunately, the victim's desire for justice is almost inevitably frustrated. If they're lucky, victims will have close family and friends who can support them during the crisis. Among the strangers beyond, however, the victim can encounter indifference or even hostility. Much of the business of "cleaning up" after the crime requires victims to deal with people who may not show any special consideration at all: in the police station, the hospital emergency room, the insurance office, the courtroom, even in the crime-victim compensation office.

More often than not, the criminal-justice system and most of the other institutions that are supposed to serve victims are bureaucracies—large, proliferating hierarchies with many rules and few ways to make exceptions.[2] (See diagram on page 105 for a general view of the system.) Although attention to the needs of victims has at last become a real priority in many of the bureaucratic systems that crime victims encounter, change in such systems is inevitably slow. The stimulus of victim advocacy groups and public policy changes have had a modifying effect on victim services, but much remains to be done. Many of these bureaucracies are still staffed by people who are unable or unwilling to be responsive to the victim's needs.

The victim's own condition also helps to increase the probability

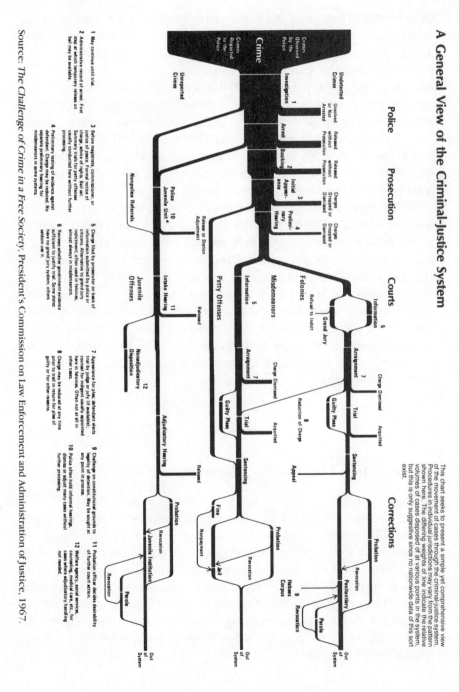

A General View of the Criminal-Justice System

of further injustice after the crime. During the impact stage of crisis, many crime victims suffer significant emotional and social disability. They may have trouble understanding their own intense feelings—waves of guilt or shame or rage or fear. Victims may be unable to handle uncertainty, frustration, unfamiliar situations, and rude strangers as well as other sources of anxiety outside of themselves. In this state of heightened vulnerability, they must cope not only with their everyday lives but also with a whole new set of problems created by the victimization. Ironically, victims have to deal with these new difficulties at precisely the time when they are least well-equipped emotionally to do so.

When they have negative experiences with the people who are supposed to be in charge of order and available to help them, victims suffer what psychiatrist Martin Symonds has called "the second injury . . . the victim's *perceived* rejection by—and lack of expected support from—the community, agencies, and society in general, as well as family or friends."[3] Because of the victim's heightened vulnerability, this second wound is a further violation of self, in some ways more egregious because it comes on top of an existing injury. It is not surprising, then, that recent crime victims often feel an increased sense of injustice as they try to handle the aftermath of their victimization.

Opting Out: The Costly Alternative

Some crime victims avoid the whole business of trying to get satisfaction from strangers; they opt out by never reporting their victimization to the police. Nonreporting victims outnumber victims who do report in many jurisdictions. The National Crime Survey has found that only a third of all the crimes it measures are ever brought to the attention of law-enforcement officials.[4] The reporting rate is highest for thefts of large sums of money and for crimes that result in physical injury to the victim, but many crimes, even very serious crimes, go unreported.

The reasons for nonreporting are complex and vary from victim to victim.[5] Many victims, including victims of physically violent crimes, say that they did not report the crimes to the police because they were "private/personal matters." It seems reasonable to assume that most of these are nonstranger-to-nonstranger crimes involving victims and offenders who know each other. Another large group of nonreporting victims said that they believe "nothing could be done" about the crimes in which they were involved. Some of these are probably making a realistic appraisal of minor theft losses or attempted crimes; in other cases, these victims seem to reflect a lack of faith in the police and the courts. Still others fail to report because they fear retaliation from the criminal or his friends if they go to the police.

Some victims make a conscious decision to "cut their losses" by staying out of the criminal-justice system. They believe that their participation will cost more in inconvenience, lost wages, and frustration than the outcome will be worth.[6] Many people think that there just isn't enough to be gained from reporting a crime to the police, and it is certainly possible to support such a position. Most victims who *do* report their crimes never see anybody arrested. Of the eight FBI Index Crimes reported to the police (and remember these are only about a third of the crimes committed), fewer than 25 percent result in the arrest of any suspect who is charged with the crime.[7] (But notice that this does not mean that most people who commit crimes get away with it, since most criminals commit more than one or two crimes and thus increase the chance that sooner or later they will be caught.)

From the point of view of the frustrated crime victim, the courts do not do much better. If a suspect is arrested and charged, the victim cannot look forward with any certainty to a conviction. Safeguarding the rights of the accused, which is an absolute necessity rightly guaranteed by our Constitution, often seems more important than safeguarding the rights of the victim. Victims are often dissatisfied with the sentence imposed, and convicted felons regularly fail to serve the maximum time.[8] All of this makes it seem somewhat futile for victims to become involved in the criminal-justice system at all.

There is only one argument in favor of reporting crime to the police, but it is an extraordinarily compelling one: Reporting the crime is the only way the victim or the society can hope to achieve justice. Victims who do not report their crimes are essentially admitting defeat. They are letting the criminal win without even putting up a fight. They are encouraging the criminal to repeat the act of violation. The police can't do anything about crimes unless they know about them. So unless victims report crimes, even more criminals are certain to get away with what they do. It's that simple.

Nonreporters sometimes defend their decision by saying that the criminal-justice system is ineffective. But victims who opt out of the system are adding to its ineffectiveness. Their behavior is self-fulfilling; if no victim or witness ever reported a crime, the criminal-justice system would be reduced to handling only the very small percentage of crimes that are actually witnessed by the police. Police and prosecutors need aggressive, committed victim-witnesses to build a strong case. It is often impossible to get a conviction without this commitment. Cases are dropped in court every day because victims don't show up to testify.

Everyone acknowledges the failures of the criminal-justice system, but the fact remains that it is the only system we have. Unless people are ready to return to vigilante "justice," in which each person handles his or her own grievances, we need to give active support to the existing criminal-justice system—even as we are critical of it and work to reform it. The rule of law is a tedious, inefficient, time-consuming process, but the alternative is chaos. Whenever the community takes the law into its own hands, a lot of innocent people are hurt—witness Ireland, witness Lebanon, witness disputes over busing to achieve school integration in neighborhoods across the nation. People who want law and order have a social responsibility to participate in the criminal-justice system, a responsibility that includes reporting crimes to the police.

A victim who does not report is likely to experience negative repercussions on a personal level. He or she is left with no legal way of getting satisfaction. Nonreporting may add to the victim's feelings of helplessness and deepen his or her mistrust of society. It can add to the sense that nobody cares, that nothing can be done. Crime victims in crisis need to have their sense of trust and their autonomy confirmed; not reporting the crime is likely to have the opposite effect.

Victims who fail to contact the police may be unable to achieve a sense of resolution about their experience. The unreported victimization remains an open-ended issue, a piece of unfinished business. Nonreporting victims sometimes have a lingering sense that they could have done something more about the crime, that it isn't over. This accurate perception can gnaw at the victim, delaying or preventing a resolution of the crisis. Thus nonreporting can be emotionally costly for the victim as well as weakening the criminal-justice system and the society that system strives to serve.

Some victims never struggle with the question of whether or not to report the crime. Many victims contact the police because they feel it's what they're supposed to do. Most victims who report are probably also angry and want revenge. Many call the police because they are hurt and need help. For victims of property crime, reporting may be a practical matter—some insurance companies require a police report as evidence of theft or damage before they will pay a claim. Those who wish to apply for crime-victim compensation may also be required to report the crime to the police. Compensation programs vary, but most legislation stipulates that the victim must report (within forty-eight hours in some states) and cooperate with the police in order to qualify for benefits.

There are also victims, most notably among the ethnic minority poor, who will avoid any involvement with the police or the courts because of previous negative experiences with the criminal-justice system. From the perspective of such victims, reporting the crime would just add another complication to their already difficult lives. Like any other crime victim, these people may need help after the crime, but they may not be able to get it. Indeed, one study has shown that victims with lower socioeconomic status had more difficulty getting their needs met than other victims.[9] In communities in which the only victim services available are those sponsored within the criminal-justice system, people who do not report fall outside of the service system and are, in effect, disenfranchised. Whatever a person's reasons for not wanting to report a crime to the police, he or she may still need victim services. It is more likely that these services will reach those who need them if at least some of the programs in each community are situated outside of the criminal-justice system and do not require reporting as a precondition for getting help.

When a victim feels ambivalent about reporting, a friend or relative can be supportive by listening while the victim works the decision through. The person who wants to help can encourage the victim to explore his or her feelings about contacting the police, suggest what the consequences of various alternatives might be, and offer to assist the victim in his or her dealings with the police and the courts. Victims who are reluctant to report may have good reasons for staying out of the system, but this choice should never be made lightly. Loved ones can help by supporting the decision-making process, but they should avoid pressuring the victim one way or the other. Reporting a crime and following through can be difficult for the victim, as we shall see, and no other person can make the decision.

If the victim does decide to report, a friend or relative can be available to act on the victim's behalf. Some victims want the police to know about the crime but feel unable to deal with them directly. One rape victim didn't contact the police because she couldn't bear the thought of having to describe to a stranger what had happened to her. She regretted the decision later: "After I pulled myself together, I felt empty and sad because I hadn't done anything to stop the rapist." A sensitive friend might offer to make the phone call and do the talking in such a situation.

Reporting the crime, cooperating with the police, working with the prosecutor, and taking the case to court can be positive experiences for crime victims. Working within the criminal-justice system allows the victim to be directly involved in society's efforts to stop crime. It gives victims a way to fight back, to do something to achieve the satisfaction they need and deserve.

And there is really nothing to match the feelings of a victim who *does* achieve what he or she feels is justice. Susan Chang was raped by a man who climbed in her bedroom window at 3:00 A.M. She was so enraged and so determined to put him behind bars that she began to prepare his prosecution while he was still in her apartment. Feigning friendliness, she offered the rapist a drink and handed him a bottle of scotch because she had heard that glass surfaces hold fingerprints well. The prints were used as evidence and helped to convict the rapist.

During the police investigation, Susan learned that he had raped fourteen or fifteen other women in her same neighborhood, including a woman who lived next door. (Most of the women had never reported the rapes to the police, and most of them were not willing to testify in court.) The trial was an extremely painful experience for Susan, but after it was over she felt a deep sense of satisfaction that left her at peace with the world. She knew that she was personally responsible for taking a terribly dangerous man off the streets. After all, as she said, "Who of my friends might have been next?"

It is unusual for a victim to experience such a high level of satisfaction with the criminal-justice system. But the possibility is available only to those victims who enter the system by reporting the crimes to the police.

Toward Realistic Expectations

Victims who decide to become involved with the criminal-justice system will be more effective and feel better about their experiences if they know what will happen at each step along the way. Police and court procedures are often puzzling, and the victim can feel lost and neglected if the system is not explained. Victims and their loved ones are often frustrated and disappointed because they do not get what they expect from the criminal-justice system. If they understand the realities of the system, they will be in a much better position to cope.

The information in this chapter and Chapter 7 is designed to fill some of that need. We will explain how the system works, where the difficulties are likely to lie, and what victims and their advocates can do to make the system work better for them.

The Police Investigation

The police are responsible for investigating the victim's complaint, gathering evidence to support it, and arresting any suspect to whom the evidence leads. Once a crime has been reported, the police are obligated to make an investigation, although in some cases all they can do is question the victim and make a formal record of the crime. Usually the crime is first reported to a uniformed police officer—the person who responds to the victim's phone call or personal request for help. This officer asks the first questions and files the initial report of the crime at the police station. Further investigation of the crime may be handled by another officer, an investigator who has special expertise in certain kinds of crime.

The victim needs to know the names and identification numbers of the responding officers and others who are involved in the case so that the victim or a relative can call the police station later to find out how the investigation is progressing. In most jurisdictions, the police also assign a case number to each reported crime; this number is used to locate the case report in the police files and may be needed by the victim for filing insurance and other compensation claims. The police officers who first respond to the victim's call may offer this information, or the victim may ask for it.

Every victim who reports a crime will be questioned at least once by a police officer. The questioning may be conducted by phone, at the scene of the crime, in the victim's home, at the police station, or at the hospital. Victims in crisis often require some time to pull themselves together, especially if their violation has been severe. Victims of physical assault, rape, and other serious crimes may need the presence of supportive friends or relatives in order to be able to answer any questions at all. Other victims of equally serious crimes prefer to be questioned alone. Loved ones who are present when the police arrive should take their cues from the victim. Usually the easiest thing to do is ask, "Would you be more comfortable if I stayed here with you?"

If the victim has been physically injured, the police will take him or her to get medical attention, usually in the emergency room of a nearby hospital. All rape victims should be offered medical assistance, whether they are visibly injured or not, including tests several weeks after the rape for possible venereal disease and pregnancy. If a rape victim wishes to prosecute the rapist, her court case will be strengthened if physical evidence of the rape is collected as soon as possible. Commonly this evidence includes a sperm sample taken by a doctor, the clothing the victim was wearing during the rape, and photographs of her injuries. Any victim who has been physically injured may be asked to permit a police photographer to record the injuries. These photographs can then be used as evidence in court after the actual physical injuries have healed.

During questioning, the victim may be asked things that seem irrelevant or unnecessarily personal. The victim should feel free to ask police officers about anything he or she does not understand, including matters of procedure and the meaning of unfamiliar terms. Sometimes an officer will seem reluctant to answer questions or seem annoyed by them. The police can forget that what is routine for them can be puzzling or upsetting for a crime victim. Occasionally a victim's questions are experienced as second-guessing by the officer. These attitudes may be understandable, but they should not dissuade the victim from seeking clarification.

It is important for the victim to be truthful even about facts that are embarrassing or things that make him or her look bad. The police will not conduct the best investigation if they doubt the victim's credibility. When victims exaggerate their losses—falsifying claims of property value in order to collect higher insurance payments, for example—they may reinforce police cynicism and contribute to an indifferent investigative effort. A young man's car was stolen from a dark street in front of a local social club where he had stopped to see some friends. His parents disapproved of the club, so he lied to the responding officer about where the car had been when it was taken. The officer suspected that he didn't have the whole story. He questioned the young man closely, and eventually the victim admitted that he had lied. The officer decided that the whole story was probably a hoax or an attempt to cheat the insurance company.

Sometimes a victim will remember something about the crime several days or even weeks after the police have asked their first questions. For example, burglary victims commonly discover, over a period of days after the crime, additional items that have been stolen. It is important to let the police know about these additional facts in the case, even if the information seems trivial. Part of the police investigation involves constructing what is called an MO (from *modus operandi*, "a method of procedure"), a description of the way particular criminals operate. By accumulating details and arranging them in a pattern, the investigators can sometimes develop a unique individual portrait of the criminal. The man who raped Susan Chang, for example, always struck around 3:00 A.M. because he got off from work then. Many criminals are repeaters. If the police have a good MO, the probability of apprehension is increased.

Victims who are badly frightened by the crime will sometimes block out most of what happened for a period of time afterward. These memory lapses can occur either during the impact phase immediately after the crime or a little later during the recoil phase when the victim first gets in touch with his or her fear. An elderly victim of robbery woke up one morning and found that he could not remember what the robber who assaulted him looked like. He had given the police a lengthy description and had subsequently recognized his assailant in a photograph, but suddenly he was drawing a complete blank. Such a lapse can be frustrating and frightening to the victim, but it is usually temporary and passes as the crisis reaction subsides. It is not helpful for a victim who has forgotten details to be pressured or scolded. The memory lapse is almost always involuntary, and most victims eventually recover their memories if they are treated with gentleness and respect.

Rape crisis centers often suggest to victims that they keep a diary in which they write down everything they can remember about the rape and what happened afterwards. Some victims use a cassette tape recorder instead of a diary. This technique may be helpful to any crime victim in crisis. It is a good way to ventilate feelings. It will often serve to jog the victim's memory and to help him or her keep the facts straight. The record can be a crucial refresher for the victim who testifies in court since hearings and trials are sometimes delayed for months after the crime. Keeping a record will also allow the victim to see how his or her feelings change as the crisis resolves, which can be especially helpful in the discouraging days when it seems that things will never be all right again.

Several outcomes are possible as a result of the initial police investigation: The police may decide that there are no legal grounds on which to pursue the victim's complaint; they may be unable to accumulate enough evidence to make an arrest; or they may gather evidence and make one or more arrests on the basis of their investigation. Victims often report crimes and then never hear from the police again. Recent judicial reform in the area of victim's rights has included provision in some states that crime victims be notified of the results of the police investigation, but such mandatory notification is still the exception rather than the rule. Of course, any one who has reported a crime to the police may subsequently contact the department to find out how the case is progressing, but different departments handle such requests in widely different ways.

Victims may be asked to help with the police investigation in a number of other ways. They may be asked to look at mug shots (photographs of people who have been arrested in the past for crimes similar to the victim's) or to help construct a composite drawing of the criminal. They may be asked to come to the police station to view a lineup, a group of people or photographs of people among whom the criminal may appear. Victims sometimes are asked to visit the scene of the crime in an attempt to reconstruct what happened. And, of course, if a suspect is arraigned, the victim will be asked to meet with the prosecutor and perhaps to testify at one or more court hearings and at the trial. Building the chain of evidence is the responsibility of the police. The prosecutor's job is to construct a case from the evidence that will convince the judge or jury of the guilt of the accused person.

Under even the very best of circumstances, participating in a police investigation can be experienced by the crime victim as a further violation. Most investigations do not result in an arrest. The victim may feel neglected and shortchanged if nothing comes of the effort. The failure to apprehend the criminal can be experienced as another violation of trust or as more evidence that the world is out of control. The victim may express anger at the police.

It *is* frustrating not to get justice. The family and friends of the victim can help ease this sort of pain by encouraging the victim to keep his or her expectations about the outcome of the investigation realistic from the beginning. Sometimes the police are willing to say what they think the probability of an arrest is in a specific case. The nationwide figures given in Appendix A of this book or, even better, local statistics showing the arrest rate for the particular crime in the victim's own area may also be used as a general guideline.

If the investigation is prolonged, the victim can encounter additional difficulties. He or she may be required to tell the story of the crime over and over. Some victims find this repetition therapeutic and enjoy the attention of repeated sessions of police questioning. But for others, an extended investigation keeps the pain of the violation raw. It imposes exterior demands on the victim that interfere with the natural internal progression of the crisis resolution. A victim who needs to put thoughts about the crime aside for a while, for example, may not be able to do so if the police are pursuing an aggressive investigation and need frequent contact with the victim.

Some repetition in questioning is inevitable, especially if the case goes to the prosecutor's office and then to trial. The responding officer, the investigator, the prosecutor, and the judge and jury will all need to hear the victim's story. But victims are sometimes subject to unnecessary interrogation in uncomfortable circumstances. Victims can protect themselves by insisting that repetition be limited as much as possible. If, for example, the victim has made a full statement to one investigator, it is appropriate to ask why the same questions need to be asked again by another investigator. A victim may also request that the police come to his or her home for questioning if that is preferable to going to the police station.

Identifying an arrested suspect is another painful task. Seeing the criminal again can be extremely upsetting to the victim. It can bring back all the fear of their first encounter. Sometimes victims are so shaken that they cannot recognize the criminal, or they may feel uncertain about the identification at first. Positive identification can be very important to building a solid court case, and the victim should have good emotional support for this task. Ideally, a friend, relative, or other victim advocate will offer to accompany the victim to the police station or courthouse for the identification.

If the crime involves stolen property which the police recover, the property may be held at the police station as evidence in the case. Procedures for its return to the victim vary, and delays are not uncommon. An elderly widow, disabled and living alone, was the victim of a burglary in which her television set was taken. The set was recovered by the police and the victim signed the release required for its return, but a week passed and the set was still not back in her home. She ordinarily watched television almost all day long, and so she was quite upset. Finally her community visiting nurse complained to the police, and they arranged to have the set brought back. Victims who need their recovered property should not hesitate to ask the police about the best way to have it returned quickly. Prompt return of property taken as evidence is another common provision in victim rights legislation.

The Police Role in Crisis Intervention

Victims who report crimes to the police are often in the initial stage of crisis during the first police interview. The responding officer is usually seen as a person of authority, and he or she is often the first person the victim talks to after the crime. Under the stress of the crime's impact, the victim may be unusually vulnerable during this initial interview, and the behavior of the first officer on the scene has an unusually strong effect. Ordinary acts of competence and kindness can help to restore the victim's faith in humanity during this crucial period. When the police are responsive to the victim's needs—when they arrive quickly, listen carefully, and appear to be concerned—the victim will often feel significantly comforted and reassured.

The victim advocate's movement has had a profound impact on law enforcement. Indeed, it is our impression that the greatest influence of the movement on the criminal-justice system has been felt among the police. They have come to see the victim as a singularly important person in furthering the investigation of the crime. As a result, police behavior has changed dramatically for the better in communicating support and concern for victims. Basic elements of crisis intervention training have been incorporated into the training of countless police officers, and many victim support services are located within or directly supported by local police departments. Victims in crisis are often helped to weather the first impact by the reassurance of the responding officers. Donna Amanti is taking courses at a major metropolitan university for a master's degree in business administration. Her purse was snatched one afternoon as she came home from registration for the fall semester. She had just stood in line for four hours to get the courses she wanted, and all of the papers were in that purse. By the time Donna got home and called the police, she was practically hysterical.

> I hadn't been hurt and there wasn't very much money in the purse, but I just couldn't stop crying. I kept thinking there was no way I was going to be able to get into any of those courses because they'd be all filled up before I could get back down there. And it was like the whole semester was going to be shot. I was still crying when the cops came, and they were just terrific about it. They sat down with me and listened to the whole story. By the time I finished telling it I had finally gotten myself under control. And, you know, I'll never forget those guys. One of them even lent me his handkerchief so I could blow my nose. They were really there when I needed them.

A rape victim whose assailant has never been apprehended was asked a year after the crime how she felt about the police. She said that she had gone through a lot of angry feelings because the police had never caught the man who raped her, but now the anger had subsided. "The only thing that stands out for me now is how kind the officers were when they got there. They couldn't have been nicer. They were sympathetic. I really felt I was being taken care of." A positive experience with the police can do a lot to help foster long-term healing.

Unfortunately, the opposite is also true: A negative experience with the police can be quite damaging to a crime victim. If the officers are delayed in responding to the call, if they are brusque or seem bored, if they are impatient or perfunctory in their questioning—the victim may experience the "second injury" discussed earlier, a further and compounded violation of self.

A newly married couple came home from their three-week honeymoon to find their house broken into and vandalized. All of their wedding presents had either been stolen or smashed. Dazed, they called the police and then sat down in the living room in the middle of the wreckage. The officer who answered the phone told them not to touch anything so they just sat and waited. An hour and ten minutes later a patrol car pulled into the driveway. When the officer came to the door, they asked what had taken him so long. He snarled, "You're lucky we came at all."

A fifteen-year-old girl, the victim of rape, was brought to the police station by her mother. The girl had been attacked on her way home from the beach. She was wearing a pair of jeans and a halter top. The detective assigned to the case came into the room, took one look at her, and exploded. "No wonder you got raped," he said. "With your tits hanging out like that, what do you expect?"

Added pain. Additional suffering. Sometimes it's nothing as dramatic as direct, angry confrontation. Sometimes it's just bureaucratic procedures or even a well-meaning little white lie. Marjorie Beauchant's car was stolen. The police told her that they had a 97 percent recovery rate, and since she needed the car to get to work, she was anxious to find out whether or not they had found it.

> I had a weird time with the cops. I called every day for a while. I had the extension and everything all down, and I always talked to this one guy. I would call and the guy would say, "Hold on for a minute," and go away for a while. They were running it through a little computer or something, I thought. And then I hadn't called for two or three days, and I called and got some new guy, and he said, "I'm sorry, miss. We don't have any way to check on that here." And I thought: My God, they've been feeding me a line all this time, putting me on hold and answering the other phone, and coming back on to say, "We've checked it. It's not here."

One of those two police officers was lying, teaching Marjorie that she can't trust cops, adding to the fundamental violation of having her car stolen.

What's Happening Behind the Badge?

It's difficult for victims to understand a police officer who treats them with indifference or hostility. Such behavior is always reprehensible, but many aspects of police work militate against human sensitivity. Every thoughtful officer has to do a constant juggling act in which complex and sometimes contradictory demands are made by the various roles that a police officer is expected to assume. We do not mean to excuse police insensitivity—there is no excuse for it—but it is useful for victims to realize what is going on in the person behind the badge.

Working in a world that is often a combination of tragic personal suffering, real danger and hostility on the streets, and periods of crushing boredom, many police officers develop a tough exterior as a kind of armor to protect themselves from the emotional demands of their work. Like the people who work in hospital emergency rooms, police officers see people in pain every day, sometimes all day. They may very well have to screen some of it out. The emotional hazards of police work have been well summarized by psychiatrist Martin Symonds:

> The job of being a policeman is unique. It is one of the few occupations in which one is feared, sometimes hated, occasionally reviled, or even assaulted in the ordinary performance of one's duties. When we consider that most people need and want to be liked, and that the young patrolman starts his career by seeing himself as an individual who will help and protect others, we can understand what an emotional strain is placed upon him. . . .[10]

Crime victims often comment that the responding officer didn't seem terribly interested in what they had gone through. Like the famous Joe Friday, many police seem indifferent and distant—"Just the facts, ma'm." They may just be protecting themselves.

At its worst, this protective armor becomes inflexible and impenetrable. The officer is truly indifferent to the victim's plight. He or she depersonalizes victims, treats them as objects to be processed as quickly as possible. A self-protective officer can become entirely detached from any human feeling for the victim. Since the victim is a person who has recently been treated like an object by the criminal, this behavior on the part of a police officer is sure to make the victim feel even more violated.

The victim's suffering may actually provoke hostility. When a police officer who sees victims all the time feels unable to help them, the officer may become antagonistic. Turning on another person to relieve oneself of unacceptable emotions has long been recognized in psychoanalytic theory, where it is identified as a defense mechanism called *projection.* Projection is commonly used to defend against guilt: If a person thinks he or she has done something bad, that person may project the guilt outward and accuse another.

Police are especially vulnerable to this form of victim denial. For a police officer, every crime victim represents a professional failure, an instance in which the police were unable to protect a citizen from crime. The officer knows how little the police and the courts can do to assure the victim any sense of justice. Feelings of helplessness and guilt can cause these professionals in the criminal-justice system to treat a victim with anger—again as a way of handling their own feelings.

As the public has become more aware of the crime victim's dilemma, pressure on the police system has intensified, often in the form of attacks on police competence and demands for more sensitive service. This public response is understandable, but it has the unfortunate effect of forcing the police into a position from which they feel obliged to counterattack by defending their present policies. A more constructive reaction results when the complexities of police work are acknowledged and provisions are made for better training so that police officers can be prepared for the many and difficult roles they must fill.

In the New York City Police Department, for example, a special Sex Crimes Analysis Unit was established in 1972 in response to a 37 percent increase in reports of forcible rape from 1971 to 1972. Investigators assigned to the unit receive training designed to increase their understanding of the rape victim's feelings and to give them better interviewing and crisis-intervention skills. The results have been satisfying for both victims and police officers.

Numerous complainants who might otherwise have been uncooperative have responded favorably to the presence of investigating detectives who present themselves as sympathetic, understanding, supportive authority figures. In addition to being of immeasurable value to the future psychological well-being of the victim, this training has had a direct impact on the apprehension rate for sex criminals.

Victims have confidence and trust in detectives who display sympathetic attitudes and skillful interview techniques, and as a result valuable information which might otherwise have been withheld is provided to the officer, which affords him the means [to conduct] a thorough, quality investigation and, ultimately, to effect an arrest. After an arrest has been made, the support and encouragement provided by these detectives has caused a greater number of victims to remain in the system and to prosecute.

Through practical experience and training programs, sex crimes investigators have developed an expertise which is reflected dramatically in arrest figures. In 1974, 2,147 arrests for forcible rape were effected, as opposed to 1,721 arrests for the year 1973, an increase of 24.8 percent. This increase is due in great measure to better quality investigations resulting from greater complainant cooperation.[11]

This program, the first of its kind, has become a model for others around the country. Now in operation for more than ten years, it is still a part of the training of every detective in the New York City Police Department. Police are also being trained in conflict management, hostage negotiation, death notification, and other skills that emphasize the interpersonal aspects of their work. Resistance within the police system to the needs of victims has been significantly lessened by this kind of training.

The Court System

If the police are successful in their investigation, they will arrest the person to whom the evidence points. After the arrest, the accused person will be processed through the courts, and the case is turned over to a prosecutor.[12] The prosecutor is a lawyer who represents the People—according to our law, a criminal offends the entire society, not just the victim, and the accused is prosecuted in the name of all the People. The prosecuting attorney works in the court system of the government whose law is alleged to have been broken. It may be a village, town, city, county, state, or federal court.

The prosecutor's job is to take the evidence gathered by the police, determine the specific charge to be filed against the accused, construct a convincing case, and argue that case before a judge and, perhaps, a jury in order to convict the person charged. Unlike the judge, who must remain neutral, the prosecutor takes the side of those who believe that the accused is guilty.

People who are arrested and accused of committing a crime have a right to defend themselves against the charge—hence, they are called *defendants* in court. The accused has a right to his or her own lawyer, the defense attorney. The United States Constitution specifies that defendants have certain other essential rights, among them the right to a speedy and public trial, the right to be informed of the charges against them, and the right to be free from excessive bails and fines.

Recent years have seen the emergence of the concept of a parallel set of rights for crime victims. About a dozen states have thus far enacted some form of legislation called a Victim's Bill of Rights. The American Bar Association, the National Judicial College, and the National District Attorney's Association have issued recommendations to their constituencies about the fair treatment of victims and witnesses. Stimulated by the victim advocacy movement, judges and lawyers are paying more attention to the needs of crime victims for information, participation in the criminal-justice system, and services. This effort is intended, as the National Conference of the Judiciary noted, "not to reduce the rights guaranteed defendants but rather to assure the rights of victims and witnesses."[13]

Legal proceedings vary enormously from one jurisdiction to another.[14] Our forefathers believed that local autonomy would help to insure justice, and so every state has its own criminal-justice system. Different jurisdictions may use different terms and follow different procedures in the prosecution. We will sketch out only the barest frame of the possibilities here. There are a few procedures that are generally standard in all systems, and there are a few problems which almost all victims encounter. These we will mention. Beyond this, the victim's access to information and help within a specific court system depends upon the availability of victim-witness services or, in their absence, the victim's ability to form a relationship with the prosecutor handling his or her case.

Where Victim's Bill of Rights legislation has been enacted, crime victims may find a victim-witness advocate within the prosecutor's office whose job is to keep victims and witnesses informed about each step in their cases. New laws also provide for victim participation at various points in criminal-justice proceedings. For example, some states require a victim impact statement—a written description of the medical, financial, and emotional injury caused by the offender—before sentencing. In many jurisdictions, however, there are no special provisions for victims' rights, and here the victim has to depend on the prosecutor (or someone else in the prosecutor's office) for information and assistance. Although the prosecutor is not a victim advocate, he or she is responsible for the victim's case. Where no other resources are available, victims should make every effort to find some person in the prosecutor's office who can answer questions and keep the victim informed about the progress of the case.

As soon as the accused person has been formally charged with the crime, he or she may be temporarily released on bail or on his or her own recognizance. Any person who has been accused but not convicted of a crime in this country has the right by law to be released from jail. This constitutional safeguard assumes that the accused is innocent until proven guilty. When a victim knows that the person accused is the criminal, it may be extremely difficult for the victim to accept this part of the law. Victims who are afraid of retaliation or are threatened by the criminal should report these fears and threats immediately to the police. Protection from pre-trial intimidation and post-trial retaliation are basic victim rights.

Most court cases are settled without a trial. The defendant pleads guilty—often to a lesser crime than the one for which he or she was originally charged. Through an arrangement called *plea-bargaining* the prosecutor may agree to reduce the charge, to dismiss other charges pending against this defendant, or to make some other concession in exchange for the guilty plea. A trial is unnecessary when the defendant enters a guilty plea because the purpose of a trial is to determine the innocence or guilt of the accused.

The practice of plea-bargaining is often criticized by victims, police officers, and others opposed to leniency for criminals because it usually results in a conviction for a less serious offense. Prosecutors plea-bargain for many reasons. Sometimes they are aware of mitigating circumstances that call for leniency in a particular case. The prosecutor may believe that the evidence is insufficient to sustain one charge but sufficient to sustain a lesser charge, in such cases, he or she may plea-bargain to insure a conviction. But plea-bargaining is probably most often an attempt to reduce the number of cases going to trial because the system cannot accommodate all of them. Some jurisdictions forbid plea-bargaining in certain circumstances, typically in the crimes seen as most terrible, such as the murder of a police officer. In others, plea-bargaining admits input from the victim. Nevada, for example, requires that victims be given an opportunity to be involved in plea-bargaining agreements. Other states require only that the victim be informed if there is a plea bargain. Whenever a victim's case is plea-bargained, he or she should be informed by the prosecutor of the reasons and of the final outcome.

Unless and until the defendant pleads guilty, various preliminary hearings—including in some cases a grand jury—will be held before the trial. Victim testimony is sometimes required at these hearings. Whenever the victim is required to appear in court he or she will be informed in advance, usually by a subpoena, a written order stating the time and place of appearance.

The trial is an examination of questions of fact or law before a judge and, in some cases, a jury. During the trial various witnesses, including the victim, testify by answering questions put to them by the prosecutor and the defense attorney. If and when the case goes to trial, the victim will testify as a witness for the prosecution. Defendants are not required to testify during either a hearing or a trial. If time and case load permit, the prosecutor will meet with the victim before the trial to go over the facts of the case and to help the victim understand what will happen during the trial.

After all the witnesses have testified, the judge or the jury, if there is one, decides on the verdict—whether the defendant is guilty or not guilty. Defendants who have been convicted are sentenced by the judge, who takes the offender's past behavior and circumstances into consideration when he or she imposes the penalty. In jurisdictions in which victim involvement in sentencing has been mandated, the judge will get some sort of written or oral statement from the victim. Sometimes it is a victim impact statement, sometimes a victim statement of opinion, in which the victim expresses his or her views about the most appropriate sentence in the case.

The offender may be sentenced to a prison or jail term, in which case the court usually indicates a maximum and sometimes a minimum time to be served. The sentence may be suspended so that the offender can be placed on probation. Fines are also sometimes levied in criminal cases, including restitution in money to the victim of the crime. Judges have always had common law authority to order restitution, and under the influence of the crime victims' movement, this form of victim reparation has become more common. A few states now require the judge to order restitution or to give a written reason for not doing so.

Young people who are accused of crime are not handled in the adult court system. From the time they are arrested, a different set of rules and procedures pertains. Their cases are heard in a juvenile system, where the penalties that can be imposed are different from those imposed on adults. The theory behind a separate juvenile system is that young people who commit crimes are thought to be less responsible for their behavior than adults and to be more in need of help. The age at which a person no longer merits this special treatment varies from jurisdiction to jurisdiction. Juvenile records and hearings are usually considered confidential by law and are not open to the public.

Lost in the Shuffle

Coming to the courthouse to testify for the first time can be a frustrating and frightening experience for the crime victim. Even the most competent person is likely to feel lost and intimidated, especially if the court building is large and information centers are inadequate. There are usually lots of people milling around—court officials and police officers, lawyers and defendants, and witnesses. One victim said that coming down to the courthouse was like walking into a big, unfriendly junior high school in the middle of the school year as a new student—nobody talks to you, everyone else seems to know where to go, and you're sure that the bell is going to ring, all the doors are going to close, and you're going to be left alone in that big corridor, hopelessly lost and late for your first class.

People who work in the courthouse are so familiar with the procedures and the physical layout of the place that it may not occur to them to explain. Defendants often have a guide; either they are in police custody or their defense attorney has arranged to meet them. Many defendants have been arrested previously and know the ropes. The victim is often the only person involved in the case who has never been in court before, and a busy prosecutor may neglect to tell the victim what he or she needs to know in order to feel reasonably secure. Where victim-witness services are available, the difficulties outlined below may be minimized, but in many districts victims and witnesses are still lost in the shuffle.

When victims are not adequately informed before they go to court, they may become so rattled that their ability to testify is impaired. They may even give up and go home, losing the case by default. It is a good idea for the victim to go to court with someone else, a victim advocate or friend or family member who can also help the victim to find out as much as possible beforehand about what will happen. Questions about procedures addressed to someone in the prosecutor's office, and they can be quite specific: Exactly where is the courthouse? What's the best way to get there? What parking facilities are available and how much do they cost? Which door should I go in? What room should I go to? What will I be asked? How long do you think it will take?

All too often, the court system is not arranged to make things easy for victims and other witnesses.[15] They are regularly asked to come to court first thing in the morning, for example, when their testimony may not be required until late in the afternoon. There is little recognition that serving as a witness can be time-consuming and expensive. Victims and other witnesses may incur transportation costs, child-care expenses, and the loss of wages from time missed at work.

Witness fees are available in some jurisdictions, but they are ordinarily only a token sum and often no one even mentions the fact that they are available.

Frequently, no provision is made for the witnesses' physical comfort or safety. Victim-witnesses sometimes meet the accused, out on bail, in the corridors outside the courtroom. One victim was followed around all day by the defendant's weeping wife, who pleaded with the victim to drop the charges. In another case, a victim was threatened by several members of the defendant's family who had come to the courthouse with him.

More and more court systems do provide services for victims and other witnesses. Witness-alert systems have been set up in some jurisdictions to telephone witnesses when it is time for them to give their testimony so they don't have to sit around the courthouse all day. Some jurisdictions provide reception areas where victims and other witnesses can wait in a reasonably comfortable and sheltered place. Volunteers have been trained in some areas to help victims by answering their questions, escorting them to and from the court, providing transportation and child care, reporting the progress and outcome of the various court procedures, and so on. Some of these programs are organized and staffed by the police or the prosecutor's office; others are sponsored by a variety of private groups. Sometimes victims in jurisdictions with victim-witness services are unaware of these programs. It's a good idea to ask the police or the prosecutor if such service is available.

Among the most discouraging and infuriating aspects of the court system for victims is the ease with which proceedings can be delayed. Sometimes a victim will take time off from work, come down to the courthouse, wait around for the hearing or trial to begin, and then learn that the judge has granted a continuance. Repeated delays are common in many systems. It is rare for a criminal case to be concluded in a few weeks or even a few months in some jurisdictions. The Constitution requires a speedy trial and some local laws now stipulate a particular time period within which certain kinds of cases must be tried. But the court process will almost inevitably take longer than the victim wishes it would.

Even if the victim has been informed of the delay beforehand by a conscientious prosecutor, it is still psychologically wearing to prepare oneself to testify and then to have the proceeding postponed. A victim is naturally nervous about appearing in court; having the proceeding put off will increase this nervousness. Again, the extended process of criminal prosecution imposes external timetables on the victim's own internal recovery process and may add to the victim's sense of violation.

These delays are almost always beyond the control of the victim and often beyond the control of the prosecutor. It is helpful if the victim can anticipate them by asking the prosecutor early on how much time he or she expects each step in the process to take. Victims who have been subpoenaed as witnesses can call the prosecutor's office the day before the time indicated on the subpoena to find out if the proceeding has been delayed.

Victim-witnesses commonly feel ambivalent about participating in the court process. They may be afraid they will make a mistake in their testimony, or that they will appear foolish on the witness stand. Some fear that they will be personally attacked in the defense attorney's cross-examination. Many victims have reservations about sending anybody to prison because they believe that prison conditions are brutalizing and encourage criminal behavior.[16] Victims sometimes begin the prosecution with a lot of energy and zest, strongly motivated by their anger at the criminal, and then become less and less enthusiastic as the case drags on. They may feel caught in a catch-22, unwilling to drop out of the process but unhappy about staying in it.

Giving testimony can be an upsetting experience. The judge is supposed to forbid harrassing questions, and the prosecutor can object if the victim-witness is being attacked by the defense attorney. It is helpful for the victim to know beforehand what the defense attorney might ask, but of course the prosecutor will not always know. Sometimes it helps to have friends and family attend the trial. Every criminal trial in this country is public by constitutional law, and anyone can attend. This is another time, however, when the victim's loved ones should be sure they know what the victim wants. Some people feel better about testifying if nobody they care about is in the courtroom.

Victim advocates and loved ones can also help by listening to the victim's fears and sometimes by serving as an audience while the victim rehearses his or her testimony. But family members and friends who want to help the victim should avoid giving advice about what the victim might say in court. Giving legal testimony can be a highly intricate business. However well-intentioned a layperson might be, his or her advice can easily be harmful. It is better to seek information from those who have the training and experience to be helpful. Victims who feel inadequately prepared for giving testimony can seek help from a victim advocate or victim counselor. If none is available, the prosecutor should be asked for help.

Blind Justice

The rule of law imposes certain restrictions on the citizen who is the victim of a personal crime. In most contemporary societies, individuals have given up the right to settle their own scores. In exchange, they are supposed to be protected by the state. Thus where once the victim could gather family and friends and go with them to exact retribution directly from the offender, now victims must rely on the intervention of the criminal-justice system. Human civilization is clearly advanced by this arrangement. Few people would suggest that we return to the era of personal retaliation and tribal vengeance. But from the victim's perspective, turning one's grievance over to the strangers who represent the People is surely a less satisfying way of redressing the emotional injury suffered.

The justice of the state is, by definition, dispassionate. Often depicted as a blindfolded figure holding a scales in which only the facts are weighed, this justice is deliberately removed from the emotions and the personal circumstances of the case. As such, it is very different from the justice to which the victim feels entitled. In a trial the guilt or innocence of the accused is the only matter of question; the victim's plight is not a factor. The judge cannot be partisan. His or her job is to determine the facts of the case.

This high ideal can account for a very painful experience in court: the victim's sense that the judge does not care what happened. For the victim, "what happened" includes the violation of self, an emotional injury that echoes through the victim's life like a series of shock waves. The court does not care about that injury. The court's business is weighing questions of law and matters of fact.

In practice the requirements of neutrality on the part of the judge can encourage reprehensible behavior and patronizing attitudes. The family of a young woman who was murdered during a robbery followed the prosecution with intense interest, coming to court every day for weeks to get information and to press for justice. The murderer was convicted but given a light sentence, and the sister of the victim became extremely bitter:

> All they care about in the trial is witnesses and factual information. They didn't want my father at that trial. They asked him not to go. To the grand jury, too; he waited outside the door to see if the indictment would come down. They never questioned him at the grand jury. But if the defendant had a character witness, they would have had him there. And then my father asked for an appointment with the judge, to talk with the judge. And he said, "What do you mean by this sentence?" And the judge said, "Well I have this and I have that...." So my father says, "You never asked me what it did to my family." And the judge said, "That's not important. All that is important is that this man is sentenced and he pays for his crime." My father wrote to the appellate judge and received a letter that it was not in his jurisdiction. And it's all a big, legal, red-tape hassle.

In 1983, a National Conference of the Judiciary on the Rights of Victims of Crime met to discuss the treatment of crime victims by the criminal-justice system and to consider ways to minimize victims' burdens and trauma. The recommendations from that historic conference include many reforms which have already been enacted in areas where the crime victims' movement has been a moving force. Among these are such obvious victim rights as "ensuring that victims and witnesses are treated with courtesy, respect, and fairness" and such essential services as information about the victim's case, separate waiting areas for victims and the accused, victim-witness protection from intimidation, child care services, restitution, crime-victim compensation, and crisis intervention and counseling.

Victim participation is urged "at all stages of judicial proceedings," including "1. pre-trial release or bail hearings; 2. the propriety and conditions of diversion; 3. the scheduling of court proceedings; 4. continuances or delays; judges should state on the record the reason for granting a continuance; 5. plea and sentence negotiations; 6. sentencing; 7. victim-offender mediation in nonviolent cases, when appropriate."[17] These Recommended Judicial Practices represent an enormous step forward for victims of crime. The recommendations also speak eloquently by inference about the shortcomings of judicial practices in the past. Too frequently, victims have had no way to let the judge know how the crime has affected them. And many judges still believe that they service justice better by remaining "objective."

Winning the Fight Against Crime

Unlike the judge, police officers and prosecutors can be fiercely partisan, especially when they are young and still idealistic. Some of them are passionately devoted to stamping out crime. This attitude is gratifying, of course, for a victim who sees his or her own outrage mirrored in it. But victims may also feel pushed aside by the enthusiasm of the zealous crime fighter when all of the energy is being focused on the hunt and the kill.

Both the police and the courts are mainly concerned with criminals. Their professional business is catching and convicting the bad guys, putting evil behind bars where it belongs. Most police officers remain convinced that their main job is apprehending criminals, despite studies that show that more than 80 percent of their time is spent providing services.[18] Police training and police operations stress the law-enforcement function, and television reinforces the myth.

Winning each skirmish in the war on crime provides the police officer and the prosecutor with positive status and a sense of professional achievement. Being sensitive to the victim's needs often carries no professional satisfaction; it can even be a liability. A prosecutor is admired when he or she wins a case, not when the prosecutor's office is willing to answer every victim's question carefully. There's not a whole lot of drama in the care and tending of victims.

Some law-enforcement professionals see themselves as the "thin blue line," defending the community against the criminal. They may actually feel as if they are locked in life-and-death combat with a resistant and evil enemy. The fight against crime has the quality of a civil war for these people: It is inbred and totally consuming. There are no small-scale ways to wage this war. Destructiveness is met with destructiveness: an eye for an eye; a tooth for a tooth.[19] Nothing is more important than winning the battle.

Police officers and prosecutors who see themselves as crime fighters can become totally preoccupied with winning. And they are likely to feel that "all's fair" in the war. If they have to invade the privacy of a witness or hurt the feelings of a victim to get the criminal, it will be done. Police officers who are urged to be more sympathetic and helpful to the victim may protest; they signed up to fight crime, not to hold hands. The victim is simply not very interesting or important to such an officer because the victim is not the threat. The officer is engaged in a combat mission and, like any soldier, he or she is most interested in defeating the enemy.

The hard, combat-oriented role needed to fight the criminal may not allow much room for feelings of compassion and sympathy. An officer who identified strongly with the victim might be unable to perform his or her main work role—and even the most liberal reformer doesn't want the cop to be *just* a social worker. Emotional and functional economy requires many criminal-justice professionals to maintain a certain amount of insensitivity in order to perform their jobs. Most people can't be both empathic counselors and combat soldiers unless they have been trained for both roles.

The police officer or prosecutor who is naturally good at both aggressive crime fighting and compassionate identification with victims is rare. Many people who work in criminal justice feel that they have to make a choice; their professional training and the policies of their systems often encourage them to give the victim low priority. By seeing their job as making war on criminals, they can add drama and intensity to work that is often boring. They avoid the possibility that they will be identified with the victim/loser. From the point of view of their own ability to function, this strategy may work very well. But it has the unintended side effect of creating further difficulties for many victims of personal crime.

Facing the Outcome

When the case of a personal crime victim goes to trial, the victim is faced with the possibility that he or she may lose again. In spite of everyone's best effort, the evidence may not be compelling enough to get a conviction. The victim, the police, and the prosecutor may all be quite convinced of the guilt of the accused, but the law requires more than personal opinion. The law requires persuasive evidence—"beyond a reasonable doubt."

Four years ago last September Judy Bowles was assaulted and raped by a man who surprised her in the kitchen of her apartment while she was making supper. He rang the doorbell and forced his way into the house by threatening Judy's roommate with a gun when she answered the door. Three weeks later he tried to rob another woman at gunpoint on the same street; one of her neighbors saw him and called the police. He was arrested, and because Judy had given the police such a good physical description, they immediately suspected that he was her assailant as well.

Judy made a positive identification of the suspect by picking him out of a police lineup. She met with the prosecutor, who told her they had a good chance of getting a conviction, and she agreed to be the prosecution's chief witness. Over the next eighteen months Judy testified at a preliminary hearing, before a grand jury, and during two jury trials. The first trial ended in a hung jury: nine for conviction, three for acquittal. During the second trial, she was on the stand for four days straight. The second jury deadlocked ten to two.

Judy believes that the police and the prosecutor mishandled her case. She is sure that the defendant in her case is the same man who raped her, and she is bitter about her experience in court:

> Before I was raped I really did feel that the law would protect me, but now I know that's not the case. Everything is a technicality. It seems that there's no common sense. . . .
>
> When you go to trial, sit back in your chair because you're going to get knocked back. So much of the defense attorney's questioning is really a form of harrassment. You do have some limited freedoms in the court-room—very few. And those that you have no one wants you to know about.
>
> I do not view the court as my friend. Because you have to remember that nine times out of ten the defendant is not going to take the stand. You're the one that's on trial. Anybody who tells you differently is lying. You have to have credibility. You have to convince twelve good men and true beyond a reasonable doubt that what you say happened did happen. The whole trial is on your shoulders.
>
> Here's your day in court. Ha. Fat chance. When you go, you're scared. And who's been trained? I mean, I took speech class in high school, but you're not trained to speak in front of an audience. You're not trained to answer questions or to observe things so carefully when they happen. And I must say that my powers of observation have just degenerated to nothing since this happened. Because next time I go to court, I want to be able to say, "I don't know what happened. I don't remember a thing. I couldn't identify anybody." I don't want to be involved in this business again. Because it's a bummer. I don't need the aggravation. Nobody needs the aggravation. But, at the same time, somebody better be aggravated because we've got a lot of problems.
>
> I think very little of the system. The more I learned about it the less I thought of it. I don't think anybody's protected by it. Except maybe the judge and the lawyers on both sides. It's so institutionalized that the institution lives to feed the institution. And as far as justice goes—don't even say *law* and *justice* in the same sentence. . . . You come up empty no matter what happens.

Forcible rape is the most painful violation of self that a person can endure and still live. Anyone who has been hurt so badly is going to be especially vulnerable and sensitive for a long time afterward. Add to that, in this case, the pain of losing again, of feeling further violated by the injustice of the courts. Judy's angry feelings are certainly understandable.

Miscarriages of justice are inevitable in any human system. But the attitudes that Judy encountered in the courtroom are becoming less prevalent. Twenty years ago almost every rape victim suffered further violation in the hands of the authorities. Today the tide is turning. The influence of the women's movement and of the courageous rape victims who have protested these injustices is finally being felt. As people in the criminal-justice system become more aware of the psychological consequences of victimization, their attitudes are changing. The system will never be perfect, but it is demonstrating that it can become more sensitive to victims—and without compromising the ideal of justice on which it is based.

Our law requires evidence of guilt. It requires the presumption of innocence for the accused. It surrounds defendants with safeguards so that they cannot be deprived of their freedom capriciously. These are necessary and proper rules. But all the intellectualizing in the world cannot prevent crime victims from feeling terribly wronged when the criminal-justice system fails to satisfy their need for justice. There just isn't any way to soften the blow.

And still—the rule of law is terribly important to our survival as a species. In *A Man for All Seasons*, Robert Bolt's wonderful play about Sir Thomas More, there is a speech in which More passionately defends the law, saying that the devil himself is entitled to its benefits. His prospective son-in-law, Will Roper, replies that he would cut down every law in England to get at the devil, and More turns on him in a fury:

> Oh? And when the last law was down, and the Devil turned round on you—where would you hide, Roper, the laws all being flat? This country's planted thick with laws from coast to coast—man's law, not God's—and if you cut them down—and you're just the man to do it—d'you really think you could stand upright in the winds that would blow then? Yes, I'd give the Devil the benefit of law, for my own safety's sake.[20]

If our world is to be fit to live in, its citizens must maintain certain codes of behavior. We can't go around maiming and robbing and raping each other because if we do no one will be safe. By the same token, we can't lock up or execute every person accused of violating the law. The law is meant to provide all of us with the measure of safety we need to function. And no matter what its imperfections, it is the best we have. Those who disregard it tear at the very foundations of our civilization.

NOTES

1. See the discussion in chapter 5 of Melvin J. Lerner's "just-world" theory.

2. The criminal-justice system includes police, prosecution, courts, and corrections. The chart on page 00 shows the movement of a case through the system.

3. Martin Symonds, "The 'Second Injury' to Victims," *Evaluation and Change: Services for Survivors* (Minneapolis, Minn., Minneapolis Medical Research Foundation, Inc., 1980), p. 37.

4. Bureau of Justice Statistics, *Report to the Nation on Crime and Justice: The Data* (Washington, D.C.: Government Printing Office, 1983), pp. 24-25.

5. For a consideration of some of the factors involved in the victim's decision about reporting the crime, see Robert F. Kidd and Ellen F. Chayet, "Why Do Victims Fail to Report? The Psychology of Victimization," *Journal of Social Issues* 40 (1984), and Martin S. Greenberg, R. Barry Ruback, and David R. Westcott, "Seeking Help from the Police: The Victim's Perspective," in Arie Nadler, Jeffrey D. Fisher, and Bella M. DePaulo, eds., *New Directions in Helping*, Vol. 3 (New York: Academic Press, 1983).

6. Richard D. Knudten et al, *Victims and Witnesses: Their Experience with Crime and the Criminal-Justice System. Executive Summary* (Washington, D.C.: Government Printing Office, 1977), p. iv.

7. The eight Index Crimes are murder, forcible rape, robbery, aggravated assault, burglary, larceny-theft, motor vehicle theft, and arson. See Appendix A for a discussion of the limitations of criminal-justice statistics collected by the F.B.I. The rate of arrests is higher for certain very serious crimes–76 percent of murder and nonnegligent manslaughter cases and 52 percent of forcible rape cases reported were cleared by arrest in 1983. However, only 26 percent of robberies and 15 percent of burglaries were cleared that year. U.S. Department of Justice, Federal Bureau of Investigation, *Crime in the United States: 1983 Uniform Crime Reports* (Washington, D.C.: Government Printing Office, 1984).

8. We are especially grateful to Jim Garofalo, Director of the Hindelang Criminal Justice Research Center at SUNY Albany, for his comments on this section, which enabled us to correct several factual errors in the first edition and also reminded us that the question of how "successful" the police and the courts and the prisons are needs always to be illuminated by the clear light of First Amendment concerns, even though a crime victim who has been disappointed by the criminal-justice system cannot be expected to see it that way.

Victims who want to compare their own experience with national statistics for arrest and conviction have some resources from which to draw, although *local* data are likely to be more meaningful for comparison since laws, agencies, standards, and procedures vary so much. National data showing the clearance rate for each personal crime are given in Appendix A at the end of this book. The *Uniform Crime Reports*, which is available in many public libraries, publish local clearance rates for offenses known to the police in cities and towns with populations of 10,000 or more.

On the difficulty of generalizing about conviction rates and comparing the criminal-justice system in one jurisdiction with another, see *Report to the Nation on Crime and Justice: The Data*, p. 45.

The performance of the courts and the prisons has been the subject of many studies. Two useful, and opposing, views are expressed in Karl Menninger's *The Crime of Punishment* (New York: The Viking Press, 1968) and Ernest van den Haag's *Punishing Criminals: Concerning a Very Old and Painful Question* (New York: Basic Books, 1975).

9. Kenneth Friedman *et al*, *Victims and Helpers: Reactions to Crime*, Victim Services Agency, New York City, New York, 1982, p. 175.

10. Martin Symonds, "Emotional Hazards of Police Work," *American Journal of Psychoanalysis* 30 (1970): 155.

11. Mary L. Keefe and Harry T. O'Reilly, "Rape: Attitudinal Training for Police and Emergency-Room Personnel," *The Police Chief*, November, 1975, p. 37.

12. The legal terms used in this book are all defined in the glossary in Appendix B at the back of the book. Legal terminology varies somewhat from one jurisdiction to another. A prosecutor, for example, may also be called a U.S. Attorney (in federal court); a district attorney; a state's attorney; a county, state, or federal prosecutor; and so on. We use the terms recommended by the SEARCH Group, Inc., in *Dictionary of Criminal Justice Data Terminology*, Second Edition (Washington, D.C.: Government Printing Office, 1981).

13. National Conference of the Judiciary on the Rights of Victims of Crime, *Statement of Recommended Judicial Practices* (Washington, D.C.: Government Printing Office, 1983), p. 6.

14. For a broad overview of the structure and function of most criminal-justice systems in the United States, see Appendix B at the back of this book.

15. Richard D. Knudten and his colleagues at the Marquette University Center for Criminal Justice and Social Policy found, in a study of Milwaukee victims and civilian witnesses, that most had some problem in their dealings with the criminal-justice system. The difficulties most often mentioned included transportation and parking expense, time loss, uncomfortable conditions, difficulty finding out what to do, income loss, long waiting time, unnecessary trips, exposure to upsetting or threatening persons, difficulty finding the right place to go, property kept as evidence, difficulty arranging child care, and difficulty arranging transportation. Knudten et al, *Victims and Witnesses: The Impact of Crime and Their Experience with the Criminal-Justice System* (Milwaukee, Wisc.: Center for Criminal Justice and Social Policy, Marquette University, 1976), table 3.5, p. 32.

16. Readers who are interested in prison conditions might read Tom Wicker's *A Time to Die* (New York: Quadrangle Books, 1975), which is about the inmate rebellion at the Attica State Prison in upstate New York, for a passionate indictment of those conditions. A different view of prisons is found in Susan Sheehan's *A Prison and a Prisoner* (New York: Houghton Mifflin, 1978).

17. National Conference of the Judiciary on the Rights of Victims of Crime, *Statement of Recommended Judicial Practices*, p. 10.

18. For a discussion of some of the implications of this confusion about role, see Morton Bard and Robert Shellow, *Issues in Law Enforcement: Essays and Case Studies* (Reston, Va.: Reston Publishing Company, 1976).

19. The recurrent public debate about capital punishment reflects this primitive perception of the crime problem as a war between criminals and decent citizens.

20. Robert Bolt, *A Man for All Seasons*, in Robert W. Corrigan, ed., *The New Theatre of Europe* (New York: Dell Publishing Company, 1962), p. 81.

7

Getting Help: Resources and Strategies

> There was no one to turn to. Every time I tried to get help
> I just got more trouble. I had a screaming fight with some
> cop on the phone because they wouldn't come to the house
> to take the report. The insurance company lost my claim
> form, and they didn't give me half of what the stolen stuff
> was worth. The new lock I bought didn't fit right. There
> just didn't seem to be any way to get through.
>
> —Burglary victim

People in trouble have to overcome three difficulties: their problem, whatever it is; their "natural" reluctance in this society to accept the identity of a needy person; and the indifference of the systems that are supposed to help them. Our cultural aversion to helplessness is clearly reflected in our helping institutions. Collecting unemployment compensation or welfare is generally considered to be shameful, for example. The conviction that most people who accept this help are lazy good-for-nothings is widespread and deeply rooted. Welfare and unemployment services are often delivered by staff people who can barely conceal their contempt for their clients. Humiliation and suspicion are built into the routines of these bureaucracies.

All of the systems that are supposed to serve crime victims are vulnerable to the same weakness: The stigma of the loser clings to them, sapping their sensitivity and efficiency. Many victims first encounter difficulty when they contact the police. Delays in response, indifference to the victim's fear and pain, lack of communication, and a general reluctance to acknowledge the victim's needs are characteristic of too many police officers. Prosecutors and others in the criminal-justice system can be just as bad.

In hospital emergency rooms, where most crime victims with physical wounds go to be treated, injured victims sometimes wait alone for several hours before a doctor finds time to see them. One woman who had been raped reported that the worst part of her experience was the casual attitude of the emergency-room nurse who chatted with friends on the phone and snapped her chewing gum while she filled out the victim's admitting forms. Crime victims who try to claim insurance, workmen's compensation, or victim-compensation benefits may encounter long lines, complicated forms, rude clerks, and exasperating waiting periods. Over and over again the victim can get the message: "You are a loser, and nobody gives a damn." Such an insult to the self would be difficult enough to bear for a person with intact defenses; it can produce additional damage in a crime victim made vulnerable by crisis.

Getting help can be hardest when the crime victim needs it most. Navigating through a resistant system—finding your way to the person who can help and getting that person to help you—often requires toughness, resilience, and good organization. Some bureaucracies have become so indifferent that they have to be approached with aggressive persistence. Personal crime victims in the first stage of crisis are singularly lacking in all of these qualities.

People need each other to survive. We all depend on others, emotionally as well as in other ways. But in a society that values independence and personal strength, human interdependence is often camouflaged. When people are feeling good, they can usually hide their neediness pretty well. A person in trouble may not be able to indulge in this pretense. Crime victims are sometimes so needy that they can't hide it. Because of the social norms, victims also anticipate rejection, and this expectation can add to their inability to get help.

Many people find it extremely difficult to express their needs, even to those they love. A person who is usually self-reliant may have a lot of trouble asking for help or even focusing on what he or she needs. One victim said, "I couldn't find any words for it." At the opposite extreme are people who feel inadequate all the time and are always asking for help. When these people are victimized, they may discover that no one will listen to them or take their needs seriously. Victims may also deny their needs because helplessness feels so threatening. They may insist that they are all right, and they may seem to be.

The most helpful thing for another person to do is to create a climate in which the victim can express whatever his or her needs are. Accepting victims wherever they are can be enormously reassuring. Full acceptance includes allowing the victim to deny the need and being sensitive to indirect requests for help. The day after Melinda Jefferson had been mugged, she said she felt perfectly fine. But about five o'clock, she became restless and began to complain that she couldn't think of anything to fix for dinner. Melinda's husband suggested that they go out for dinner. They went to a favorite place, and neither of them said a word about the crime all during the evening. Several days later, when she *did* feel like talking about it, Melinda's husband listened sympathetically. She was grateful for his sensitivity to her needs on both occasions.

You're Entitled

It's natural for victims to be upset after a crime. Most of them don't need a therapist, but any person who has been violated does need support. Usually family and friends are the best source for this help—they know and care about the victim.[1] Outside intervention from professional helpers may be needed if the violation has been very serious or if appropriate early help is not given. But most victims are strong and resilient, and they will recover their equilibrium without professional counseling.

In the early stages of the crisis, when the victim is feeling most disorganized and helpless, loved ones can provide support by accepting the victim's neediness and responding to his or her requests for help. The victim's ability to trust will be renewed when other people can make themselves available to give whatever is needed.

Renewing the victim's sense of autonomy requires a different kind of support. The helper needs to allow the victim to express his or her own strengths so that self-esteem and a sense of control return. Autonomy will be regained when victims feel that they can handle things again. This means that helpers should support victims while they get to their feet, hold on while they regain their balance, and then *let go* so that the victim can walk unaided.

Labeling a victim "helpless" or "weak" or "sick" further diminishes his or her self-esteem. Such labels encourage self-blame and self-doubt. They can leave the victim feeling paralyzed, unable to work at getting things back together. When the victim's difficulties are accepted as a natural and temporary reaction to a significant emotional injury, they are more likely to be seen as problems that can be solved.[2] Such a perspective will foster recovery because it encourages victims to see themselves as capable and because it externalizes the problem. Victims are entitled to help, not because they are inadequate people but because they have suffered a grievous injury.

Crime-Victim Compensation and the Victim Rights System

Since 1965, when the state of California launched the first statewide victim-compensation program, 40 states and the federal government have enacted compensation programs for crime victims.[3] The laws, which vary from state to state, provide public compensation in the form of a financial award to certain victims (and, in some cases, surviving families of victims) for medical expenses, loss of earnings, loss of support, funeral expenses, counseling, disability, rehabilitation, and other expenses. Victim compensation awards throughout the nation totaled $34 million in 1980.

Seventeen states have enacted a Victim Bill of Rights, focusing primarily on the needs of crime victims in relation to the criminal-justice system and including provisions for such rights as victim and witness notification, protection from intimidation and revenge by the offender, return of property taken for evidence, intervention with employers and creditors on the victim's behalf, and victim participation in criminal-justice proceedings. Statewide funding has also been provided for victim and witness services in 18 states since 1980. Some of these services include counseling, legal aid, medical aid, and restitution by the offender to the victim. Nineteen states now fund programs for victims of sexual assault, and 42 states fund domestic violence shelters.

All of these legislative advances complement and reinforce the network of publicly and privately funded victim assistance programs in existence throughout the nation. In December, 1984, the new National Victim Resource Center listed over 1200 such programs. Some are sponsored by local police departments and prosecutor's offices. Others have come out of existing social service agencies. Still others are grassroots initiatives by private groups. They are organized in different ways,[4] and their effectiveness varies, but the proliferation of services for crime victims is surely cause for celebration.

The National Organization for Victim Assistance (NOVA) is a private, nonprofit organization of victim and witness practitioners, criminal-justice professionals, researchers, former victims, and others who are committed to the recognition of victim rights. NOVA performs an essential service: It sustains the helpers, those who are directly responsible for delivering services to crime victims. Many victim assistance systems developed without much structure or organization, staffed by service givers who had little formal training and no professional support system of their own. As the movement developed, these victim advocates needed a forum for professional growth, mutual support, information exchange, training, and protection against "burn out" and other professional hazards. NOVA has provided this support system, along with a strong national voice for victim advocacy in public policy.

A schematic developed by NOVA (see pages 146-147) shows the various stages of the crime victim's experience and notes the kinds of interventions that may be needed to meet the victim's needs and secure his or her rights at each stage.

Recent advances in crime victim legislation and the realization of basic victim rights carry with them a new responsibility. The government agencies, social service organizations, and victim advocates who have begun to provide for victims' needs must not falter in their continuing efforts. Just as the reestablishment of trust is of primary importance in the individual victim's reparative process, so it is for crime victims as a class. These recent initiatives inspire greater social trust because they express an important shift in the values and attitudes of society—a shift away from blaming and ignoring the victim. Failure to build on the advances already achieved will threaten disillusionment, cynicism, and further social harm to those among us who have been the targets of the criminal offender.

The next challenge is to begin to meet the needs of crime victims who are disenfranchised in the current crime victim's movement: those millions whose victimizations go unreported. Many of those who fail to report do so because they lack trust in the criminal-justice system. Most of them are people who occupy the most victimized stratum of society—poor, inarticulate, uneducated, and defeated. The accomplishments of the victim's movement have tended thus far to represent the more affluent and better educated crime victims, those whose expectations had led them to hope for fairness and justice from the system. The pressure for change occurred when the hopes of these victims were shattered by reality. But there is a large population of victims who are essentially without hope and whose prior experiences with the system have inspired little trust in our institutions. They represent the work still to be done.

Many more victim services should be made available outside agencies of criminal justice. It may well be that the availability of such services will have the long-term effect of restoring trust and increasing the expectation of justice among these disenfranchised victims, ultimately bringing them into the formal justice-seeking system. In any case, a responsible society must continue to seek ways to assist these millions of victims.

Needs and Resources

One of the most important and continuing needs of many crime victims is the need for information.[5] First of all, victims need to know what is happening to them emotionally and in their relationships as a result of the crime. This book attempts to provide that information. Victims and other witnesses who become involved in the criminal-justice system need to understand the proceedings at each stage. They may be puzzled by legal terminology and procedures. They may want to follow the progress of the investigation. If the case goes to court, the victim-witness will need to be carefully briefed about his or her role in giving testimony. Police who take the time to keep victims informed about their cases and victim advocates and prosecutors who help to demystify the criminal-justice system do crime victims an enormous service.

Some victims want to learn how to prevent crime so that they can take action to protect themselves. Others need information about how to apply for insurance reimbursement, victim compensation, or other benefits. Still others need legal advice or psychological counseling or extended medical care.

Knowledge about the resources that are available is a crucial first step in the victim's problem-solving process. Although more than 40 states now provide some form of financial compensation for certain crime victims and about 20 states have enacted other provisions for victim rights and services, most crime victims in most communities do not have access to separate, comprehensive victim assistance. However, other existing public and private agencies may be able to provide some of the needed help—a victim who needs counseling for emotional problems, for example, can get a referral from his or her local department of mental health. Many people are unaware of these agencies, and the agencies may not reach out to crime victims or even see victims as part of their responsibilities.[6] At the back of this book, in Appendix C, is a general guide to locating and gaining access to such resources.

Many crime victims also need money to help them repair the damages done by the crime. Compensation for stolen or damaged

The Victim

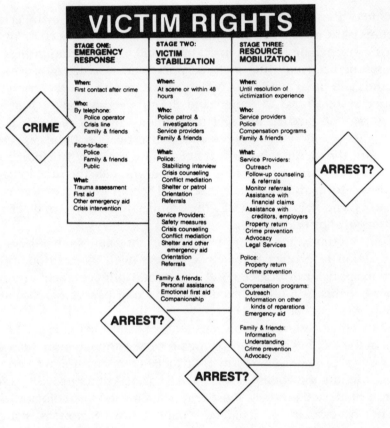

Source: National Organization for Victim Assistance, *The Victim Service System: A Guide to Action*, 1983.

Rights System

VICTIM AND WITNESS RIGHTS				
STAGE FOUR: **AFTER** **ARREST**	**STAGE FIVE:** **PRE-COURT** **APPEARANCE**	**STAGE SIX:** **COURT** **APPEARANCE**	**STAGE SEVEN:** **PRE-SENTENCE**	**STAGE EIGHT:** **POST-SENTENCE**

When:
First contact after arrest
 	
Who:
Prosecutor
Police
Service providers
Family & friends
 	
What:
Prosecutor:
  Consultation in
    charging decisions
  Consultation on bail
  Consultation on future
    scheduling
  Protection or
    relocation
 	
Service Providers:
  Start or continue with
    Stages II and III.
 	
Police:
  Protection or
    relocation
  Crime prevention
  Advocacy
 	
Family & friends:
  Peer self-help
  Crime prevention
  Advocacy
	When:
	Prior to hearing/trial
	
	Who:
	Prosecutors
	Service providers
	Family & friends
	
	What:
	Prosecutor:
	  Criminal justice
	    orientation
	  Scheduling and
	    hearing notification
	  Case status
	  Information
	  Preparation of
	    testimony
	  Witness preparation
	  Employer intervention
	  Consultation on plea
	    bargaining
	  Counseling
	  Advocacy
	
	Service providers:
	  Criminal justice
	    orientation
	  Scheduling and hearing
	    notification
	  Case status
	    information
	  Witness preparation
	  Employer intervention
	  Consultation on plea
	    bargaining
	  Counseling
	  Advocacy
	
	Family & friends:
	  Peer self-help
	  Advocacy
		When:
		Day of hearing or trial
		
		Who:
		Prosecutor
		Service providers
		Family & friends
		
		What:
		Prosecutor:
		  Transportation
		  Reception
		  Escort
		  Counseling
		  Childcare
		  Witness fees
		  Preparation for
		    outcomes
		  Advocacy
		
		Service providers:
		  Transportation
		  Reception
		  Escort
		  Counseling
		  Childcare
		  Witness fees
		  Preparation for
		    outcomes
		  Advocacy
		
		Family & friends:
		  Peer self-help
		  Advocacy
			When:
			After conviction or entry
			of guilty plea
			
			Who:
			Probation
			Prosecutor
			Judiciary
			Service providers
			Family & friends
			
			What:
			Probation:
			  Notice of outcome
			  Notice of sentencing
			    hearing
			  Victim impact
			    statement
			  Restitution plan
			  Counseling
			
			Prosecution:
			  Notice of outcome
			  Notice of sentencing
			    hearing
			  Victim impact
			    statement
			  Restitution plan
			  Counseling
			
			Judiciary:
			  Victim statement
			  Restitution plan
			
			Service providers:
			  Victim impact
			    statement
			  Restitution plan
			  Counseling
			  Information on civil
			    entitlements
			
			Family & friends:
			  Peer self-help
			  Advocacy
				When:
				After sentencing
				
				Who:
				Probation, corrections
				  && parole
				Service providers
				Prosecutor
				Family & friends
				
				What:
				Probation, corrections
				  && parole:
				Victim impact
				  statement for
				  parole hearing
				Victim input to
				  revocation hearings
				Notice on hearing
				  outcomes
				
				Prosecutor:
				  Victim impact
				  statement for
				  parole hearing
				  Victim input to
				  revocation hearings
				  Notice on hearing
				    outcomes
				
				Service Providers:
				  Victim impact
				    statement for
				    parole hearing
				  Victim input to
				    revocation hearings
				  Notice on hearing
				    outcomes
				  Counseling
				  Legal services
				
				Family & friends:
				  Protection
				  Advocacy

property is usually available only if the property was insured. Burglary victims and people whose keys have been stolen often need to replace locks. The victim may want to purchase other hardware for crime prevention such as window gates or burglar alarms.

Victims who have been physically injured need money to pay their medical expenses. If a victim requires psychological counseling, he or she will also need the money to pay for it. When the physical or emotional injury is serious and the victim loses time from work, he or she may need extra money to recover lost wages. Some victims are permanently disabled as a result of the crime; these people need long-term financial assistance.

Cooperating with criminal-justice officials can also cost the victim money. He or she may lose time from work during court appearances and incur child-care and transportation expense. In criminal proceedings, the government pays the prosecutor, but if the victim institutes a civil suit as a result of the crime, the lawyer's fees will be an additional expense.

Sometimes people of middle-class means fail to appreciate the position of a victim whose financial resources are more limited. Poor people are more likely to be victimized by crime and also more likely to be unable to meet the resulting expenses. One elderly woman whose apartment was burglarized found herself in a terrible dilemma. Because her social-security pension barely covered her living costs, she was unable to afford to get her lock fixed. "I've either got to stop eating for the next two weeks or live in constant fear."

Financial assistance from crime-victim compensation, where it is available, is typically limited to victims of violent crime and sometimes also to cases where "financial hardship" can be shown. Other public resources are sometimes available to meet some of these financial burdens, but it often takes weeks to qualify and actually receive payment. Many victims are reluctant to seek any public aid because of the stigma attached to it. Even unemployment compensation, an insurance for which every qualified person pays all during his or her working life, is often viewed by the unemployment agency and the recipient as if it were a dole.

In simple societies, assistance to those in need is usually provided by the family or the extended family. In complex societies, where family ties can be more easily loosened or broken, the responsibility for helping the needy is transferred to institutions. The quality of the help often suffers, but the resources available are still an expression of the most fundamental social responsibility. Each person in a society contributes to the common good, and each is entitled to benefit from society's resources in times of need. Victims of personal crime have suffered injury because society has failed to protect them. They are surely entitled to whatever compensation the society provides.

When Professional Counseling Is Needed

Victims and their loved ones sometimes have difficulty deciding whether they might benefit from professional counseling after the crime. In many cases outside therapeutic intervention is clearly not needed. Some crimes are less serious than others. A burglary victim who has reasonably good family support, for example, will probably resolve whatever problems arise without professional help. But the survivor-victims of a murder are much more likely to need some outside support.

During the period immediately after the crime, the victim will suffer some disruption—perhaps something as minor as a lost night's sleep. The seriousness of the victim's reaction usually depends on the seriousness of the crime. Many victims feel depressed or edgy, ashamed or fearful for a period of time after the crime. They may seem irritable and have trouble getting along with other people. These problems are to be expected and do not by themselves indicate the need for professional counseling.

Ongoing support from loved ones is the best remedy for the emotional strains of the impact phase. When this support is absent, the victim may benefit from the help of a professional counselor. And, of course, some victims are more troubled by their reactions than others. If a victim expresses the wish for professional help, he or she may be reassured by a counseling session.

The disruptions of the impact phase will give way to a gradual and uneven recovery of functioning in a good crisis resolution. If significant dysfunctioning persists or returns, the victim may need professional help. Maladaptive changes in the victim's behavior that continue for some time after the crime are another indication of a lack of resolution. A mugging victim who is still afraid to go outside alone a month after the crime will probably benefit from the intervention of a trained counselor. When the crisis has been satisfactorily resolved, victims feel as if the experience is over, and they function at least as well as they did before the crime.

The decision to see a professional counselor is a very personal one, and it can be made only by the person who needs the help. Loved ones who insist that a reluctant victim seek professional help do both the counselor and the victim a disservice. Victims have a right to resist such intrusion, and pressure will often simply harden their resistance. Sometimes a friend or family member feels deeply troubled by the victim's behavior. When this happens, the loved one may benefit from counseling; he or she should probably seek a professional for help in sorting the feelings out.

Francine Jacobson has lived in San Francisco for more than fifty years. She married, raised a family, and still keeps house in the same little apartment. Her husband Sam owns the drugstore across the street. Four years ago Sam was robbed and pistol-whipped in his store. His wife came to the living-room window and saw the ambulance and the police cars. She ran across the street just as they were putting Sam into the ambulance.

The doctor put twenty-three stitches in Sam's head and kept him in the hospital for a week. One of his eyes had been injured and they wanted to be sure his sight was intact. He recovered from his physical injuries, spent another week at home, and then had the stitches out and went back to work. Francine seemed to be all right. She visited him every day in the hospital and took care of him while he convalesced at home.

But when Sam came home for dinner after his first day back at work, he noticed that his wife was acting strangely. She didn't eat very much, and she seemed very sad and uncommunicative. He tried to talk to her, but she just brushed him off. As the days went on, she seemed to get worse. She was sleepless and irritable most of the time. By the third week, Sam was really concerned. The changes in his wife were more than he could understand or deal with.

Finally one day a doctor friend called the store to order a prescription, and Sam talked with him about Francine. The doctor recognized the symptoms of depression and when Sam told him about the crime, he explained that Francine was probably suffering from a delayed reaction that surfaced when Sam went back to work. So long as Sam was in the hospital or at home, she knew he was safe, but when he went back to the store he was in danger again. This time he might be killed, leaving her alone. The depth of her depression indicated to the doctor that she would benefit from professional counseling. He suggested that Sam go to see Dr. Connors, a woman psychologist whom he recommended, about the best way to approach Francine. He offered to call Dr. Connors and tell her that Sam would be getting in touch with her.

The next day Sam made an appointment, and two days later he went in to talk with the counselor. She agreed with her colleague that Francine needed help, but she said that the idea would have to be presented to her with care. Dr. Connors also asked Sam how *he* was feeling, and he was able to admit that he hadn't been doing so well either. He was really worried about his wife, but he also felt angry because he had to deal with her problems while he was still struggling with his fear of strange customers and other residual reactions from the crime.

Dr. Connors suggested that both Sam and his wife could benefit from counseling. She advised him to go home and tell his wife that he had decided to work with a psychologist because he had unresolved feelings about the assault. She also recommended that he tell his wife that the psychologist thought Francine might want to come to the counseling sessions.

The fact that Sam was able to acknowledge his own problems made it easier for Francine to admit to hers when he talked with her about his visit to Dr. Connors. They went together to the next session, and they both began to talk about the feelings that had been bottled up. Francine's depression eased, and her husband became less angry and also less fearful. The support of their doctor friend who made the referral and the tact with which Dr. Connors was able to include Francine in the counseling process were both crucial in the final resolution of this couple's crisis.

Bureaucracies and Band-Aids

Trying to deal with an unresponsive bureaucracy is a familiar struggle in any complex society. Most people know from painful experience what it is to be enmeshed in bureaucratic coils. For some the frustrations are minor—standing in lines at the bank or the post office. Others confront "the system" when they try to collect on their medical insurance or when they have to get a car license. For many, surviving their years in school means confronting the arbitrary rules of a resistant institution. If a person is poor, he or she must cope with clinics, welfare forms, red tape, and nastiness as a matter of course.

In any bureaucratic system, the individual is reduced to a number. People feel as if they have no personal identity, no power, no way to influence the decisions that affect them. The rules are made by someone else. The bureaucratic mechanism reinforces helplessness and the loss of autonomy—you can't get service unless you do it their way.

People use their "connections" to get around the bureaucracy when they can because this is the only way to become a person in the system. If you know somebody or you *are* somebody—a celebrity or politician—you become worthy of attention, consideration, and explanation. Otherwise you're just one of the crowd, and you have to pay your fine or wait for your turn or stay after school.

Crime victims who seek help from bureaucratic institutions are especially vulnerable to their dehumanizing effects. Like the criminal, many of these systems humiliate victims by requiring them to relinquish control of their lives. Bureaucracies can be capricious and victims may feel as if they are out of control, again calling up echoes of the experience with the criminal. These associations prevent many victims from getting the help they need.

The effects of bureaucratic indifference can also be devastating in themselves. Rita Morgan's experience with the police system set her back in a particularly cruel way. Her husband was killed in a chance encounter with a stranger. They had stopped in Tony's Bar on their way home after a weekend move. Rita and Tony had gone to school together, and many of their friends were regulars at this place. This particular night, Jeff got into an argument with a stranger at the bar. Usually Jeff was a quiet, easygoing person, but this guy said something nasty to Rita and Jeff found himself getting very angry. Unfortunately the stranger was drunk and he had a gun. He pulled it out suddenly, shot Jeff in the chest, and killed him.

Rita spent about four months in virtual seclusion after her husband's murder. For part of that time she was unable to care for their two small children, who were sent to live with their grandmother. Jeff had been adequately insured, but the first checks were delayed and his family was without cash for several months. Their first Christmas after the murder was a nightmare.

By the following spring things had begun to improve. Rita found a social worker at the local hospital who was able to help her begin to work through her grief. The children came home to stay in June, and in September Rita went back to work. She began to see her old friends again. She began to smile again.

The night that Jeff died his wedding band, wallet, keys, and the other things found on his body were impounded by the police as evidence. About a year later, when his assailant had been sentenced and the case was finally closed, these personal effects were taken out of storage and returned to the victim's family. They simply arrived in the mail one day, sealed in a large manila envelope. Rita opened the package, reached into it, and pulled out her dead husband's wallet. It was still covered with his blood.

How does such a bizarre thing happen? A tired detective tosses the evidence into an envelope, seals it up, and sends it down to the property office. Months later, the property clerk gets an order, pulls out the envelope, addresses it to the victim's next of kin, and drops it in the mail. And a young widow is plunged back into agony. Just as she is beginning to recover her equilibrium, she is violated again. Nobody meant any harm, but from Rita's point of view, sending that package was like scraping open a wound that had just begun to heal. The system that allows such an injury to happen is dangerously removed from human feeling.

Victims are often angered or confused by the indifference of those who work in bureaucracies. These people are supposed to be helpers; their job is giving assistance to those in need. But the structure of many bureaucracies militates against their helping function. There is no excuse for what they sometimes do to victims, but there are several explanations.

People who work in such systems are often as helpless as the victims themselves. Many bureaucracies are essentially dysfunctional: inadequately funded, housed in barren offices, glutted with paperwork and indifference—the kind of place where it takes six months to get a new stapler. It's hard to be giving and caring when you're stuck in the middle of an uncaring system. If nobody's nourishing you, how can you nourish someone else? Ineffective bureaucracies victimize those who work in them as well as those who should be served by them.

Many of the people who are supposed to help crime victims lack the power to do so. Their helping systems just don't work. An insurance clerk cannot make the company process claims faster, but he or she is the focus of the victim's rage when the money isn't available soon enough. The emergency-room doctor may not have any control over the number of staff assigned to work with him or her. The prosecutor can't tell the judge how to run the courtroom. People who work in bureaucracies often need to protect themselves from the stupidities of systems they cannot control. Under these circumstances it is not surprising that those who deal with crime victims seem callous to the victim's needs.

Those who try to help the victim can also acquire a stigma by association—"it takes one to love one." Certain helping agencies have acquired the taint of the loser. Social work is a good example—almost everybody makes fun of social workers, the "little old ladies in tennis shoes." Most medical doctors and psychiatrists are exempt because their helping behavior is well paid, but many people feel there is something not quite normal about helpers whose contributions seem selfless. A priest or a lawyer who works with the poor or a volunteer who answers the phone at a rape crisis center is as likely to be viewed with suspicion as with admiration.

Like the crime victim, these helpers can be threatening because they raise uncomfortable questions. People who show compassion for a loser—an alcoholic, a runaway kid, an assault victim—complicate things. They aren't observing the social taboo, they're not helping to keep the unpleasantness out of sight. Their helping behavior is an indictment of those who stigmatize the losers and ignore their pain. And so the helper may share the stigma of the victim.

Some of those who work with victims disassociate themselves from the victim's needs to avoid the loser stigma. They derive little or no positive status from the helping function in their work—being nice to losers is hardly a valued occupation. Most police officers, for example, are more than willing to tell you that they're not social workers.

Trying to help victims of personal crime can be a frustrating and painful experience. Sometimes even the victim's family and friends are unable to show compassion and concern, and it is quite common for a victim to feel neglected or abused by a stranger who works in one of the systems that serve victims. Often the victim is seen within these systems as a nonperson—like Ralph Ellison's hero, the crime victim becomes invisible. Because he or she is not a person of significance, the system reacts to the victim with indifference. It is not so much irresponsible as unresponsive.

Stigmatization and indifference can produce a secondary trauma in crime victims in crisis. They may feel the neglect of bureaucracies very deeply, attributing the lack of attention to their own unworthiness— "They're ignoring me because I'm a bad person." Or the victim may become enraged with the system—"They're ignoring me so they're bad." In either case the neglect is likely to be taken personally and to complicate the victim's recovery.

When a victim encounters frustration in trying to navigate a bureaucracy, he or she may react by giving up. This will confirm the victim's sense that nobody cares. Victims sometimes become argumentative and difficult in a protective attempt to shield themselves from the ineffectiveness of bureaucratic systems. This behavior can be self-fulfilling when those who work in the system react to the victim's defensiveness. Some victims become "stupid," relinquishing even their common sense in an attempt to follow the line of least resistance, but this response is costly because it is personally debasing.

Most victims need only common, ordinary human decency from the strangers they meet in the systems that serve victims. The average victim who encounters a police officer or a nurse, a welfare case worker or a prosecutor, needs the attention of someone who expresses competence and concern. What the victim wants is a person who cares and who knows what he or she is doing. But their fairly straightforward need is often not met by the existing service systems.

It *is* possible to overcome the indifference of many bureaucratic systems, but it takes a level head and a certain stubbornness. Victims in the early stages of crisis will probably be unable to muster the energy needed to beat the system. But if they or their loved ones can gather themselves together to make the effort at a later stage, some person within the institution may well prove to be responsive after all.

Strategies

One of the most effective ways to deal with any bureaucracy is to establish a relationship with some person inside the system who can serve as a liaison. Dealing with an institution is difficult for those on the outside, partly because they don't know how to make the system work. A staff person can be an invaluable ally if he or she can be persuaded to help the outsider interpret regulations and ask the right questions.

Finding a liaison depends on the outsider's ability to establish himself or herself as a person, another human being whose feelings and needs become important to the liaison. It's certainly fair to use a connection if you can. A crime victim who has a cousin on the police force can sometimes establish an identity in dealing with the officers who are handling his or her case by simply asking if they know the cousin. It's important to avoid the suggestion of intimidation—the idea is to be as unthreatening as possible, to suggest that you sympathize with the inside person because you know someone else in his or her position.

Lacking a specific personal connection, a victim can often personalize himself or herself by being friendly and talking a little bit about interests, hobbies, and so on. Establishing some common ground is always a first step in making friends with another person, and the victim need not feel manipulative or insincere. Most people who work in bureaucracies are treated as if they are less than human by many of those who make demands on them; a friendly face is a welcome change.

It usually makes sense to approach any stranger in an easy, relaxed way and to be as pleasant as possible. This might be called "the honey strategy," after the old saying that a person will catch more flies with honey than with vinegar. Common courtesy and a little patience can go a long way in distinguishing a victim from most of the people who pass by the desk each day. If you want to be remembered when you come back in two weeks, it probably pays to be as nice as you can.

Once a victim has established a liaison person in the system, he or she can encourage that person to be accountable, again in a friendly and nonthreatening way. If the prosecutor's secretary has chatted with a victim on the phone, she will probably be willing to answer a question or two when the victim calls back. A victim can say, "I'm going to need to know what time to go to court. Is it okay if I call you?" Dealing with the same person gives the victim a wedge, a way to get the answers he or she needs.

Victims need to present themselves to their liaisons as people with problems that the insider can help to solve, not as helpless incompetents who need to have their hands held. A person with the power to help will often feel pleased to exercise that power if he or she is appreciated and if the victim is not so needy that the request is experienced as a hysterical demand. When the inside person sees the victim as one who is temporarily troubled because of something for which he or she is not responsible, the request for help becomes less threatening because the problem is seen as external. The victim is not to blame. If, on the other hand, the liaison sees the victim as a crazy person who will always have lots of difficulties, the burden of accepting the responsibility to help may feel too great.[7]

Assertiveness is an effective weapon against bureaucratic indifference. Victims need to ask for what they need, to find out where the best sources of help are. The people inside the system know this information but they may not volunteer it. Many police officers fail to inform victims about compensation and victim-advocate programs unless they are required by law to do so, for example, but they will respond to a direct question. People who work in bureaucracies often see themselves as helpers and want to help. If the victim can break through the veneer of their indifference and appeal to the helping image, he or she is more likely to get the needed information. It is useful to be specific about what you want to know and to anticipate that the first person you ask may not have the answer.

Persistence is crucial in dealing with bureaucracies. The person the victim needs to talk to may seem to be eternally out of the office; phones may be busy more often than not. The victim can sometimes enlist a friend or relative to help keep at the problem, chipping away at the system's resistance. Taking someone else along when you have to stand in line can help you keep your good humor. If the victim can accept the reality that most bureaucracies are inefficient and slow to respond, he or she may be able to feel that special stubbornness that makes a person stay with a problem until it finally yields.

Anger can also be an effective weapon, but victims need to control their outrage if they expect the system to help them. Angry people are so familiar in many bureaucracies that strong expressions of rage go practically unnoticed. If you alienate everybody in the place, it is unlikely that you will be able to get what you need from them. When a victim has to make a complaint about the performance of someone in a bureaucracy, the best first step is to approach someone else of the same rank. If a worker in the crime-victim office refuses to answer questions, for example, the victim might try first to be reassigned to another worker. Another strategy is to take one of the troublesome person's colleagues into your confidence and ask how best to approach the problem. "I just can't seem to get through. What can I do to make it easier?"

Failing that, the next step is to talk to the immediate supervisor of the resistant person. Again, asking how you can change to make the system work better is less threatening and probably more effective than coming on with a lot of accusations. If nothing else works, the victim can always go to the top and demand to see the chief of police or the hospital's chief resident or the president of the insurance company. But going to the top is bound to be seen as troublemaking by the staff people in the system, and a person usually sacrifices their confidence when he or she pulls rank on them. A victim who has to lodge a formal complaint should realize that this probably will prevent his or her ever getting support from the colleagues of the person who is the object of the complaint.

Getting through to the people who can help is often a time-consuming and enervating struggle. But achieving satisfaction can be enormously gratifying for a crime victim because it confirms a person's sense of power and reinforces self-esteem. Victims who felt helpless and ineffective in the encounter with the criminal may be able to repair that injury to self if they can break down a bureaucracy's resistance and get what they need from the system.

Getting Even

Someone has said that living well is the best revenge. When a crime victim makes a good recovery and comes out of the crisis with renewed strength, he or she has achieved the ultimate victory over the criminal. The destructive effects of the violation of self can be transformed into a constructive sense of oneself as a strong and resourceful person.

Many victims feel a kind of survivor's pride in their ability to recover from the victimization. They have faced a terrible thing, and they have a new appreciation for their own inner resources. A crisis can bring out the worst in a person, but it also calls forth the best in many people. Crime victims ofen experience their crisis resolution as a maturing and toughening experience. They end up feeling less vulnerable and more capable of handling stress.

Victims often feel that their sense of the world is more realistic after the crime. They may become more cynical, but they may also become aware of their human limitations in a healthy way. After the criminal strikes, you know it *can* happen to you. Many victims express a new acceptance of themselves as vulnerable beings.

New strengths often emerge out of adversity. The victims of the more serious crimes are sometimes dramatically changed. A woman who had been raped was able to confront herself as a result of the crime.

> I can see that I've grown beyond that age that I was when I was raped. I was a really immature woman—very naïve and very trusting and very dependent. Really different from the person I am now. The rape was a terrible experience, and I'm certainly not recommending rape as a therapy, but it did take me right down to the essence of myself. I got rid of all this being a nice little girl stuff, wanting to please everyone. It's only since the rape that I've really been able to see who I am.

Another victim, who had been robbed, was able to use the experience to confirm his commitment to the city he lives in.

> At first, I wanted to get out of here. I was very ambivalent. All of a sudden the grubby aspects of the city began to drain on me. It was very difficult to deal with my own paranoia. If I walked down the street at night and I saw a black kid with tennis shoes on, I didn't even want to be on the same side of the street with him. Late at night when I went into my building, I would check the street, check the lobby. It's all a terrific pain. I mean why the hell should I have to do this in order to live?
>
> Finally, I said to myself, "God damn it, *nobody* is going to drive me out of this city. I have every right to be here, just as much as the next person. And I also felt that I had survived so many terrible things that it came down to: You're just not going to drive me out. It was a new kind of rage. I still felt angry, but it was much more positive. I *belong* here. This is my city.

I ended up with this feeling that the city is now the frontier in our society. This is where you carve out a new kind of existence somehow. This was my resolution of the whole problem of victims, crime, people preying on each other. It's a do-or-die situation, but like somebody on the frontier, this is where I want to be. And I am going to survive here.

People are far more resilient than they think. It is a fact of life that most of us will suffer and most of us will survive. We're not teetering on the edge of breakdown and despair. Most of us have strong resources. With decent support and the healing effects of time, most crime victims come back together whole—perhaps a little more sober, a bit more realistic than before. No one wants to be a victim, but there is something to be said for surviving such an experience well.

NOTES

1. In a study of the resources people draw on for help in life crises, Vernoff, Douvan, and Kulka found that informal support systems of friends, relatives, neighbors, and co-workers are a critical resource for contemporary Americans (J. Vernoff, E. Douvan, and R. Kulka, *The American Experience: Portrait Over Two Decades* (New York: Basic Books, 1980).

2. The importance of seeing a victim's difficulties as problems that have solutions is admirably explored in Barbara Cooper, *Wife Beating: Counselor Training Manual #2, Crisis Intervention* (Ann Arbor, Mi.: NOW Domestic Violence Assault Fund, Inc., 1976). This discussion is indebted to Ms. Cooper's analysis.

3. For an overview of current federal and state victim rights and services legislation, including crime-victim compensation, see the latest issue of *Victim Rights and Services: A Legislative Directory* by the National Organization for Victim Assistance, 717 D St., N.W., Washington, D.C. 20004.

4. For a brief history of the victim advocacy movement and a description of three different models for organizing victim services, see John H. Stein and James H. Ahrens, *Criminal Justice and the Elderly: How To Win Law-Enforcement Support for Victim Services Projects* (National Council of Senior Citizens, Criminal Justice and the Elderly Program, Washington, D.C., 1980).

5. We are grateful to James Rowland, Director of the California Youth Authority, for helping us to focus on the central importance of information needs.

6. In one 1980 study of victims, for example, the majority (81 percent) were unaware of *any* agency that could provide support, despite the fact that the study was done in New York City where, at the time, there were both a City Victim Services Agency and a State Crime Victim Compensation Board. Thirty percent of the victims in this study said that they did not receive all of the help they needed, and only 15 percent had sought agency support. (Kenneth Friedman, et al, *Victims and Helpers: Reactions to Crime*. Victim Services Agency, New York, 1982). Another study demonstrated that existing public and private agencies could have handled

most victim needs, but the victims did not realize that the agency help was available. Richard D. Knudten et al, *Victims and Witnesses: The Impact of Crime and Their Experience with the Criminal-Justice System* (Milwaukee Wisc.: Marquette University, Center for Criminal Justice and Social Policy, 1976), p. 44.

7. One study of the relationships among attributions, dependency, and help-giving found that help is more likely to come from a powerful person if the one seeking help is perceived as dependent because of external, environmental factors. The researchers explained their results by proposing that internally determined dependence does not arouse the norm of social responsibility because the needy one is seen to be responsible for his or her trouble. J. Schopler and M. Matthews, "The Influence of the Perceived Causal Locus of Partner's Dependence on the Use of Interpersonal Power," *Journal of Personality and Social Psychology* 2 (1965): 609-612.

Appendix A

Crimes Against People

Most crime victims are interested in what has happened to other victims like themselves. Hearing another person describe his or her victimization can help to cut the sense of isolation and the feeling of being "crazy" that many victims experience. In rape crisis centers, groups of rape victims often meet together over a period of time in order to find mutual support. Victims of other personal crimes, especially the survivor-victims of homicide, may also benefit from this kind of sharing, although few organizations sponsor such groups for them.

Unfortunately, direct support from other victims is not always available. Throughout this book we have tried to provide alternatives to that close personal contact; this appendix is a supplement to the victimization experiences reported in the book itself.

Most of the information here is derived from national crime statistics. It includes the number of people victimized nationwide by each personal crime, some characteristics of each type of crime, and some characteristics of victims, including the percentage who report the crime to the police. These facts will give the victim some sense of how his or her experience compares with those of other victims across the nation.

We have also included the national data available about arrest rates for each crime, but here the victim is likely to find local information more useful. Crime rates, the ability of the police to apprehend criminals, and the success of prosecutors in obtaining convictions vary widely from one jurisdiction to another. Victims who can learn from their local police and prosecutors about the conditions in their own community will have a better perspective than can be provided by nationwide statistics. Arrest and conviction data can help victims to maintain realistic expectations about their own cases.

Readers who want to learn more about crime and criminal justice may want to order a copy of *Report to the Nation on Crime and Justice: The Data.* This report from the Bureau of Justice Statistics presents a comprehensive picture of crime and criminal justice in the United States in a readable form. Single copies are available free from the National Criminal Justice Reference Service, Box 6000, Dept. F, Rockville, Md. 20850; ask for publication NCJ-87068.

Where Do the Numbers Come from?

Crime statistics are regularly quoted in the media with great authority, as if the numbers were absolutely accurate, but the quality of such statistics varies a great deal.[1] The average person is not usually aware of important limitations imposed by the methods used to collect this data. The distinction between crimes committed and crimes reported to the authorities, for example, is rarely emphasized. The information that follows here is designed to help the reader understand where the numbers come from and what their limitations are.

Crime statistics for the United States as a whole are compiled in two Department of Justice programs: The Federal Bureau of Investigation publishes a yearly tabulation called *Crime in the United States: Uniform Crime Reports,*[2] and the Bureau of the Census conducts a continuous survey of crime victims, called the National Crime Survey,[3] for the Bureau of Justice Statistics.

The information provided by the FBI and the National Crime Survey is different in several important ways. The FBI *Uniform Crime*

Reports, which have been published annually since 1930, are compiled from the reports of local and state law-enforcement agencies. These agencies count and classify the crimes reported to them by victims, witnesses, and law-enforcement officers. The agencies also tabulate the number of crimes cleared by arrest and in some jurisdictions the results of prosecution. The program is voluntary; the contributing law-enforcement agencies are responsible for collecting their own data and submitting it to the FBI.

Eight crimes are classified by the FBI as Crime Index offenses —murder, forcible rape, robbery, aggravated assault, burglary, larceny-theft (theft in which no force or threat is used; this category includes pocket picking and purse snatching, although the vast majority of larceny-thefts involve unattended property), motor-vehicle theft, and arson. Reports of these crimes are used to calculate Crime Index rates in the United States, which are expressed in the *Uniform Crime Reports* in terms of the number of crimes per 100,000 inhabitants. In 1983, for example, the FBI recorded 78,918 cases of forcible rape in the United States, a crime rate of 33.7 per 100,000 inhabitants.

The *Uniform Crime Reports* are our oldest and most-often cited source of national crime statistics, but the program has been widely criticized and it has several limitations. In the first place, the FBI and other law-enforcement agencies have a vested interest in the crime statistics they report. Their funding, judgments of their competency, the public sense of the need for continued and increasing law-enforcement activity, and other matters of central concern to these agencies may be based in part on the *Uniform Crime Reports.* It is likely, for this reason, that at least some of the reports are biased.

An even more serious limitation is the fact that the *Uniform Crime Reports* ignore all of the crimes that are not reported to the authorities. Other studies have established that more than half of the personal crimes committed in this country are never reported, so the FBI crime rates are based on only a portion of the victim population.

Because the UCR relies on voluntary participation by local agencies, it must keep its demands to a minimum and, therefore, requests only the barest essentials so that UCR data are lacking in detailed information about crime incidents. Additional difficulties arise because of the definitions used. The 1983 *Uniform Crime Reports* rate for forcible rape of 33.7 per 100,000, for example, excludes all male victims because the crime of rape is defined by the FBI as "the carnal knowledge of a female, forcibly and against her will." Further, the crime rate for rape is calculated by the FBI from the total population, both male and female, not just the female population, which would give a more accurate rate by their definition.

The National Crime Survey program is a continuous nationwide survey in which a representative sample of individuals and households is interviewed. The program began to gather information in 1972 about rape, robbery, assault, burglary, larceny (including pocket picking and purse snatching), and motor-vehicle theft victimization. About one-quarter of a million interviews are conducted annually in the NCS program. Only residents age twelve and over are surveyed. Because the interviewers talk directly to the victims, the surveys include both reported and unreported crimes.

The personal crime rates in the National Crime Survey are expressed in terms of victimization per 1,000 inhabitants age twelve and over. Burglary and motor-vehicle theft are classified as household crimes, and these rates are expressed as victimizations per 1,000 households. Each individual or household victimization is counted, unlike the FBI method in which each reported crime is counted. The National Crime Survey data is an estimate rather than an actual count because only a sample of the population is interviewed. However, Survey statistics come from carefully designed studies, and the expected amount of error due to using a sample rather than the entire population is relatively small. We have used these data as the primary source in this appendix because the National Crime Survey seems to be generally more accurate than the *Uniform Crime Reports* although the NCS also has shortcomings. It tends to undercount crimes in which the victim and the offender are not strangers to each other, for example, particularly when they are related or married to each other (since NCS interviews are conducted in the household).

Unfortunately, the Survey does not collect data for homicide, and we have used the *Uniform Crime Reports* statistics in discussing that crime. The FBI data for homicide are generally thought to be a more accurate measure of actual incidence than the data for other Index Crimes, however. Homicide is reported to the police more often than other crimes; it is a very serious offense and difficult to keep from the other authorities because the body of the dead victim is not easily concealed. The *Uniform Crime Reports* also request more detailed information from local and state agencies about homicide than about most other crimes.

The information about arrests in this appendix is also based on FBI statistics, which are the only available source for this information nationwide. An offense is counted as "cleared by arrest" if at least one person is arrested, charged with committing the offense, and handed over to the court for prosecution. Police can clear a crime by arrest even if the person is never charged with that crime. It is not unusual, for example, for the police to arrest someone for a specific burglary and, after questioning, "clear" a whole group of prior burglaries that they believe the person committed, even though the person may never be charged with those other burglaries. Also counted as "cleared" are crimes in which the victim refuses to co-operate in prosecution or in which the offender is prosecuted for a lesser offense, as often occurs in plea-bargaining.

Pocket Picking and Purse Snatching

Pocket picking and purse snatching are classified together as "personal larceny with contact" by the National Crime Survey. Pocket picking has the following definition:

Cash or a wallet was taken by stealth directly from the victim.
The offender did not have a weapon.
The victim was not threatened or attacked.

In purse snatching:

A purse was taken by stealth directly from the victim.
The offender did not have a weapon.
The victim was not threatened or attacked.

Although the definition of purse snatching as a form of personal larceny seems clear, purse snatching is really a borderline crime that can be classified as a personal larceny or as a robbery depending on how the incident unfolds. If the purse is simply snatched and then the offender runs, it's a personal larceny. If the victim holds on to her purse and then the offender threatens her and pushes her down, the crime is a robbery or, arguably, a robbery with assault.

In 1980 in the United States there were 546,000 personal larceny with contact victimizations, including 352,000 pocket pickings and 194,000 purse snatchings and attempted purse snatchings. The victimization rate (number of victimizations per thousand inhabitants twelve or older) was 2.0 for pocket picking and 1.1 for purse snatching. Of all purse snatching victims, 47.3 percent reported the crime to the police; 29.5 percent of pocket picking victims reported the crime.

Table A-1 shows some characteristics of the 1980 victims of purse snatching and pocket picking, compared with victims of robbery and rape. The two personal larceny crimes together were less than half as common as robbery and more than three times as common as rape.

More women than men were victims of personal larceny with contact in 1980. More than twice as many black people as whites were victims of these crimes. Young people age sixteen to nineteen had the highest rate of victimization (3.8 per thousand) of any age group, and people fifty to sixty-four had the lowest rate (2.6). The victimization rate varied dramatically according to the annual family income of the victim: Among victims with family incomes under $3,000.00, the rate for personal larceny with contact was 6.7 per thousand while the rate was only 1.9 per thousand for victims with family incomes over $25,000. Victimization rates were highest for people living inside the central cities of large metropolitan areas (12.2 per thousand in cities of over one million residents), lower for those living outside of central cities but still in metropolitan areas (3.6 per thousand outside of central cities of over one million residents), and lowest of all for residents of nonmetropolitan areas (0.9 per thousand).

In the FBI data from which arrest figures are taken, the category "larceny-theft" includes any stealing of property that is neither burglary, robbery, or motor-vehicle theft. Thus the FBI larceny-theft category includes shoplifting, for example, as well as pocket picking and purse snatching. In 1983, of all the larceny-thefts reported to the police, 19 percent were cleared by arrest.

Motor-Vehicle Theft

Motor-vehicle theft is classified as a crime against a household (not against an individual) by the National Crime Survey. It includes the theft and attempted theft of a car or other motor vehicle.

In 1980 in the United States there were 1,355,000 motor-vehicle theft victimizations, of which 435,000 were attempts and 920,000 were completed thefts. The victimization rate (number of victimizations per thousand *households*) was 16.7, 11.4 for completed thefts and 5.4 for attempted thefts.

Motor-vehicle theft is reported to the police more often than many other crimes, probably because most vehicles are insured and reporting the theft is required to collect insurance compensation. In 1980, 69.3 percent of attempted and completed vehicle thefts were reported to the police; 86.6 percent of completed thefts were reported.

Table A-2 shows some characteristics of the households victimized by motor-vehicle theft in 1980. Among the ethnic groups surveyed, households with white heads had the lowest victimization rate (15.6 per thousand), while households headed by blacks had the highest rate (25.1 per thousand). Victimization rates rise with annual family income, presumably because affluent families have more cars (and cars that are more attractive to thieves) than poorer families. Rates are consistently higher for residents inside central cities than in areas

TABLE A-1

1980 Victimization Rates: Selected Personal Crimes with Contact
(Victimization per 1,000 Inhabitants Age 12 and Over)

Victimizations	Personal Larceny with Contact		All Robbery (includes attempts)	Robbery with Injury (includes attempts)	Rape (includes attempts)
	Pocket Picking (includes attempts)	Purse Snatching (includes attempts)			
Total number of victimizations	352,000	194,000	1,179,000	405,000	169,000
Victimization rate (per 1,000 inhabitants age 12 and over):					
For all victims	2.0	1.1	6.5	2.3	0.9
For all male victims	2.2		9.0	2.9	0.3
For all female victims	3.8		4.2	1.7	1.6
For all white victims	2.6		5.7	2.0	0.9
For all black victims	6.2		13.9	4.3	1.1
For all victims:					
Age 12-15	2.9		8.8	2.0	0.7*
Age 16-19	3.8		11.1	3.0	2.9
Age 20-24	3.3		10.6	3.7	2.4
Age 25-34	2.9		7.2	2.6	1.3
Age 35-49	2.8		4.7	1.9	0.4
Age 50-64	2.6		4.4	1.9	0.0*
Age 65 and over	3.7		3.5	1.3	0.1*
Victim's annual family income:					
Less than $3,000	6.7		14.3	5.7	2.9
$3,000-$7,499	4.8		10.6	3.9	1.5
$7,500-$9,999	2.8		7.2	2.1	1.3
$10,000-$14,999	3.3		6.3	2.1	1.2
$15,000-$24,999	2.5		4.9	1.5	0.4
$25,000 and over	1.9		4.8	1.5	0.6

Victim's place of residence:				
Metropolitan areas with central cities of 1,000,000 or more:				
Inside central city	12.2	21.9	6.6	1.8
Outside central city	3.6	7.4	2.0	0.5*
Metropolitan areas with central cities 500,000 to 999,999:				
Inside central city	4.5	12.7	6.1	1.4
Outside central city	2.0	4.9	1.9	1.5
Metropolitan areas with central cities 250,000 to 499,999:				
Inside central city	4.9	9.4	3.6	0.9*
Outside central city	2.4	4.4	1.3	1.0
Metropolitan areas with central cities 50,000 to 249,000:				
Inside central city	2.7	7.1	2.5	0.9
Outside central city	1.7	3.9	1.7	0.8
Nonmetropolitan areas	0.9	2.6	0.8	0.7

*Indicates a victimization rate based on about ten or fewer cases that is, therefore, statistically unreliable.

SOURCE: Table constructed by the authors from data in United States Department of Justice, Bureau of Justice Statistics, *Criminal Victimization in the United States*, 1980.

TABLE A-2
1980 Victimization Rates: Motor-Vehicle Theft (Victimizations per 1,000 Vehicles owned) and Residential Burglary (Victimization per 1,000 Households)

Victimizations	Motor-Vehicle Theft (Includes Attempts)	Residential Burglary (Includes Attempted Forcible Entry)
Total number of victimizations	1,355,000	6,817,000
Victimization rate (per 1,000 households):		
For all households	16.7	84.2
For all households with white head	15.6	80.6
For all households with black head	25.1	114.7
Annual family income		
Less than $3,000	7.7	111.7
$7,500-$9,999	16.2	76.9
$15,000-$24,999	19.4	79.7
Place of residence:		
Metropolitan areas with central cities of 1,000,000 or more:		
Inside central city	34.2	113.7
Outside central city	24.7	86.4
Metropolitan areas with central cities of 500,000 to 999,000:		
Inside central city	25.9	122.3
Outside central city	21.5	79.2
Metropolitan areas with central cities of 250,000 to 499,999:		
Inside central city	20.4	114.6
Outside central city	16.7	86.5
Metropolitan areas with central cities of 50,000 to 249,000:		
Inside central city	15.6	105.9
Outside central city	11.0	72.9
Nonmetropolitan areas	7.9	60.5

SOURCE: Table constructed by the authors from data in United States Department of Justice, Bureau of Justice Statistics, *Criminal Victimization in the United States*, 1980.

outside of central cities and lowest of all (7.9 per thousand) in nonmetropolitan areas.

In 1983, of all the motor-vehicle thefts (including thefts of commercial vehicles) reported to the police, 15 percent were cleared by an arrest.

Burglary

Like motor-vehicle theft, burglary is classified by the National Crime Survey as a crime against households rather than individuals, and victimization rates are expressed as the number of victimizations per households. Burglary is defined by the Survey this way:

> The offender illegally enters, or attempts to enter, a residence or a place of business.
> The offender may or may not use force (for example, breaking down the door) to gain entry.
> The illegal entry is usually, but not necessarily, attended by theft.

Some local jurisdictions call burglary "breaking and entering."

There were 6,817,000 residential burglaries in the United States in 1980, of which 1,440,000 were unsuccessful attempts to gain entry by force. The burglary victimization rate per thousand households was 84.2. Of all burglaries and attempts, 51.3 percent were reported to the police; successful burglaries involving forcible entry were reported in 72.9 percent of the cases.

Households headed by a black person were victimized by burglary at a rate (114.7 victimizations per thousand) that is almost one and one-half times the rate for households headed by a white person (80.6 per thousand). Families with incomes of less than $3,000 were victimized more often (at a rate of 111.7 per thousand households) than more affluent families. If a person is poor and nonwhite, he or she is more likely to be a victim of burglary.

In metropolitan areas with central cities of a million or more inhabitants, the burglary rate was higher (113.7) outside the city than inside it (86.4). Again, the lowest victimization rate (60.5) was found in nonmetropolitan areas.

Of all burglary cases (including burglaries of businesses) reported to the police, 15 percent were cleared by arrest in 1983.

Assault

Assault is defined by the National Crime Survey as a crime in which
>   The victim suffers an unlawful physical attack.
>   The offender may or may not have used a weapon.

Assaults cover a broad range of encounters, ranging from minor threats to incidents that bring the victim close to death. The degree of physical harm and the presence or absence of a weapon govern the classification of assaults. *Simple assault* is an attack without a weapon resulting in minor injury (bruises, black eyes, cuts, scratches, swelling). *Aggravated assault* includes any attack with a weapon and also an attack without a weapon that results in serious injury (broken bones, loss of teeth, internal injuries, loss of consciousness).

If a victim is attacked by an offender who also commits another crime—say, robbery—the attack will not be classified as an assault by the National Crime Survey because the Survey rates robbery as "more serious" than assault, and because it counts only the more serious offense. Thus, crimes counted as assaults never include the physical threat or harm done in the course of a robbery or a sexual assault.

Assault is the most common violent crime. According to NCS data, in 1980 there were 3,905,000 assaults in the United States, of which 1,334,000 were aggravated assaults and 2,571 were simple assaults. The rate of assault (victimizations per thousand inhabitants age 12 and over) in 1980 was 25.7 for all assault, 9.2 for aggravated assault, and 16.4 for simple assault. Of all 1980 assaults found by the Survey, 45 percent had been reported to the police. The rate is significantly higher—60 percent—for aggravated assault with injury.

Almost half of all assaults reported to the Survey in 1980 involved people who knew each other, and there is reason to believe that assault between nonstrangers is underreported since the Survey is conducted in the victim's home. According to the 1980 NCS data, 43 percent of assaults involved nonstrangers. More than 80 percent of 1980 assaults that occurred inside the victim's own home were incidents between people who knew each other; by contrast, of the assaults that occurred on the street (including the playground, the schoolyard, and parking lots) in 1980, 74 percent involved strangers.

The rate of assault victims among men and boys in 1980 was about twice the rate for women and girls (35 per thousand for males and 17 per thousand for females). Young people are more likely to be assaulted than older people—the rate in 1980 was highest for 20–24 year olds (56 per thousand), almost as high for 16–19 year olds (55 per thousand), and lowest for the oldest group in the sample (3 per thousand among those 65 years old and older). There is very little difference in the overall 1980 NCS assault rate of whites and blacks; black victims have a higher rate for aggravated assault, and white victims have a higher rate for simple assault. The poorest people suffer the highest victimization rates for assault—in the 1980 NCS data those with incomes of less than $3,000 have a rate of 47 assaults per thousand while all others have rates of less than 30 per thousand, and the rate improves as income rises. Again in 1980, the rate for assault was highest inside the central cities, lower outside the central cities, and lowest in nonmetropolitan areas.

The Uniform Crime Reports gather information about aggravated assault only. In 1983, the clearance rate for aggravated assault was 61 percent.

Robbery, Including Robbery with Assault

The crime of personal robbery has the following elements according to the National Crime Survey:

Property or cash was taken directly from the victim.
The offender used force or the threat of force.
The offender may or may not have used a weapon.

There were 1,179,000 personal robbery and attempted robbery victimizations in the United States in 1980. Of these, 405,000 were robberies in which force was used and the victim was injured. The victimization rate (victimizations per thousand inhabitants) for all robbery was 6.5; for robbery with injury, the rate was 2.3. Of all personal robbery victimizations in 1980, 56.9 percent were reported to the police. Seventy percent of personal robbery victimizations with injury were reported to the police.

For crimes in which there is direct contact between the victim and the offender, the National Crime Survey distinguishes victimization by strangers (in which the victim said the offender was a stranger to him or her, or the victim did not see or did not recognize the offender) from victimization by nonstrangers (in which the victim was related to, well known to, or acquainted with the offender). In personal robbery, 83 percent of the victimizations involved strangers. The Survey also collects information about the percentage of personal crimes of violence in which a weapon is present. In 1980, a weapon was present in 44.8 percent of the incidents of personal robbery. Of those robbers who were armed, 33 percent used a firearm and 39 percent used a knife.

The victimization rate for all personal robbery varied significantly according to sex and race in 1980. The rate for all male victims was 9.0; for female victims, it was 4.2. This same pattern appears in personal robbery with injury victimizations (2.9 to 1.7). Black people were victimized by personal robbery at more than twice the rate of white people (13.9 to 5.7).

The relationship between the victim's annual family income and the 1980 personal robbery victimization rate is clear: The poorest families had the highest victimization rates (14.3); the richest families had the lowest victimization rates (4.8); and the rate declined as the income went up at every step. There is tragedy as well as irony in these figures since poor victims can least afford the monetary loss involved. The same pattern is found in personal robbery with injury—the rate for victims from the poorest families was 5.7; for victims from the richest families it was 1.5.

As we have already seen in other personal crimes, personal robbery victimization rates for people living inside central cities in 1980 was higher than for those living outside the central city. In metropolitan areas with central cities of one million or more inhabitants, the rate inside the city was 21.9; outside the city, it was 7.4, less than half. In nonmetropolitan areas, the rate dropped to 2.6.

Of all robberies (including robberies of banks and other commercial establishments) reported to the police in 1983, 26.0 percent were cleared by the arrest of at least one person.

Sexual Assault

The National Crime Survey uses the term *rape* or *forcible rape* for sexual assault. According to the Survey, rape occurs when—

> The offender achieves or attempts carnal knowledge of a male or female victim.
> The offender uses force or the threat of force.

Sexual assault of wives by their husbands is included in this definition, and sexual assaults other than forcible sexual intercourse may be included if the victim believes he or she has been forcibly raped. Statutory rape (without force) is excluded.

In 1980, there were 169,000 rape and attempted rape victimizations in the United States. The victimization rate (per thousand male and female inhabitants) was 0.9. Since sexual assault is predominantly a crime in which girls and women are victimized, a clearer sense of the actual incidence is shown by the victimization rate for females. In 1980, the victimization rate per thousand female inhabitants was 1.6.

Fewer than half (41.5 percent) of the rape victimizations reported to the National Crime Survey in 1980 were reported to the police.

The rates for rape victimizations by strangers and nonstrangers in

1980 show that 28 percent of sexual assaults occurred between a victim and an offender who knew each other. A weapon was present in 21.6 percent of the incidents of rape recorded in 1980. Of armed rapists, almost half (46.0 percent) used a knife.

Black victims had a slightly higher rate (1.1) of sexual assault victimization in 1980 than did white victims (0.9). Among victims of all ages over 11, the highest victimization rate (2.9) occurred in the 16 to 19 age bracket, and the next highest (2.4) in the 20 to 24 age bracket.

The highest victimization rates for rape were found among victims with the lowest annual family income—victims from families with annual incomes of less than $3,000.00 had a rate of 2.9 per thousand inhabitants, compared with a rate of 1.3 for victims from families with annual incomes from $7,500.00 to $9,999.00, and a rate of 0.4 for victims from families with incomes from $15,000.00 to $24,999.00.

Rape victimization rates in 1980 were unevenly distributed among central cities and the areas outside of them. The highest rate (1.8) was found within the city in metropolitan areas with the largest central cities (one million or more inhabitants). The rate in non-metropolitan areas (0.7) was lowest of all.

Of the cases of forcible rape of women reported to the police in 1983, 52 percent were cleared by arrest.

Homicide

As noted earlier, the only nationwide statistics available for homicide are *Uniform Crime Reports* figures. Criminal homicide includes three categories of crime: murder, nonnegligent (voluntary) manslaughter, and negligent (involuntary) manslaughter. Of these, murder and nonnegligent manslaughter are a Crime Index offense defined as "the willful killing of another." The data that follow includes only murder and nonnegligent manslaughter reported to the FBI by local and state police authorities.

There were 19,308 reported cases of murder and nonnegligent manslaughter in 1983 in the United States. The victimization rate was .083 per thousand inhabitants of all ages.

Approximately three-fourths of the victims of reported cases of murder and nonnegligent manslaughter in 1983 were male. (Note that slightly less than half of the national population is male.) For every one hundred victims, approximately 55 were white and 43 were black. (Note that about 11 percent of the national population is black.) Thirty-three percent of victims were between the ages of 20 and 29.

The circumstances surrounding cases of murder and nonnegligent manslaughter in the United States in 1983 indicate that in these crimes many of the victims and offenders know each other. In 9.4 percent of the reported cases, a spouse killed a spouse. Three percent of the cases involved parents killing children. In six percent, other relatives were both the offender and the victim. Some kind of argument was the motive for 43.7 percent of the cases reported in 1983. Another 18 percent of murders and cases of nonnegligent manslaughter were known to involve other crimes, such as rape, robbery, and narcotics offenses.

Firearms were used in 58 percent of the reported cases of murder and nonnegligent manslaughter in 1983. Fourty-four percent of these crimes were committed with handguns.

Of all cases of murder and nonnegligent manslaughter known to the police in 1983, 76 percent were cleared by arrest.

NOTES

1. Readers who are interested in the difficulties that arise when a person tries to draw conclusions from available crime statistics might read the meticulous and detailed examples in James Q. Wilson and Barbara Boland, "Crime," in William Gorham and Nathan Glazer, eds., *The Urban Predicament* (Washington, D.C.: The Urban Institute, 1976).

2. Data from the *Uniform Crime Reports* used in this appendix is taken from United States Department of Justice, Federal Bureau of Investigation, *Crime in the United States: Uniform Crime Reports* (Washington, D.C.: Government Printing Office, 1984).

3. Data from the National Crime Survey used in this appendix is taken from United States Department of Justice, Bureau of Justice Statistics, *Criminal Victimization in the United States*, (Washington, D.C.: 1982).

Appendix B

The Legal Labyrinth

The criminal-justice system often poses unnecessary difficulties for victims of personal crime. Legal terminology and the procedures of the system are two of the greatest stumbling blocks. In this appendix, a general overview of the system is presented in the first section, which has been reprinted in slightly edited form from the report of the President's Commission on Law Enforcement and Administration of Justice.

This is followed by a glossary which defines commonly used legal terms in nontechnical language. The precise definition of these legal terms varies from jurisdiction to jurisdiction, and the glossary is not intended to be an adequate substitute for the explanations that a police officer or prosecutor can give the victim. It is simply an indication of the general meaning of these terms throughout the United States.

America's System of Criminal Justice[1]

The system of criminal justice America uses to deal with those crimes it cannot prevent and those criminals it cannot deter is not a monolithic, or even a consistent, system. It was not designed or

181

built in one piece at one time. Its philosophic core is that a person may be punished by the government if, and only if, it has been proved by an impartial and deliberate process that he or she has violated a specific law. The entire system represents an adaptation of the English common law to America's peculiar structure of government, which allows each local community to construct institutions that fill its special needs. Every village, town, county, city, and state has its own criminal-justice system, and there is a federal one as well. All of them operate somewhat alike; no two of them operate precisely alike.

Any criminal-justice system is an apparatus society uses to enforce the standards of conduct necessary to protect individuals and the community. It operates by apprehending, prosecuting, convicting, and sentencing those members of the community who violate the basic rules of group existence. What most significantly distinguishes the system of one country from that of another is the extent and the form of the protections it offers individuals in the process of determining guilt and imposing punishment. Our system of justice deliberately sacrifices much in efficiency and even in effectiveness in order to preserve local autonomy and to protect the individual. Sometimes it may seem to sacrifice too much.

The criminal-justice system has three separately organized parts—the police, the courts, and corrections—and each has distinct tasks. However, these parts are by no means independent of each other. What each one does and how it does it have a direct effect on the work of the others. The courts must deal, and can only deal, with those whom the police arrest; the business of corrections is with those delivered to it by the courts. How successfully corrections reform convicts determines whether they will once again become police business and influences the sentences the judges pass; police activities are subject to court scrutiny and are often determined by court decisions.

The diagram on page 105 sets forth in simplified form the process of criminal administration and shows the many decision points along its course. Since felonies, misdemeanors, petty offenses, and juvenile cases generally follow quite different paths, they are shown separately.

The popular, or even the lawbook, theory of everyday criminal process oversimplifies in some respects and overcomplicates in others what usually happens. That theory is that when an infraction of the law occurs, a police officer finds, if he or she can, the probable offender, arrests the suspect, and brings him or her promptly before a magistrate. If the offense is minor, the magistrate disposes of it forthwith; if it is serious, he or she holds the defendant for further action and admits him or her to bail. The case then is turned over to a prosecuting attorney who charges the defendant with a specific statutory crime. This charge is subject to review by a judge at a preliminary hearing of the evidence and in many places, if the offense charged is a felony, by a grand jury that can dismiss the charge or affirm it by delivering it to a judge in the form of an indictment. If the defendant pleads "not guilty" to the charge, he or she comes to trial; the facts of the case are marshaled by prosecuting and defense attorneys and presented, under the supervision of a judge, through witnesses, to a jury. If the jury finds the defendant guilty, he or she is sentenced by the judge to a term in prison, where a systematic attempt to convert the criminal into a law-abiding citizen is made, or to a term of probation, under which the criminal is permitted to live in the community as long as he or she behaves.

Some cases do proceed much like that, especially those involving offenses that are generally considered "major": serious acts of violence or thefts of large amounts of property. However, not all major cases follow this course and, in any event, the bulk of the daily business of the criminal-justice system consists of offenses that are not major—of breaches of the peace, crimes of vice, petty thefts, assaults arising from domestic or street-corner or barroom disputes. These and most other cases are disposed of in much less formal and much less deliberate ways.

The theory of the juvenile court is that it is a "helping" social agency, designed to prescribe carefully individualized treatment to young people in trouble, and that its procedures are therefore non-adversary. Here again there is, in most places, a considerable difference between theory and practice. Many juvenile proceedings are no more individualized and no more therapeutic than adult ones.

What has evidently happened is that that transformation of America from a relatively relaxed rural society into a tumultuous urban one has presented the criminal-justice system in the cities with a volume of cases too large to handle by traditional methods. One result of heavy caseloads is highly visible in city courts, which process many cases with excessive haste and many others with excessive slowness. In the interest both of effectiveness and of fairness to individuals, justice should be swift and certain; too often in city courts today it is, instead, hasty or faltering. Invisibly, the pressure of numbers has effected a series of adventitious changes in the criminal process. Informal shortcuts have been used. The decision-making process has often become routinized. Throughout the system the importance of individual judgment and discretion, as distinguished from stated rules and procedures, has increased. In effect, much decision making is being done on an administrative rather than on a judicial basis.

The Police

At the very beginning of the process—or, more properly, before the process begins at all—something happens that is scarcely discussed in lawbooks and is seldom recognized by the public: Law enforcement policy is made by the police officer. For police officers cannot and do not arrest all the offenders they encounter. It is doubtful that they arrest most of them. A criminal code, in practice, is not a set of specific instructions to the police but a more or less rough map of the territory in which police officers work. How an individual police officer moves around that territory depends largely on his or her personal discretion.

Police duties compel the officer to exercise personal discretion many times every day. Crime does not look the same on the street as it does in a legislative chamber. How much noise or profanity makes conduct "disorderly" within the meaning of the law? When must a quarrel be treated as a criminal assault: at the first threat or at the first shove or at the first blow, or after blood is drawn, or when a serious injury is inflicted? How suspicious must conduct be before there is "probable cause," the constitutional basis for an arrest? Every police officer, however complete or sketchy his or her education, is an interpreter of the law.

Every police officer, too, is an arbiter of social values, for he or she meets situation after situation in which invoking criminal sanctions is a questionable line of action. With juveniles especially, the police exercise great discretion.

Finally, the manner in which an officer works is influenced by practical matters: the legal strength of the available evidence, the willingness of victims to press charges and of witnesses to testify, the temper of the community, and the time and information at the officer's disposal.

The Magistrate

In direct contrast to the police, the magistrate before whom a suspect is first brought usually exercises less discretion than the law allows him or her. Magistrates are entitled to inquire into the facts of the case, into whether there are grounds for holding the accused. They seldom do. They seldom can. The more promptly an arrested suspect is brought into magistrate's court, the less likelihood there is that much information about the arrest other than the arresting officer's statement will be available to the magistrate. Moreover, many magistrates, especially in big cities, have such congested calendars that it is almost impossible for them to subject any case but an extraordinary one to prolonged scrutiny.

In practice the most important things, by far, that a magistrate does are to set the amount of a defendant's bail and in some jurisdictions to appoint counsel. Bail is a device to free an untried defendant and at the same time make sure he or she appears for trial. That is the sole stated legal purpose in America. The Eighth Amendment to the Constitution declares that it must not be "excessive." Appellate courts have declared that not just the seriousness of the charge against the defendant, but the suspect's personal, family, and employment situation, as they bear on the likelihood of his appearance, must be weighed before the amount of bail is fixed. Yet more magistrates than not set bail according to standard rates: so and so many dollars for such and such an offense.

The persistence of money bail can best be explained not by its stated purpose but by the belief of police, prosecutors, and courts that the best way to keep a defendant from committing more crimes before trial is to set bail so high that he or she cannot obtain release.

The Prosecutor

The key administrative officer in the processing of cases is the prosecutor. Theoretically the examination of the evidence against a defendant by a judge at a preliminary hearing, and its reexamination by a grand jury, are important parts of the process. Practically they seldom are because a prosecutor seldom has any difficulty in making a prima facie case against a defendant. In fact, most defendants waive their rights to preliminary hearings and much more often than not grand juries indict precisely as prosecutors ask them to. Prosecutors wield almost undisputed sway over the pretrial progress of most cases. They decide whether to press a case or drop it. They determine the specific charge against a defendant. When the charge is reduced, as it is in as many as two-thirds of all cases in some cities, the prosecutor is usually the official who reduces it.

In the informal, noncriminal, nonadversary juvenile-justice system there are no "magistrates" or "prosecutors" or "charges," or, in most instances, defense counsel. An arrested youth is brought before an intake officer who is likely to be a social worker or, in small communities, before a judge. On the basis of an informal inquiry into the facts and circumstances that led to the arrest, and of an interview with the youth, the intake officer or the judge decides whether or not a case should be the subject of formal court proceedings. If he or she decides it should be, a petition is drawn up describing the case. Bail in very few places is a part of the juvenile system; a youth whose case is referred to court is either sent home with orders to reappear on a certain date, or he or she is remanded to custody. This decision, too, is made by the screening official. Thus though these officials work in a quite different environment and according to quite different procedures from magistrates and prosecutors, they in fact exercise the same kind of discretionary control over what happens before the facts of a case are adjudicated.

The Plea and the Sentence

When a prosecutor reduces a charge it is ordinarily because there has been "plea bargaining" between the prosecutor and a defense attorney. The issue at stake is how much the prosecutor will reduce his or her original charge or how lenient a sentence he or she will recommend, in return for a plea of guilty. There is no way of judging how many bargains reflect the prosecutor's belief that a less charge or sentence is justified and how many result from the fact that there may be in the system at any one time ten times as many cases as there are prosecutors or judges or courtrooms to handle them, should every one come to trial. In form, a plea bargain can be anything from a series of careful conferences to a hurried consultation in a courthouse corridor. In content it can be anything from a conscientious exploration of the facts and dispositional alternatives available and appropriate to a defendant, to a perfunctory deal.

Plea bargaining is not only an invisible procedure but, in some jurisdictions, a theoretically unsanctioned one. In order to satisfy the court record, a defendant, his or her attorney, and the prosecutor will at the time of sentencing often ritually state to a judge that no bargain has been made. Plea bargaining may be a useful procedure, especially in congested urban jurisdictions, but neither the dignity of the law, nor the quality of justice, nor the protection of society from dangerous criminals is enhanced by its being conducted covertly.

In the juvenile system there is, of course, no plea bargaining in the sense described above. However, the entire juvenile process can involve extrajudicial negotiations about disposition. Furthermore, the entire juvenile process is by design invisible. Though intended to be helpful, the authority exercised often is coercive; juveniles, no less than adults, may need representation by counsel.

In perhaps nine-tenths of all cases there is no trial; the defendants are self-confessedly guilty. The sentencing decision of a judge is enormously consequential. The law recognizes the importance of fitting sentences to individual defendants by giving judges, in most instances, considerable latitude, although new legislation in some areas is setting mandatory minimum sentenes and imposing restraints on felony plea-bargaining. Even when a judge has presided over a trial during which the facts of the case have been carefully set forth and has been given a probation report that carefully discusses a defendant's character, background, and problems, he or she cannot find it easy to choose a sentence.

In the lower or misdemeanor courts, the courts that process most criminal cases, probation reports are a rarity. Under such circumstances judges have little to go on and many sentences are bound to be based on conjecture or intuition. When a sentence is part of a plea bargain, which an overworked judge ratifies perfunctorily, it may not even be the judge's conjecture or intuition on which the sentence is based, but a prosecutor's or a defense counsel's. But perhaps the greatest lack judges suffer from when they pass sentence is not time or information, but correctional alternatives. Some lower courts do not have any probation officers, and in almost every court the caseloads of probation officers are so heavy that a sentence of probation means, in fact, releasing an offender into the community with almost no supervision. Few states have a sufficient variety of correctional institutions or treatment programs to inspire judges with the confidence that sentences will lead to rehabilitation.

Corrections

The most striking fact about the correctional apparatus today is that, although the rehabilitation of criminals is presumably its primary purpose, the custody of criminals is actually its major task. On any given day there are well over a million people being "corrected" in America, two-thirds of them on probation or parole and one-third of them in prisons or jails. However, prisons and jails are where four-fifths of correctional money is spent and where nine-tenths of correctional employees work. Furthermore, fewer than one-fifth of the people who work in state prisons and local jails have jobs that are not essentially either custodial or administrative personnel. Of course many jails are crowded with defendants who have not been able to furnish bail and who are not considered by the law to be appropriate objects of rehabilitation because it has not yet been determined that they are criminals who need it.

What this emphasis on custody means in practice is that the enormous potential of the correctional apparatus for making creative decisions about its treatment of convicts is largely unfulfilled. This is true not only of offenders in custody but of offenders on probation and parole.

Except for sentencing, no decision in the criminal process has more impact on the convicted offender than the parole decision, which determines how much of the maximum sentence a prisoner must serve. This again is an invisible administrative decision that is seldom open to attack or subject to review. It is made by parole-board members who are often political appointees. Many are skilled and conscientious, but they generally are able to spend no more than a few minutes on a case.

Most authorities agree that while probationers and parolees need varying degrees and kinds of supervision, an average of no more than 35 cases per parole officer is necessary for effective attention; 97 percent of all officers handling adults have larger caseloads than that.

In sum, America's system of criminal justice is overcrowded and overworked, undermanned, underfinanced, and very often misunderstood. It needs more information and more knowledge. It needs more technical resources. It needs more coordination among its many parts. It needs more public support. It needs the help of community programs and institutions in dealing with offenders and potential offenders. It needs, above all, the willingness to reexamine old ways of doing things, to reform itself, to experiment, to run risks, to dare. It needs vision.

A Glossary of Legal Terms[2]

abscond—to be intentionally absent or to conceal oneself illegally in order to avoid a legal process.

accused—formally charged but not yet tried for committing a crime; the person who has been charged may be called *the accused.*

acquittal—a judgment of a court, based on the decision of either a jury or a judge, that a person accused is not guilty of the crime for which he or she has been tried.

adjudication—the judicial decision that ends a criminal proceeding by a judgment of acquittal, conviction, or dismissal of the case.

adjudicatory hearing—a hearing by a judicial officer in a juvenile court to determine if there is enough evidence to support the claims made in a petition. *See* petition.

affidavit—a written statement which the writer swears is true.

alleged—said to be true, but not yet proven to be true; until the trial is over, the crime may be called "the alleged crime," for example.

appeal—a request by either the defense or the prosecution that the results of a decision on certain motions or of a completed trial be reviewed by a higher court.

appearance—coming into a court and submitting to the authority of that court.

arraignment—the appearance in a court of an accused person at which the court may inform the accused of the charges against him or her, advise the accused of his or her rights, appoint a lawyer for the accused, and/or hear the plea of the accused. The meaning of arraignment varies widely among jurisdictions.

arrest—to take a person suspected of committing a crime into legal custody for the purpose of charging him or her with committing a specific crime or for the purpose of beginning juvenile proceedings if the suspect is a juvenile.

arrest warrant—a document issued by a judicial officer which directs a law-enforcement officer to arrest a person accused of committing a crime.

assault—an illegal and intentional physical attack or attempted or threatened attack by one person against another. Assaults are commonly divided in the law into aggravated assault, which is generally, a physical attack in which serious bodily injury is inflicted or there is a threat or attempt to inflict serious bodily injury with a deadly weapon, and simple assault, in which a threat, attempt, or actual attack is made without serious bodily injury or the use of a deadly weapon.

attorney—a person trained in law and authorized to advise, represent, and act for others in legal proceedings. An attorney may also be called a *lawyer,* a *counsel,* or an *advocate.*

auto theft—*see* motor-vehicle theft.

bail—money or property promised or given to the court as security when an accused person is released before and during his or her trail with the agreement that the accused will return to court when ordered to do so or forfeit the bail.

bailiff—a uniformed officer who keeps order in a courtroom.

bench—the judge; also the place where the judge sits during court proceedings.

bench trial—a trial in which the accused does not want a jury and asks the judge to hear the case and decide if the accused is guilty or not.

bench warrant—an order issued by a judge to bring to court an accused person who has been released before trial and does not return to court when ordered to do so or a witness who has failed to appear in court when ordered to do so.

beyond a reasonable doubt—the degree of proof needed for a jury or judge to convict an accused person of a crime.

booking—an official police record of the arrest of a person accused of committing a crime which identifies the accused, the time and place of arrest, the arresting authority, and the reason for the arrest.

breaking and entering—*see* burglary.

burglary—the act of illegally entering or attempting to enter any fixed structure or a vehicle or vessel used for residence, industry, or business with or without force with the intent of committing a felony or larceny.

charge—an allegation that a specific person has committed a specific crime; the filing of the charging document may be called *pressing charges*.

citation—a written order by a law-enforcement official that requires a suspect to appear in a certain court at a stated time and place to answer a criminal charge.

civil court—a court that hears cases concerned with the alleged violation of civil law; not a criminal court.

civil law—the law relating to private, not criminal, matters in which one party sues another for remedy.

complainant—the person who makes a formal criminal complaint; also, the victim of the crime described in the complaint.

complaint—a formal written statement made by any person, often a prosecutor or a victim, and filed in court to accuse a specific person of committing a specific crime.

continuance—a delay or postponement of a court hearing; the case is said to be "continued" when it has been delayed or postponed.

conviction—a judgment of the court, based either on the decision of a jury or a judge or on the guilty plea of the accused, that the accused is guilty of the crime for which he or she has been tried.

corroborating witness—a person who is able to give information that supports the statements made by either the victim or the accused.

counsel—*see* attorney.

count—each separate offense listed in a complaint, information, or indictment accusing a person of committing a crime.

court—an agency of the judicial branch of the government authorized by statute or constitution to decide controversies of law and disputed matters of fact brought before it.

criminal—a person who has been convicted by a court of committing a crime.

criminal court—a court that hears cases concerned with the alleged violation of criminal law.

criminal-justice system—the government agencies charged with law enforcement, prosecution of alleged violations of the criminal law, public defense services for accused or convicted persons who are unable to hire private counsel, the court hearing of charges against the accused, and the punishment and supervision of those convicted.

criminal law—the law whose violation is considered an offense against the state that is punishable upon conviction by imprisonment and other penalties for adult offenders and by action of a juvenile court for juvenile offenders.

defendant—a person who has been formally charged with committing a crime.

defense attorney—the lawyer who represents the defendant in a legal proceeding. Victims are generally not required to talk to the defense attorney except in court.

dismissal—a decision by a judicial officer to end a case for legal or other reasons.

disposition—the final judicial decision which ends a criminal proceeding by a judgment of acquittal or dismissal, or which states the sentence if the accused is convicted.

district attorney—*see* prosecutor.

double jeopardy—putting a person on trial more than once for the same offense. Double jeopardy is forbidden by the United States Constitution.

evidence—testimony and objects used to prove the statements made by the victim and the accused.

eye witness—a person who saw the crime take place.

felony—a serious crime for which the punishment is imprisonment, usually in a state or federal prison, usually for one year or more.

grand-jury hearing—a legal process in which citizens selected by law and sworn to investigate criminal activity and the conduct of public officials and to hear the evidence against accused persons sit as a jury to decide if there is enough evidence to bring the accused to trial; unlike court trials, grand jury hearings are generally closed to the public and their proceedings, by law, are secret.

guilty—a verdict of a judge or a jury that a person accused of committing a specific crime did commit it.

guilty plea—a formal response by a person accused of committing a specific crime in which the accused says that the charges are true and he or she did commit a crime.

habeas corpus—a written order challenging on constitutional grounds the right of the state to continue to detain or imprison a person.

hearing—a legal proceeding in which arguments, witnesses, and/or evidence are heard by a judicial officer or an administrative body.

homicide—any killing of one person by another without justification or excuse.

hung jury—a jury whose members cannot agree whether the accused is guilty or innocent.

indictment—a formal written accusation, made by a grand jury and filed in a court, alleging that a specific person has committed a specific crime.

indigent—an accused person who has been found by the court to be too poor to pay for his or her own attorney. The court provides an attorney for indigents.

information—a formal written accusation, made by a prosecutor and filed in a court, alleging that a specific person has committed a specific crime.

initial appearance—the first appearance of the accused in the court which has jurisdiction over his or her case; the appearance may include a formal reading of the charges, the plea and/or the setting of bail, but the accused may merely be informed of his or her rights and asked if he or she has a lawyer. Different jurisdictions have different policies at the first appearance. *See* arraignment *and* preliminary hearing.

innocent—*see* not guilty.

investigation—the gathering of evidence by law-enforcement officials and in some cases prosecutors, for presentation to a grand jury or in court, to prove that the accused did commit the crime.

jail—a confinement facility; technically, a jail is usually administered by a local law-enforcement agency for adults and sometimes juveniles who have been accused of committing a crime but whose trials are not yet over and/or persons who have been convicted in a trial and sentenced to imprisonment for one year or less. *See* prison.

judge—a judicial officer who has been elected or appointed to preside over a court of law.

jury—a group of citizens who are selected by law and sworn to determine certain facts by listening to testimony in order to decide whether the accused is guilty or not. The jury in a trial is called a *petit jury. See* grand-jury hearing.

jury selection—the process by which the judge, the prosecutor, and the defense attorney screen citizens who have been called to jury duty to determine if they will give a fair hearing in a particular trial.

juvenile—a person accused of an offense who is too young at the time of the alleged offense to be subject to criminal court proceedings and is handled in the juvenile justice system. The upper age limit for juveniles in most states is the eighteenth birthday.

larceny—stealing other than motor-vehicle theft that does not involve either force or illegal entry; for example, pocket picking is a larceny.

lawyer—*see* attorney.

lineup—a group of people who are viewed by the victim or witness to identify a person who committed a crime.

manslaughter—causing the death of another person either unintentionally but because of recklessness or gross neglect (involuntary or negligent manslaughter) or intentionally but with provocation that a reasonable person would find extreme (voluntary or nonnegligent manslaughter).

misdemeanor—a crime that is less serious than a felony and for which the punishment is usually imprisonment for one year or less, usually in a jail or other local facility.

motion—a verbal or written request made by the prosecutor or the defense attorney before, during, or after a trial that the court issue a rule or an order.

motor-vehicle theft—unlawful taking or attempt to take a motor vehicle owned by another person.

mugging—an assault, usually with the intent to rob the victim.

mug shots—pictures of people who have been arrested for a crime and photographed by the police.

murder—intentionally causing the death of another person without extreme provocation or legal justification, or causing the death of another while committing or attempting to commit another crime.

nolo contendere—a defendant's formal answer in court to the charges in which the defendant states that he or she does not contest the charges. The nolo contendere plea is not an admission of guilt but it carries the same legal consequences as a guilty plea.

not guilty—a verdict by a judge or a jury that a person accused of a crime did not commit it or that there is not enough evidence to prove beyond a reasonable doubt that the accused committed the crime.

not guilty plea—a formal response by a person accused of committing a specific crime in which the accused says that the charges are not true and he or she did not commit the crime.

notice—a written order to appear in court at a certain time and place.

offender—an adult who has been convicted of a crime.

offense—a crime; technically, in some jurisdictions, only the most minor crimes are called offenses.

parole—the conditional release of a convicted offender from a confinement facility before the end of his or her sentence with requirements for the offender's behavior set and supervised by a parole agency.

penitentiary—a state or federal prison.

perjury—deliberate false testimony under oath.

perpetrator—a person who commits a crime.

personal recognizance—the promise of an accused person to the court that he or she will return to court when ordered to do so; given in exchange for release before and during his or her trial.

petition—a document filed in a juvenile court alleging that a juvenile should come under the jurisdiction of the juvenile court for some offense or asking that the juvenile be transferred to criminal court for prosecution as an adult.

plea—a defendant's formal answer in court to the charge that he or she has committed a crime.

plea bargaining—an agreement between the prosecutor and the defense attorney that the defendant will plead guilty to a crime in exchange for some concession, commonly a lesser charge, the dismissal of other pending charges, or a recommendation by the prosecutor for a reduced sentence.

pocket picking—theft of a wallet or cash directly from the victim by stealth, without the use or threat of force.

predisposition report—a document which details the past behavior, family background, and personality of a juvenile offender and is prepared by a probation agency or other authority after an investigation in order to assist a juvenile court in determining the most appropriate action to be taken. A predisposition report for a juvenile corresponds to a presentence report for an adult.

preliminary hearing—a legal proceeding before a judicial officer in which arguments, witnesses, and/or evidence are presented to determine if there is sufficient cause to hold the accused for trial. Sometimes called a *probable-cause hearing* or a *pretrial hearing*.

presentence report—a document which details the past behavior, family circumstances, and personality of a convicted adult offender and gives information about the crime he or she committed. It is prepared by a probation agency or other authority in order to assist the court in determining the most appropriate sentence.

pretrial hearing—*see* preliminary hearing.

prison—a state or federal confinement facility for adult offenders, usually those sentenced for one year or more. *See* jail.

privileged relationship—a special relationship whose confidences may not be violated, such as the relationship between a husband and wife, a priest and a penitent, or an attorney and his or her client. An attorney is not generally required to reveal information given to him or her by a client.

probable cause—the degree of proof needed to arrest and begin prosecution against a person suspected of committing a crime; the evidence must be such that a reasonable person would believe that this specific crime was committed and that it is probable that the person being accused committed it.

probable-cause hearing—*see* preliminary hearing.

probation—conditional freedom granted to an offender by the court

after conviction or a guilty plea with requirements for the offender's behavior set and supervised by the court.

prosecutor—an attorney for the community employed by a government agency to represent the interests of the general public,
including crime victims, in court proceedings against people accused of committing crimes. Some jurisdictions use other terms
for the prosecutor, such as *U.S. Attorney* (a federal prosecutor),
district attorney, or *state's attorney*.

public defender—an attorney employed by a government agency
to represent defendants who are unable to hire private counsel.

purse snatching—the theft of a purse directly from the victim.

rape—in most laws, *rape* refers specifically to unlawful sexual intercourse or attempted sexual intercourse by a male with a female
other than his wife by force or without a legal or factual consent;
other sexual assaults, such as forced oral sex and forced anal sex,
are commonly given other names. *See* sodomy.

release on bail—the release of an accused person by a judicial
officer before and during the trial of the accused upon the promise
of the accused that he or she will pay a sum of money or property
if he or she fails to return to court when ordered to do so.

release on own recognizance—the release of an accused person
by a judicial officer before or during the trial of the accused upon
the promise of the accused that he or she will return to court
when ordered to do so.

release to a third party—the release of an accused person by a
judicial officer before and during the trial or juvenile adjudication
of the accused upon the promise of a third party that the accused
will return to court when ordered to do so.

rights of the defendant—the powers and privileges which are
constitutionally guaranteed to any person arrested and accused of
committing a crime, including the right to remain silent; the right
to an attorney at all stages of the proceeding; the right to a court-
appointed attorney if the defendant does not have the financial
means to hire his or her own counsel; the right to release on
reasonable bail; the right to a speedy public trial before a jury or
a judge; the right to the process of the court to subpoena and
produce witnesses; the right to see, hear, and question the wit-

nesses during the trial; and the right not to incriminate himself or herself.

robbery—the unlawful taking or attempt to take property in the immediate possession of another by force or the threat of force, with or without a weapon. Robberies are commonly divided in the law into armed robbery, which is generally robbery by the use or threat of a dangerous or deadly weapon, and strongarm robbery, which is generally robbery by the use or threat of force without a weapon.

robbery with assault—the unlawful taking or attempt to take property in the immediate possession of another by physical attack or attempted physical attack with or without a weapon.

sentence—the punishment imposed by the court on a person convicted of a crime.

sentencing—the legal process in which a defendant who has been found guilty of a crime hears in court what his or her punishment will be.

sexual assault—broadly, any sexual act or attempted sexual act in which the victim is forced to participate by the threat or use of force; in the law, sexual assaults are usually distinguished according to the sex and age of the victim and the nature of the act. *See* rape *and* sodomy.

sodomy—Unlawful physical contact between the genitals of one person and the mouth or anus of another person, or with the mouth, anus, or genitals of an animal. In many jurisdictions *sodomy* is the term used to designate forcible anal and oral sex in sexual assault.

state's attorney—*see* prosecutor.

subpoena—a written order by a judicial officer requiring a specified person to appear in a designated court at a specific time and place in order to serve as a witness in a case or to bring material to the court.

summons—a written order by a judicial officer requiring a person accused of a criminal offense to appear in a designated court at a specific time and place to answer the charge.

suspect—a person who is believed by criminal-justice officials to be one who may have committed a specific crime but who has not been arrested or formally charged.

suspended sentence—a court decision to postpone the pronouncing of sentence on a convicted person or to postpone the execution of a sentence that has been pronounced by the court.

testimony—statements made in court by people who have sworn to tell the truth.

trial—an examination of issues of fact and law before a judge and sometimes a jury at which evidence is presented to determine whether or not an accused person is guilty of committing a specific crime.

U.S. Attorney—*see* prosecutor.

verdict—the decision of the judge or jury at the end of a trial that the accused defendant is either guilty or not guilty of the crime for which he or she has been tried.

warrant—*see* arrest warrant *and* bench warrant.

witness—a person who has directly seen an event, such as a crime, or thing, such as a piece of physical evidence, or who has other knowledge that is related to a court case.

NOTES

1. United States President's Commission on Law Enforcement and Administration of Justice, *The Challenge of Crime in a Free Society* (Washington, D.C.: Government Printing Office, 1967), pp. 7, 10-12.
2. Most of these definitions are taken from SEARCH Group, Inc., *Dictionary of Criminal Justice Data Terminology* (Washington, D.C.: United States National Criminal Justice Information and Statistics Service, 1976) and *Dictionary of Criminal Justice Data Terminology, Second Edition* (Bureau of Justice Statistics, 1981).

Appendix C

Access to Resources

Victims of personal crime need different kinds of help. Emotional support during the crisis reaction is often best provided by selected friends and relatives who know and care about the victim, although some victims feel more comfortable with a supportive stranger because of their need for privacy. Other needs, including police assistance, medical care, legal advice, and psychological counseling, are best met by professionals who have special training. Monetary compensation for losses suffered because of a crime is also available to some victims.

In this list of resources we have indicated the best places to seek professional help and monetary compensation. The victim's immediate needs are listed first, followed by resources for help in five areas: police, medical, counseling, legal, and money. In most cases, access to these helping resources is available by telephone. This list is not exhaustive and it is general because resources vary from one part of the country to another. But we hope it will provide victims and their loved ones with ways to find the people who can help them.

201

Immediate Help

If you need:

emergency police assistance	Dial "o" for the operator. Say, "This is an emergency," give the telephone number from which you are calling, and ask for the police in the town of ——. The operator will connect you with the police.
emergency medical assistance	Dial "o" for the operator. Say, "This is an emergency," give the telephone number from which you are calling and the address where help is needed, and ask for an ambulance.

or

Go to the emergency room of the nearest hospital (listed under "hospital" in the white pages of the telephone book). If you don't know where the hospital is, call the local police (listed in the white pages under "police" or under the name of the town) and ask them for directions.

emergency emotional support	If you have any relative or friend you feel able to trust, call him or her.

or

Some communities have twenty-four-hour hotlines to handle crisis situations. Look in the white pages (under "hotline," "crisis," "rape," "suicide," "crime victim assistance," or "victim assistance.")

Weekends and nights: Call your local or county Mental Health Association (listed in the white pages under "Mental Health Association"); some associations have twenty-four-hour telephone service.

or

Call your local police and ask them where to get help.

or

Call or go to the emergency room of the nearest hospital.

or

Weekdays: See the Counseling section of this appendix.

to secure your home after a burglary or the theft of keys	If a lock must be replaced, call a locksmith (listed in the yellow pages); some locksmiths provide twenty-four-hour service. If none is available or there is damage to the building structure, call the police. Do not stay alone in an unsecured building.
to report stolen credit cards	Call the twenty-four-hour number provided by your credit-card company, if you have it. If not, call the bank, gasoline company, or store that issued the card. Confirm the notification with a letter after you call.

Help from the Police
If you need:

to report a crime	Call the local police (listed in the white pages under "police" or under the name of the town). Be sure to get the name and identification number of the responding officer(s) and the number of the police report.
to find out how the police investigation is progressing after you report a crime	Call the local police and ask for one of the officers to whom you reported the crime

protection from a suspect or accused person who threatens you after you report a crime	Call the police immediately.
information about crime prevention techniques and hardware	Call the local police and ask for the officer who specializes in crime prevention.

Medical Help

If you need:

medical care for physical injuries	Private medical care is often expensive, and many crime victims cannot afford it. If you do not have a private physician but you can afford one, or you have medical insurance to cover the expenses, or you qualify for compensation (see the Money section of this appendix), you can get a referral to a private physician by calling your local county medical society (listed in the white pages under the county name or under "Medical Society of the County of ——"). Private physicians and surgeons are also listed in the yellow pages (under "Physicians and Surgeons").
	If you cannot afford a private physician and do not qualify for compensation or insurance benefits, call the out-patient clinic of your local hospital and ask for an appointment.
medical care for physical rehabilitation following physical disability	See the listings of social service agencies in the Counseling section of this appendix.

Help With Counseling

If you need:

counseling for emotional problems such as phobias, anxiety, feelings of guilt, problems in your relationships, and other personal difficulties

There are many different kinds of counselors, and their personalities, techniques, and fees vary. If you know someone who is being counseled, you may want to ask that person about his or her counselor.

Like private medical care, private counseling can be expensive. If you can afford private care, or you have insurance, or you can qualify for compensation (see the Money section of this appendix), you can get advice and a referral to a counselor in private practice by calling your city or county Mental Health Association (listed in the white pages under "Mental Health Association" or under the city or county name).

If you cannot afford private counseling and you do not qualify for compensation, you can get advice and a referral to a clinic or other low-cost counseling facility by calling your local city or county Department of Mental Health or Mental Hygiene (listed in the white pages under the city or county name).

or

Some local hospitals have psychiatric services or mental-health clinics. Call the hospital and ask.

or

Some communities have Rape Crisis

Centers or Victim-Assistance Centers (both listed in the white pages under those names) that are staffed by trained counselors.

or

Victims who find comfort and meaning in religion may be helped by their local clergy.

counseling for help with social problems such as the need for new housing, financial support, employment counseling, vocational training after disability, and other practical difficulties

Call your local city or county Department of Social Services (listed in the white pages under the city or county name).

Legal Help

If you need:

legal assistance with questions about court procedures when your case is in the courts

Call the prosecutor who is handling your case.

or

Call your local crime-victim assistance center, if there is one in your community.

legal assistance to understand your rights as a victim, including help with compensation programs, advice about charging the criminal or others in a civil suit, and personal legal counsel if you are being sued as a result of the crime

Call the prosecutor who is handling your case.

or

Call your local crime-victim assistance center, if there is one in your community.

or

Call your local county Bar Association (listed in the white pages under the county name and in the yellow pages under "Lawyer Referral Service") for a referral to a private attorney.

or

Call your local Legal Aid Society (listed in the white pages under "Legal Aid Society"), which serves people who cannot afford a private attorney.

Help with Money

If you need:

money for medical and/or counseling expenses or for living expenses because you have been injured and cannot work

As of March, 1985, forty-one states have passed some crime-victim compensation law which provides money from the state government for certain victims of crime.

The programs vary. Most provide money to eligible victims for medical expenses, living expenses if the victim has lost earnings because of injury, and funeral expenses for murder victims.

Some programs provide money for vocational rehabilitation, psychological counseling; disability claims, short-term support of eligible survivor-victims of murder, attorney fees, rape evidence kits, and/or "pain and suffering." Almost all of the programs have upper limits for benefits, typically $10,000 to $25,000, and other restrictions. The victim may be required to show financial need.

If you live in a state that has a crime-victim compensation program, ask the police or the local prosecutor's office how to apply.

If you do not have medical insurance or your insurance does not pay for all of your medical expenses, you may be eligible for government assistance under Medicaid or Medicare. Medicaid pays for all or some of hospital and medical costs if your income is low and your resources are limited. Medicare pays a substantial part of your hospital and medical expenses if you are sixty-five or older. Call your local Medicaid or Medicare office (listed in the white pages under "Medicaid" or "Medicare") or your city or county Department of Social Services (listed in the white pages under the city or county name) for help in applying for these benefits.

A victim who is injured in a crime while he or she is working may qualify for Workmen's Compensation benefits. Call your state Workmen's Compensation office (listed in the white pages under "Workmen's Compensation") or your city or county Department of Social Services for help.

Victims who are disabled by a crime-related injury may be eligible for Social Security benefits. Call you local Social Security Administration (listed in the white pages under "Social Security") or your city or county Department of Social Services for information.

money for living expenses because you depend for your support on a victim who has been injured or killed in a crime.

Some crime-victim compensation programs (see above) include benefits for living expenses for victims' families and/or benefits for the survivors of victims who have been killed in a crime.

Workmen's Compensation (see

above) also pays benefits to eligible families of workers who are injured or killed on the job.

Social Security (see above) benefits provide a monthly income payment to widows or widowers age sixty and over whose spouses were insured workers. Social Security also pays a lump sum death benefit to whoever assumes the burial costs of insured workers.

money as compensation for property stolen or damaged in a crime

Uninsured losses over $100 from theft are deductible under certain circumstances on your federal income tax return. Call your local Internal Revenue Service (listed in the white pages under "United States—Internal Revenue Service") and ask for publication 547, which explains this deduction.

If you need:

insurance to protect your property against future burglary and robbery

The Federal Insurance Administration offers a residential crime insurance policy that cannot be canceled because of previous losses. This insurance, which is less expensive than many commercial insurance policies, is available in Connecticut, Illinois, Kansas, Maryland, Massachusetts, Missouri, New Jersey, New York, Ohio, Pennsylvania, Puerto Rico, Rhode Island, Tennessee, the Virgin Islands and the District of Columbia. Information and applications may be obtained by calling (toll free) 800-638-8780, or by writing to: Federal Crime Insurance, P.O. Box 6301, Rockville, Md. 20850

Information About Victim Rights and Victim Services

The National Organization for Victim Assistance (NOVA) is a private, nonprofit organization of victim and witness practitioners, criminal-justice professionals, researchers, former victims, and others who are committed to the recognition of victim rights. NOVA can provide many services and resources to those who want to learn about or work for victim rights, including membership in NOVA, various conferences and workshops, publications, and so on. Write to NOVA, 717 D Street, N.W., Washington, D.C. 20004 or call (202) 393-6682 for more information.

The U.S. Department of Justice has established a National Victims Resource Center which serves as a national clearinghouse for information on victim assistance and compensation programs and victim advocacy organizations, functions as a liaison to public and private organizations that assist crime victims, and provides reference services for those seeking current information about victim-related legislation and victim services. Write to the National Victims Resource Center, Office of Justice Assistance, Research, and Statistics, Washington, D.C. 20531 or call (202) 724-6134 for more information.

Appendix D

An Agenda for the Future

What follows here are excerpts from the reports of two important task forces, the President's Task Force on Victims of Crime, which published its final report in December, 1982, and the American Psychological Association Task Force on the Victims of Crime and Violence, which published its final report in November, 1984. In each case, a distinguished panel of experts has considered what more needs to be done to secure victim rights and advance victim services. Taken together, these recommendations make up a challenging agenda for the future.

**PRESIDENT'S
TASK FORCE ON
VICTIMS OF CRIME**

Task Force Members

Lois Haight Herrington,
Chairman

Garfield Bobo	**Kenneth O. Eikenberry**
Frank Carrington	**Robert J. Miller**
James P. Damos	**Reverend Pat Robertson**
Doris L. Dolan	**Stanton E. Samenow**

FINAL REPORT   **DECEMBER 1982**

Statement of the Chairman

If we take the justice out of the criminal justice system we leave
a system that serves only the criminal.

Something insidious has happened in America: crime has made victims of us all. Awareness of its danger affects the way we think, where we live, where we go, what we buy, how we raise our children, and the quality of our lives as we age. The specter of violent crime and the knowledge that, without warning, any person can be attacked or crippled, robbed, or killed, lurks at the fringes of consciousness. Every citizen of this country is more impoverished, less free, more fearful, and less safe, because of the ever-present threat of the criminal. Rather than alter a system that has proven itself incapable of dealing with crime, society has altered itself.

Every 23 minutes, someone is murdered. Every six minutes a woman is raped. While you read this Statement, two people will be robbed in this country and two more will be shot, stabbed, or seriously beaten. Yet to truly grasp the enormity of the problem those figures must be doubled, because more than 50 percent of violent crime goes unreported. The criminal knows that his risk of punishment is miniscule. A study of four major states revealed that only 9 percent of violent crimes reported were resolved with the perpetrator being incarcerated.

Victims who do survive their attack, and are brave enough to come forward, turn to their government expecting it to do what a good government should—protect the innocent. The American criminal justice system is absolutely dependent on these victims to cooperate. Without the cooperation of victims and witnesses in reporting and testifying about crime, it is impossible in a free society to hold criminals accountable. When victims come forward to perform this vital service, however, they find little protection. They discover instead that they will be treated as appendages of a system appallingly out of balance. They learn that somewhere along the way the system has lost track of the simple truth that it is supposed to be fair and to protect those who obey the law while punishing those who break it. Somewhere along the way, the system began to serve lawyers and judges and defendants, treating the victim with institutionalized disinterest.

The President created this Task Force to address the needs of the millions of Americans and their families who are victimized by crime every year and who often carry its scars into the years to come. He recognized that in the past these victims have pleaded for justice and their pleas have gone unheeded. They have needed help and their needs have gone unattended. The neglect of crime victims is a national disgrace. The President is committed to ending that neglect and to restoring balance to the administration of justice....You cannot appreciate the victim problem if you approach it solely with your intellect. The intellect rebels.

The important proposals contained here will not be clear unless you first confront the human reality of victimization. Few are willing to do so. Unless you are, however, you will not be able to understand. During our hearings we were told by one eloquent witness, "It is hard not to turn away from victims. Their pain is discomforting; their anger is sometimes embarrassing; their mutilations are upsetting." Victims are vital reminders of our own vulnerability. But one cannot turn away.

You must know what it is to have your life wrenched and broken, to realize that you will never really be the same. Then you must experience what it means to survive, only to be blamed and used and ignored by those you thought were there to help you. Only when you are willing to confront all these things will you understand what victimization means.

We who have served on this Task Force have been forever changed by the victims we have met, by the experiences they have shared, by the wisdom sprung from suffering that they imparted.... The problems we refer to unfortunately exist. They exist in every jurisdiction of the country. The examples used in this report to illustrate these problems are taken directly from victim testimony. While not every victim will face every one of these problems, our inquiry has shown that almost every victim will face some of them.

The lessons of the victims run like a thread throughout and are the foundation of all the proposals that follow. Please take the time to learn, as we have, the depth and the human aspect of this grave social problem, then join in seeking and implementing the solutions.

> Lois Haight Herrington
> Chairman

Washington, D.C.
December 20, 1982

VICTIMS OF CRIME IN AMERICA

Recommendations for Government Action

The United States is a nation of laws. If laws are to be obeyed, they must be respected; to be respected, they must be just. A system that fails to be equitable cannot survive. The system was designed to be the fairest in history, but it has lost the balance that has been the cornerstone of its wisdom.

Proposed Executive and Legislative Action at the Federal and State Levels

The legislative and executive branches, at both the state and federal level, must pass and enforce laws that protect all citizens and that recognize society's interest in assisting the innocent to recover from victimization. The recommendations that follow comprise proposals for action by both federal and state executives and legislatures.

Recommendations for Federal and State Action

1. Legislation should be proposed and enacted to ensure that addresses of victims and witnesses are not made public or available to the defense, absent a clear need as determined by the court.
2. Legislation should be proposed and enacted to ensure that des-

ignated victim counseling is legally privileged and not subject
to defense discovery or subpoena.

3. Legislation should be proposed and enacted to ensure that hear-
say is admissible and sufficient in preliminary hearings, so that
victims need not testify in person.

4. Legislation should be proposed and enacted to amend the bail
laws to accomplish the following:

   a. Allow courts to deny bail to persons found by clear and convincing evidence to present a danger to the community;

   b. Give the prosecution the right to expedited appeal of adverse
   bail determinations, analogous to the right presently held by
   the defendant;

   c. Codify existing case law defining the authority of the court
   to detain defendants as to whom no conditions of release are
   adequate to ensure appearance at trial;

   d. Reverse, in the case of serious crimes, any standard that pre-
   sumptively favors release of convicted persons awaiting sentence or appealing their convictions;

   e. Require defendants to refrain from criminal activity as a mandatory condition of release; and

   f. Provide penalties for failing to appear while released on bond
   or personal recognizance that are more closely proportionate
   to the penalties for the offense with which the defendant was
   originally charged.

5. Legislation should be proposed and enacted to abolish the exclusionary rule as it applies to Fourth Amendment issues.

6. Legislation should be proposed and enacted to open parole release hearings to the public.

7. Legislation should be proposed and enacted to abolish parole
and limit judicial discretion in sentencing.

8. Legislation should be proposed and enacted to require that
school officials report violent offenses against students or teach-
ers, or the possession of weapons or narcotics on school grounds.
The knowing failure to make such a report to the police, or
deterring others from doing so, should be designated a misdemeanor.

9. Legislation should be proposed and enacted to make available

to businesses and organizations the sexual assault, child molestation, and pornography arrest records of prospective and present employees whose work will bring them in regular contact with children.

10. Legislation should be proposed and enacted to accomplish the following:
    a. Require victim impact statements at sentencing;
    b. Provide for the protection of victims and witnesses from intimidation;
    c. Require restitution in all cases, unless the court provides specific reasons for failing to require it;
    d. Develop and implement guidelines for the fair treatment of crime victims and witnesses; and
    e. Prohibit a criminal from making any profit from the sale of the story of his crime. Any proceeds should be used to provide full restitution to his victims, pay the expenses of his prosecution, and finally, assist the crime victim compensation fund.

11. Legislation should be proposed and enacted to establish or expand employee assistance programs for victims of crime employed by government.

12. Legislation should be proposed and enacted to ensure that sexual assault victims are not required to assume the cost of physical examinations and materials used to obtain evidence.

Proposed Federal Action

The foregoing recommendations of this Task Force are meant for consideration at both the federal and state levels. Those that follow are concerned specifically with efforts most properly undertaken by the federal government; they include recommendations for Congressionally directed funding of certain types of programs and of selected areas for further study.

Recommendations

1. Congress should enact legislation to provide federal funding to assist state crime victim compensation programs.

2. Congress should enact legislation to provide federal funding, reasonably matched by local revenues, to assist in the operation of federal, state, local, and private nonprofit victim/witness assistance agencies that make comprehensive assistance available to all victims of crime.

3. The federal government should establish a federally based resource center for victim and witness assistance.

4. The President should establish a task force to study the serious problem of violence within the family, including violence against children, spouse abuse, and abuse of the elderly, and to review and evaluate national, state, and local efforts to address this problem.

5. A study should be commissioned at the federal level to evaluate the juvenile justice system from the perspective of the victim.

6. The Task Force endorses the principle of accountability for gross negligence of parole board officials in releasing into the community dangerous criminals who then injure others. A study should be commissioned at the federal level to determine how, and under what circumstances, this principle of accountability should be implemented.

Proposed Action for Criminal Justice System Agencies

The actions of certain elements of the criminal justice system—the police, prosecutors, the judiciary, and parole boards—are guided not only by law but also by rules, regulations, and procedural codes. The following recommendations of this Task Force are proposals for change at this level.

Recommendations for Police

The police are often the first on the scene; it is to them, the first source of protection, that the victim first turns. They should be mindful that, in fulfilling their obligation to solve the crime and apprehend the criminal, they must also treat victims with the attention due them. The manner in which police officers treat a victim affects not only his immediate and long-term ability to deal with the event but also his willingness to assist in a prosecution. The foundation of all interactions between police and victims should be the knowledge that it is these citizens whom the officer has sworn to serve. These recommendations are meant to ensure better treatment of victims by police.

1. Police departments should develop and implement training programs to ensure that police officers are:
    a. Sensitive to the needs of victims; and
    b. Informed, knowledgeable, and supportive of the existing local services and programs for victims.
2. Police departments should establish procedures for the prompt photographing and return of property to victims (with the prosecutor's approval).
3. Police departments should establish procedures to ensure that victims of violent crime are periodically informed of the status and closing of investigations.
4. Police officers should give a high priority to investigating witnesses' reports of threats or intimidation and should forward these reports to the prosecutor.

Recommendations for Prosecutors

The primary obligation of prosecutors is to see that truth and justice are served. The power of the prosecutor and the court system as a whole derives from the people's willingness to entrust to them the administration of justice. Prosecutors should keep their primary obligation in mind as they make decisions. In doing so they undertake the serious responsibility of serving the interests and concerns of citizens victimized by crime. These recommendations are meant to help prosecutors in this effort.

1. Prosecutors should assume ultimate responsibility for informing victims of the status of a case from the time of the initial charging decision to determinations of parole.
2. Prosecutors have an obligation to bring to the attention of the court the views of victims of violent crime on bail decisions, continuances, plea bargains, dismissals, sentencing, and restitution. They should establish procedures to ensure that such victims are given the opportunity to make their views on these matters known.
3. Prosecutors should charge and pursue to the fullest extent of the law defendants who harass, threaten, injure, or otherwise attempt to intimidate or retaliate against victims or witnesses.
4. Prosecutors should strongly discourage case continuances. When such delays are necessary, procedures should be established to ensure that cases are continued to dates agreeable to victims and witnesses, that those dates are secured in advance whenever possible, and that the reasons for the continuances are adequately explained.
5. Prosecutors' offices should use a victim and witness on-call system.
6. Prosecutors' offices should establish procedures to ensure the prompt return of victims' property, absent a need for the actual evidence in court.
7. Prosecutors' offices should establish and maintain direct liaison with victim/witness units and other victim service agencies.

Recommendations for the Judiciary

The ultimate responsibility for how the system operates rests with judges, who must reconfirm their dedication to be fair to both sides of a criminal prosecution. If they fail to do this, they do not serve the public from whom their authority is derived. In passing judgment, from initial bail hearing to the imposition of a sentence that properly reflects the seriousness of the offense, to appellate review of convictions and sentences, each jurist must act with the goal of equal justice clearly in mind. These recommendations are meant to help keep that goal clear.

1. It should be mandatory that judges at both the trial and appellate levels participate in a training program addressing the needs and legal interests of crime victims.
2. Judges should allow victims and witnesses to be on call for court proceedings.
3. Judges or their court administrators should establish separate waiting rooms for prosecution and defense witnesses.
4. When ruling on requests for continuances, judges should give the same weight to the interests of victims and witnesses as that given to the interests of defendants. Further, judges should explain the basis for such rulings on the record.
5. Judges should bear their share of responsibility for reducing court congestion by ensuring that all participants fully and responsibly utilize court time.
6. Judges should allow for, and give appropriate weight to, input at sentencing from victims of violent crime.
7. Judges should order restitution to the victim in all cases in which the victim has suffered financial loss, unless they state compelling reasons for a contrary ruling on the record.
8. Judges should allow the victim and a member of the victim's family to attend the trial, even if identified as witnesses, absent a compelling need to the contrary.
9. Judges should give substantial weight to the victim's interest in speedy return of property before trial in ruling on the admissibility of photographs of that property.

10. Judges should recognize the profound impact that sexual molestation of children has on victims and their families and treat
is as a crime that should result in punishment, with treatment
available when appropriate.

Recommendations for Parole Boards

Parole boards should be abolished. They operate in secret and without accountability; they release the dangerous, who prey upon the
innocent. (See also Executive and Legislative recommendations 6
and 7.) Post-release supervision is both inadequate and tremendously
costly. Until such time as this system is replaced, the recommendations below may help correct the more dangerous abuses.

1. Parole boards should notify victims of crime and their families in
   advance of parole hearings, if names and addresses have been
   previously provided by these individuals.
2. Parole boards should allow victims of crime, their families, or
   their representatives to attend parole hearings and make known
   the effect of the offender's crime on them.
3. Parole boards should take whatever steps are necessary to ensure
   that parolees charged with a crime while on parole are immediately returned to custody and kept there until the case is adjudicated.
4. Parole boards should not apply the exclusionary rule to parole
   revocation hearings.

Recommendations for Other Organizations

It is obvious that the criminal justice system and the actions of its agents directly affect victims. Less evident, perhaps, are the effects of agencies outside that system with which victims must also deal, particularly hospitals, the ministry, the bar, and the school system. These recommendations are meant to help those agencies assist victims of crime more effectively.

Recommendations for Hospitals

Finding oneself in need of medical treatment is always unsettling. When crime victims need medical treatment, they bring with them problems that may exceed their injuries. In addition to their physical condition, they are often fearful and insecure. Hospital staff members who are indifferent and treat the patient with insensitivity increase rather than diminish the patient's trauma, and may ultimately impede the overall healing process. The following recommendations are meant to ensure that hospitals are as helpful as possible to victims of crime.

1. Hospitals should establish and implement training programs for hospital personnel to sensitize them to the needs of victims of violent crimes, especially the elderly and those who have been sexually assaulted.
2. Hospitals should provide emergency medical assistance to victims of violent crime without regard to their ability to pay, and collect payments from state victim compensation programs.
3. Hospitals should provide emergency room crisis counseling to victims of crime and their families.
4. Hospitals should encourage and develop direct liaison with all victim assistance and social service agencies.

5. Hospitals should develop, in consultation with prosecuting agencies, a standardized rape kit for proper collection of physical evidence, and develop a procedure to ensure proper storage and maintenance of such evidence until it is released to the appropriate agency.

Recommendations for the Ministry

In hearing after hearing across the country, victims identified the religious community as a vital and largely untapped source of support for crime victims. The Government may compensate for economic loss; the state may punish; doctors may physically heal; but the lasting scars to spirit and faith are not so easily treated. Many victims question the faith they thought secure, or have no faith on which to rely. Frequently, ministers and their congregations can be a source of solace that no other sector of society can provide. It is in recognition of the unique role of the ministry that we offer the following recommendations.

1. The ministry should recognize and address the needs of crime victims.
2. The ministry should develop both seminary and in-service training on the criminal justice system, the needs of victims, and ways to restore victims' spiritual and material health.

Recommendations for the Bar

Attorneys have an obligation to their clients, to their profession, and to justice itself. They are obligated to use their expertise to guarantee that the system does not stray from the principle that lies at the heart of the law: justice for all who seek it.

1. All attorneys should recognize that they have an obligation, as officers of the court, to make certain that the justice system deals fairly with all participants in criminal litigation.
2. Prosecutors in particular should recognize their obligation to be active members of the bar at the local, state, and national levels and to represent the often unspoken needs and interests of victims.
3. Those who organize formal bar committees to deal with issues arising in the criminal justice system should ensure that the members of such groups represent a balance between the opposing parties in criminal litigation.

Recommendations for Schools

Educators carry a public trust in the instruction of children. This trust means that educators are obliged to teach shared cultural values in an environment that is both scholarly and safe. When safety is not sought, when crimes go unreported, victims are unprotected and victimizers conclude that they can escape responsibility by manipulating the system. These recommendations are meant to help educators to lessen crime's impact and reduce the number of victims.

1. School authorities should develop and require compliance with guidelines for prompt reporting of violent crimes committed in schools, crimes committed against school personnel, and the possession of weapons or narcotics.
2. School authorities should check the arrest and conviction records for sexual assault, child molestation, or pornography offenses of anyone applying for work in a school, including anyone doing contract work involving regular proximity to students, and make submission to such a check a precondition for employment.
3. Educators should develop and provide courses on the problems, needs, and legal interests of victims of crime.
4. School authorities should be mindful of their responsibility to make students aware of how they can avoid being victimized by crime.

Recommendations for the Mental Health Community

Property damage and physical injury are readily apparent, under-stood consequences of violent crime. The psychological wounds sustained by victims of crime, and the best means of treating such injuries, are less well understood. If this severe suffering is to be relieved, mental health professionals must lead the way.

1. The mental health community should develop and provide im-mediate and long-term psychological treatment programs for vic-tims of crime and their families.
2. The mental health community should establish training programs that will enable practitioners to treat crime victims and their families.
3. The mental health community should study the immediate and long-term psychological effects of criminal victimization.
4. The mental health community should work with public agencies, victim compensation boards, and private insurers to make psy-chological treatment readily available to crime victims and their families.
5. The mental health community should establish and maintain di-rect liaison with other victim service agencies.

Recommendations for the Private Sector

Crime is costly, not only to victims but also to businesses and to society as a whole. The private sector can help ease the burden carried by victims and reduce the cost of crime in several ways. Those who are victimized want to be productive in their work and responsible to their creditors; however, convalescence and court appearances may, for a time, reduce their ability to do so. If employers can be flexible in allowing absences for court appearances and medical treatment, if creditors can be more understanding in setting payment schedules, if citizens' groups can help their victimized neighbors, all will find that such forbearance will produce tangible rewards. The following recommendations offer specific suggestions for private sector action.

1. Businesses should authorize paid administrative leave for employees who must miss work because of injuries sustained in a violent crime, and for employees who must attend court hearings.
2. Businesses should establish employee assistance programs for victims of crime.
3. Creditors should make liberal allowances for persons who are unable to make timely payments because of recent victimization.
4. The private sector should encourage private contributions of money and other support to victim service agencies, whether public or private.

Model Victim/Witness Units

Experience has shown that the only way of ensuring that the needs of victims and witnesses are met is to have a separate unit solely dedicated to their assistance. Prosecutors, police, court personnel, and others in the criminal justice system are already overworked; moreover, these professionals may have to direct their primary efforts in ways not always consistent with response to victim needs.

Whether the victim/witness assistance unit is placed within some component of the criminal justice system or outside the system in a social service organization is best left to local determination. Excellent units are operating in police departments, prosecutors' offices, probation departments, and social service agencies. Some areas have excellent volunteer victim/witness assistance units. What is important is that the unit be well organized and staffed by dedicated personnel, that it be funded generously enough to provide comprehensive services, and that its actions be coordinated with those of agencies within the criminal justice system, private service groups, and business organizations.

The success of such units is measured by how swiftly and well they meet the needs of victims and witnesses. We have identified the needs that we consider most important, the ones that every victim witness unit should meet. A model victim/witness assistance unit should:

1. Assist every victim who reports a crime, whether or not an arrest is made.
2. Respond to the scene of the crime to make crisis counseling available.
3. Provide 24-hour telephone hotline service to victims and witnesses for assistance, particularly if threats or intimidation occur.
4. Make emergency monetary aid available to help needy victims make their homes secure, replace such things as glasses and hearing aids, and buy food and other necessities.
5. Refer victims to appropriate social service and victim compensation programs and assist in filling out forms for compensation.
6. Educate the public about the operation of the criminal justice system and the way it treats victims.
7. Assist in prompt return of victim's property.
8. Notify the victim of progress of the investigation, the defendant's arrest, subsequent bail determination and status of the case as it proceeds through the system.
9. Assist victims in making appropriate input on the following: bail determinations, continuances, plea bargaining, dismissals, sentencing, restitution and parole hearings.
10. Consult with victims and witnesses to facilitate the setting of convenient hearing dates.
11. Implement a victim/witness on-call system.
12. Intercede with the employers or creditors of victims or witnesses.
13. Assist the elderly and handicapped in arranging transportation to and from court.

14. Provide a translator service.
15. Coordinate efforts to ensure that victims have a secure place to wait before testifying.
16. Provide counseling or companionship during court appearances when appropriate.

VICTIMS OF CRIME AND VIOLENCE

**Final Report of the APA Task Force
on the Victims of Crime and Violence
Submitted to the Board of Directors
30 November 1984**

Task Force Members:

**Morton Bard, Ph.D., Chair
Bruce Sales, Ph.D., Vice-Chair
Irene Hanson Frieze, Ph.D.
Gary Gottfredson, Ph.D.
Martin S. Greenberg, Ph.D.
Sharon Hymer, Ph.D.
Martin Reiser, Ph.D.
Robert Rich, Ph.D.
C. Richard Tsegaye-Spates, Ph.D.**

Max Siegel, Ph.D., Board of Directors Liaison

Arnold Kahn, Administrative Officer

Executive Summary

Morton Bard, Ph.D., Chair

American psychology has taken an important step in acknowledging the existence of a large and socially disenfranchised part of our population. Victims of crime and violence, for too long nearly invisible, suffered the additional indignity of seeing an enormous investment by society in those who did harm and virtually none for those who were its object. Billions have been spent to apprehend, prosecute, incarcerate, rehabilitate, and study criminals, but almost nothing to compensate, rehabilitate, and study victims. This enormous imbalance is played out on the television screen each night during prime time. Society is intrigued by those who commit harmful acts, but so great is the aversion to learn of crime's consequences in human terms, that for television producers to portray them accurately invites a loss of audience. (There seems to be a real fascination with "aggression" and "success" even if it victimizes another.) At some level, victims are seen as having had some collusive role in the event, as somehow deserving blame or at the very least, as being weak and ineffectual.

This implied societal value has not been without its effect on psychology. Despite a distinguished history of research on aggression and violence in a variety of forms, and despite large numbers of psychologists whose interests touch upon crime related issues (forensic psychologists, community psychologists, correctional psychologists, policy psychologists, legal psychologists, etc.), literature attesting to interest in victims is sparse indeed. In fact, even psychologists interested in stress have failed to include crime victimization in the category of stressful life events. In many ways, psychology has, in the past, followed society in defining the nature of its interest.

With this report, psychology has taken stock of itself and of its sister professions. The APA Task Force on the Victims of Crime and Violence organized itself to review the state of psychological knowledge on victimization; to survey theory and approaches to interventions for helping those who have been victimized; to explore past and present public and legal policies regarding victimization, with special emphasis on the interface between psychology and law; and to make recommendations to the Board of Directors.

Recommendations

Objective 1: Psychologists involved in service delivery should acquire specific, identifiable skills in direct intervention with victims.
Training to work with victims should be a part of the graduate and postgraduate curricula in psychology.
Licensing in clinical and counseling psychology should

require a demonstration of knowledge and expertise
in service to victims.

There should be more continuing education workshops on the provision of services to victims.

Examination of training in services to victims should
be a part of the procedures for making accreditation
reviews.

Objective 2:   More psychologists should acquire specialized consultative skills to increase the capacity of indigenous
workers to help victims.

A network of psychologists interested in providing
help to victims and those who work with victims
should be established. The network should assist the
National Organization for Victim Assistance to ensure
the local availability of psychologists.

A list of speakers knowledgeable about research on the
experience of victims should be developed.

Objective 3:   More psychologists should become involved in initiating and evaluating changes in the criminal justice
system designed to ameliorate the problems victims
experience in that system.

Training models for criminal justice personnel who
work with victims of crime should be produced.

Research should be encouraged on the effects of legal
arrangements that have been created to help victims
and their families.

Continued evaluation research on victim oriented
practices within the criminal justice system should be
encouraged.

Legislation relating to research on the criminal justice
system and its activities should be monitored, and efforts should be made to maintain the adequacy of research support and to proper management of the
research functions of the pertinent agencies.

Objective 4:   More psychologists who are prepared to do so should
actually provide service directly to victims, to indigenous helping systems, and in the criminal justice system.

Training models for crisis intervention personnel should be produced.

Training modules for mental health professionals should be produced.

Objective 5: Psychologists should be more involved in gaining knowledge about the victim experience and about helpful interventions for victims.

Psychologists should be encouraged to engage in research in the following areas, which the Task Force believes to be of the highest priority:

a. Identifying the conditions under which victims seek help from others and from whom help is sought.

b. Identifying the linkages between the various sources of victim stress and the particular coping strategies utilized.

c. Exploring the dynamics of victimization within the family, including the source of stress, coping strategies employed, and the mode of effective intervention.

d. Determining the sources of stress, coping strategies employed, and the modes of effective intervention for the indirect victims of crime—the friends and family members of the primary victim.

e. Developing new techniques for the treatment of victims in different stages of response; new and existing techniques should be evaluated on the basis of knowledge to determinants of successful coping.

f. Analyzing the determinants of successful coping in victims.

g. Understanding how victimization affects the victim's self-image.

h. Understanding the long-term effects of victimization.

i. Exploring the effectiveness and usefulness of support groups as well as their use as adjuncts of psychotherapy.

Greater federal funding should be encouraged for re-search on societal reactions to victimizaton.

Research should examine the development of new therapeutic tools to meet the special needs of victims.

Objective 6: There should be greater public awareness about the mental health needs of victims and the roles of psy-chology and psychologists can serve in helping victims.

Materials should be developed to influence public per-ceptions and attitudes about victimization.

A public awareness campaign on the mental health needs of victims should be instituted.

Objective 7: The APA should endorse laws and legal arrangements that facilitate the realization of victims' interests and encourage the formal evaluation of these arrange-ments.

Greater efforts should be undertaken for new federal and state legislation that is designed to increase vic-tims' participation in the police investigation process, prosecutorial decision making, bail hearings, and trial process, sentencing, and parole hearing.

Greater efforts should be undertaken for (a) legislation to increase victims' participation in the criminal justice process and (b) legislation that establishes a victim's bill of rights.

Greater efforts should be undertaken to promote the passage of victims' rights bills that include victim no-tification, compensation, restitution, and assistance programs.

Efforts should be made to encourage federal and state funding of formal evaluation of new legislation and legal arrangements.

Efforts should be undertaken to identify ways to in-volve state associations in support for victim-related legislations in each state.

SUGGESTED READINGS

Adelson, Daniel, and Kalis, Betty L., eds. *Community Psychology and Mental Health, Perspectives and Challenges.* Scranton, Pa.: Chandler Publishing Company, 1970.

Aguilera, Donna C., and Messick, Janice M. *Crisis Intervention: Theory and Methodology.* St. Louis, Mo.: C. V. Mosby, 1974.

American Bar Association, Judicial Administrative Division, Victims of Crime: Giving Them Their Day in Court, *The Judges' Journal* 23, 1984.

American Psychological Association. Task Force on the Victims of Crime and Violence, *Final Report.* Washington, D.C.: American Psychological Association, 1984.

Bard, Morton. Psychology and the Study of Crime as a Stressful Life Event, *International Journal of Group Tensions* 10 (1980), 73-85.

Bard, Morton. Immediacy and Authority in Crisis Management, in Parad, H. et al., eds., *Emergency and Disaster Management: A Mental Health Sourcebook.* Bowie, Md.: The Charles Press, 1976.

Bard, Morton, Arnone, Harriet, and Nemiroff, David. Contextual Influences on the Post-Traumatic Stress of Homicide Survivor-Victims, in Figley, C., ed. *Trauma and Its Wake.* New York: Brunner/Mazel, 1985.

Bard, Morton, and Shellow, Robert. *Issues in Law Enforcement: Essays and Case Studies.* Reston, Va.: Reston Publishing Company, Inc., 1976.

Brodyaga, Lisa, et al. *Rape and Its Victims: A Report for Citizens, Health Facilities, and Criminal Justice Agencies.* Washington, D.C.: National Institute of Law Enforcement and Criminal Justice, 1975.

Burgess, Ann Wolbert, and Holstrom, Lynda Lytle. Rape: Sexual Disruption and Recovery, *American Journal of Orthopsychiatry* 13 (1979): 658-669.

Burgess, Ann Wolbert, and Holstrom, Lynda Lytle. Adaptive Strategies and Recovery from Rape, *American Journal of Psychiatry* 136 (1979): 1278-1282.

Burgess, Ann Wolbert, and Holstrom, Lynda Lytle. *Rape: Victims of Crisis.* Bowie, Md.: Robert J. Brady Company, 1974.

Caplan, Gerald. *Principles of Preventive Psychiatry.* New York: Basic Books, Inc., 1964.

Clark, Ramsey. *Crime in America.* New York: Touchstone Books, 1971.

Cooper, Barbara. *Wife Beating: Counselor Training Manual #2, Crisis Intervention.* Ann Arbor, Mi.: NOW Domestic Violence and Spouse Assault Fund, Inc., 1976.

Cumming, John, and Cumming, Elaine. *Ego and Milieu: Theory and Practice of Environmental Therapy.* New York: Atherton Press, 1966.

Dinnerstein, Dorothy. *The Mermaid and the Minotaur.* New York: Harper and Row, 1976.

Drapkin, Israel, and Viano, Emilio, eds. *Victimology: A New Focus—Vol. 1, Theoretical Issues in Victimology.* Lexington, Ma.: D.C. Heath, 1974.

Drapkin, Israel, and Viano, Emilio, eds. *Victimology: A New Focus—Vol. 2, Society's Reaction to Victimization.* Lexington, Ma.: D.C. Heath, 1974.

Drapkin, Israel, and Viano, Emilio, eds. *Victimology: A New Focus—Vol. 3, Crimes, Victims, and Justice.* Lexington, Ma.: D.C. Heath, 1974.

Drapkin, Israel, and Viano, Emilio, eds. *Victimology: A New Focus—Vol. 4, Violence and Its Victims.* Lexington, Ma.: D.C. Heath, 1975.

Drapkin, Israel, and Viano, Emilio, eds. *Victimology: A New Focus—Vol. 5, Exploiters and Exploited.* Lexington, Ma.: D.C. Heath, 1975.

Erikson, Erik H. *Childhood and Society,* 2d ed. New York: W. W. Norton and Company, 1963.

Frederick, C. Effects of National vs. Human-Induced Violence, in L. Kivens, ed., *Evaluation and Change: Services for Survivors*, Minneapolis, Mn.: Minneapolis Medical Research Foundation, 1980.

Friedman, Kenneth, et al. *Victims and Helpers: Reactions to Crime*. New York: Victim Services Agency, 1982.

Garofalo, James. *Introduction to the National Crime Survey—Analytic Report*. Washington, D.C.: United States National Criminal Justice Information and Statistics Service, 1977.

Garofalo, James, and Sutton, L. P. *Compensating Victims of Violent Crime—Potential Costs and Coverage of a National Program*. Washington, D.C.: United States National Criminal Justice Information and Statistics Service, 1977.

Goffman, Erving. *Stigma: Notes on the Management of Spoiled Identity*. Englewood Cliffs, N.J.: Prentice-Hall, Inc., 1963.

Gorham, William, and Glazer, Nathan, eds. *The Urban Predicament*. Washington, D.C.: The Urban Institute, 1976.

Greenberg, Martin S. and Ruback, R. Barry, eds. *Journal of Social Issues: Criminal Victimization* 40 (1984).

Greenberg, M.S., Wilson, C.E., Ruback, R.B., and Mills, M.K. Social and Emotional Determinants of Victim Crime Reporting, *Social Psychology Quarterly* 42 (1979): 364-372.

Hall, D.J. The Role of the Victim in the Prosecution and Disposition of A Criminal Case. *Vanderbilt Law Review* 28 (1975): 931-985.

Hernon, Jolene C., and Forst, Brian. *The Criminal Justice Response to Victim Harm*. U.S. Dept. of Justice, National Institute of Justice, 1984.

Hindelang, Michael J. *Public Opinion Regarding Crime, Criminal Justice, and Related Topics*. Washington, D.C.: United States National Criminal Justice Information and Statistics Service, 1975.

Hindelang, Michael J., et al. *Sourcebook of Criminal Justice Statistics—1976*. Washington, D.C.: United States National Criminal Justice Information and Statistics Service, 1977.

Hirsch, B.J., Natural Support Systems and Coping with Major Life Changes. *American Journal of Community Psychology* 8 (1980): 159-172.

Hofstadter, Richard. *Social Darwinism in American Thought*. Boston, Ma.: Beacon Press, 1955.

Hunt, Morton. *The Mugging*. New York: Atheneum, 1972.

Knudten, Richard D., et al. *Crime Victim Compensation Laws and Programs*. Milwaukee: Marquette University Center for Criminal Justice and Social Policy, 1975.

Janoff-Bulman, R., Characterological versus Behavioral Self-Blame: Inquires Into Depression and Rape. *Journal of Personality and Social Psychology* 37 (1979): 1798-1809.

Kilpatrick, D., Vernonen, L., and Resnick, P. The Aftermath of Rape: Recent Empirical Findings. *American Journal of Orthopsychiatry* 49 (1979): 658-669.

Knudten, Richard D., et al. *Victims and Witnesses: The Impact of Crime and Their Experience with the Criminal Justice System*. Milwaukee: Marquette University Center for Criminal Justice and Social Policy, 1976.

Lewis, Helen B. *Shame and Guilt in Neurosis*. New York: International Universities Press, Inc., 1971.

Lynd, Helen Merrell. *On Shame and the Search for Identity*. New York: Science Editions, Inc., 1961.

Macaulay, J., and Berkowitz, L., eds. *Altruism and Helping Behavior*. New York: Academic Press, 1970.

Madden, Denis J., and Lion, John R., eds. *Rage, Hate, Assault and Other Forms of Violence*. New York: John Wiley and Sons, 1976.

Magee, Douglas. *What Murder Leaves Behind: The Victim's Family*. New York: Dodd Mead, 1983.

Maguri, M. Impact of Burglary Upon Victims. *British Journal of Criminology* 20 (1980) 261-275.

Maslow, Abraham. *Motivation and Personality*, 2d ed. New York: Harper and Row, 1970.

McDonald, W. ed. *Criminal Justice and the Victim*. Beverly Hills, Ca.: Sage Publications, 1976.

Medea, Andra, and Thompson, Kathleen, *Against Rape: A Survival Manual for Women*. New York: Farrar, Strauss and Giroux, 1974.

Menninger, Karl. *The Crime of Punishment*. New York: The Viking Press, 1968.

Menninger, Karl, with Mayman, Martin, and Pruyser, Paul. *The Vital Balance: The Life Process in Mental Health and Illness*. New York: The Viking Press, 1963.

National Organization for Victim Assistance. *The Victim Service System: A Guide to Action 1983*. Washington, D.C.,: NOVA, 1983.

National Conference of the Judiciary on the Rights of Victims of Crime. *Statement of Recommended Judicial Practices*. Washington, D.C.: National Institute of Justice, 1984.

National Organization for Victim Assistance. *Victim Rights and Services: A Legislative Directory*. Washington, D.C.: NOVA, 1984.

Nicholson, George, Condit, Thomas W., and Greenbaum, Stuart, eds. *Forgotten Victims: An Advocate's Anthology*. Sacramento, Ca.: California District Attorneys Association, 1977.

Parad, Howard J., Resnik, H.L.P., and Parad, Libbie G., eds. *Emergency and Disaster Management*. Bowie, Md.: The Charles Press Publishers, Inc., 1976.

Pepperdine University Law Review, the American Bar Association, and the National Institute of Justice. *Special Symposium Edition on Victims' Rights, Pepperdine Law Review* 11 (1984).

Ryan, William. *Blaming the Victim*. New York: Random House, 1971.

Sales, B., Baum, M., and Shore, B. Victim Readjustment Following Assault. *Journal of Social Issues* 40 (1980): 117-136.

SEARCH Group, Inc. *Dictionary of Criminal Justice Data Terminology* Second Edition. Washington, D.C.: Bureau of Justice Statistics, 1981.

Sheehan, Susan. A prison and a prisoner. *New Yorker*, 24, 31 October 1977, 7 November 1977.

Slater, Philip. *The Pursuit of Loneliness: American Culture at the Breaking Point*. Boston: Beacon Press, 1970.

Sparks, Richard F. *Research on Victims of Crime: Accomplishments, Issues, and New Directions*. National Institute of Mental Health, Center for Studies of Crime and Delinquency, 1982.

Tyler, T.R. Perceived Control and Behavioral Reactions to Crime. *Personality and Social Psychology Bulletin* 7 (1981): 212-217.

United States Attorney General's Task Force on Family Violence. *Final Report*. Washington, D.C.: Government Printing Office, 1984.

United States Department of Justice, Bureau of Justice Statistics. *Report to the Nation on Crime and Justice: The Data*. Washington, D.C.: Government Printing Office, 1983.

United States Department of Justice, Federal Bureau of Investigation. *Crime in the United States: 1975 Uniform Crime Reports*. Washington, D.C.: Government Printing Office, 1976.

United States National Commission on the Causes and Prevention of Violence. *Crimes of Violence*. Washington, D.C.: Government Printing Office, 1969.

United States National Commission on the Causes and Prevention of Violence. *To Establish Justice, to Insure Domestic Tranquility*. New York: Bantam, 1970.

United States National Criminal Justice Information and Statistics Service. *Criminal Victimization in the United States: A Comparison of the 1974 and 1975 Findings*. Washington, D.C.: 1977.

United States National Institute of Law Enforcement and Criminal Justice. *Forcible Rape: Medical and Legal Information*. Washington, D.C.: Government Printing Office, 1977.

United States National Institute of Law Enforcement and Criminal Justice. *Forcible Rape: A National Survey of the Response by Police*. Washington, D.C.: Government Printing Office, 1977.

United States President's Task Force on Victims of Crime, *Final Report*. Washington, D.C.: Government Printing Office, 1982.

INDEX